The Emperor Has a Body

THE EMPEROR HAS A BODY

BODY-POLITICS IN THE BETWEEN

JAVELINA BOOKS

Acknowledgment is given for the following:
Excerpts from *This Sex Which is Not One* by Luce Irigaray, translated by Catherine Porter. Copyright © 1985. Used by permission of the publisher, Cornell University Press.
Excerpt from *Feminism and Philosophy: Perspectives on Difference and Equality* by Moira Gatens. Copyright © 1991. Used by permission of the publisher, Indiana University Press.

Address inquiries to:
Javelina Books
P.O. Box 42131
Tucson, AZ 85733

08 07 06 05 04 03 02 01 00 99   10 9 8 7 6 5 4 3 2 1

Library of Congress Catalog Card Number: 98-67875

ISBN 0-9654418-9-X (cloth)
ISBN 0-9654418-2-2 (paper)

Cataloging-in-Publication Data:
The emperor has a body : body-politics in the between / S. Elise Peeples.
        p.   cm.
    Includes bibliographical references and index.
    1. Feminist theory. 2. Dualism. 3. Mind and body. 4. Body image in women.
    5. Body, Human (Philosophy). 6. Culture—study and teaching.
    I. Title: The Emperor Has a Body. II. Peeples, S. Elise.

Printed in the United States of America on acid-free paper.

To the living memory of my father

*with gratitude for his resistance
and his trust*

Contents

Acknowledgments

The community of those who helped me in the writing of this book is large and its members of inestimable value. Thanks first to my parents, Ruth and Bob Peeples who encouraged me to think for myself and gave me a foundation of confidence from which to work and to my brothers (Mark and Jim) and sister (Sue) who made that absolutely necessary.

The impetus for writing this book emerged from my Masters thesis in philosophy begun in 1992. My thanks go to the San Francisco State University Philosophy Department for allowing me to pursue a feminist thesis that many institutions would have nixed as prohibitively broad and unwieldy. Thanks to my thesis committee: Kosta Bagakis who seemed pleased each time I brought him a new version, engaged fully with the ideas, and encouraged me to keep the more controversial aspects; my committee chair, Mary Anne Warren who gave me latitude and in whose classes I became inspired by feminist philosophers such as Carol Gilligan and Luce Irigaray; and Jim Syphers who patiently helped me with the critique of classical philosophy.

Thanks must also go to those who provided me with the refuge I needed—to Kosta Bagakis and Yeshi Sherover Neumann for sharing their cabin in Butler Creek Flats in Northern California and to Betsy Rannells Wood for her generous gift of time in her Inverness apartment. And to the inhabitants of both Butler Creek Flats and Inverness of which the sea and the creek and all others who live nearby figure significantly. Lucy Colvin, Claudia Wolz and Michael Haseltine read early drafts and must be commended for their input and faith through fledgling attempts. Thanks to my sister Sue Peeples, a midwife and family nurse practitioner who gave of her precious time to comment on the midwifery parts of the text. And for computer support thanks to Jason Chun and David Pierini.

Numerous groups and people listened to and commented on the Fairy Tale or the text: Ruth, Bob, Mark, Sue, Jim, Ann, Jay, Chloe and Audrey Peeples; Becky Brumberg Peeples; Marguerite Pike; Pemba, Michele, and David Pierini; Sharon Turner; Robin Gordon and Leora

Forstein; Henrietta Harris; Western Region of the Society for Women in Philosophy; Land, Air and Water Conference in Eugene, Oregon; East Bay Women's Therapy Consulting Group; Women Philosophers East Bay chapter (Marti Kheel whose support was unflagging and generous of heart, Chandrika Shah whose intelligence and friendship helped get me through graduate school, Louann Trost and Angela Greyboys); Women in Transition (especially Mary Lou Peterson who arranged for me to guest speak); IMT Associates; my women's support group (Linda Hess, Joyce Slater, Valerie Kay) and other unnamed gatherings of folk.

Mujeres Unidas Diversity Camp and its predecessor, Women's Alliance Solstice Camp transformed my life by bringing me together with countless wise women whose lessons keep teaching even when the organizations can no longer hold a center. It was at the Mujeres Unidas camp where I first tested the metaphor of the "emperor" and was overwhelmed and emboldened by the support. The image of a room full of diverse women clapping, laughing and cheering continues to bring me courage when doubts arise. I want to thank the members of the Mujeres Unidas organizing committee (Lea Arellano, Maria Gonzales Barron, Viviane June de Leon Bias, Cynthia Finley, Ellena Goodman, Judy Graboyes, Tova Green, Judy Helfand, Linda Landon, Laurie Lippen, Alissa Millman, Yeshi Sherover Neumann, Queen T'Hisha, Sharon Olivia Turner, Penny Rosenwasser, Susan Runyan, Patricia Waters, Jan Watson, and Akaya Winwood) who dedicated countless hours to each other and to the idea that diverse women working together can make the political spiritual and spiritual political. And thank you to the reunion attendees (Viviane de Leon Bias, Lucia August, Penelope Douglass, Lea Arellano, Cathy Cade, Penny Rosenwasser, Kristie Markey, Linda Landon, Mabrie Ormes) who listened to the fairy tale with magic.

Gail Bourque, Penny Rosenwasser, Viviane de Leon Bias, Laurie Lippen, Lucia August, Patricia Waters, Mary Berg, Mark Peeples and Becky Brumberg-Peeples helped me in my attempt to get endorsements for the book. Thanks to Don Johnson who treated me with great kindness and respect and generously agreed to endorse the book. And thanks to Linda Peavy who took lots of her precious time for an unknown to help me with my proposal letter.

I also want to thank Constance Hester, my good friend, colleague and partner in Minding the Body, Inc. Our numerous discussions of feminism, women and body image inspired much in those sections of the book. Additionally, our workshops together have allowed me to see the ideas in practice.

XV

Special thanks must go to my dream group (Judy Mueller and Valerie Kay) without whose unflinching support of me, my ideas and my dreams, this book could never have been written. And thanks to Catalina Durazo, my sister in spirit who believes in me unconditionally. Without this cheering section, I would never have maintained the courage to complete the book.

Though many writers complain of their treatment by editors and publishers, I have nothing but praise for my editor and publisher Caitlin Gannon who risked her reputation and press on an unknown. I appreciate her critical eye, her superb editorial insight and her out-on-a-limb enthusiasm for the book. I cannot imagine a better person to enter into the Between with on the publication of a book. And thanks also to aire design company whose creative and daring collaborative imaginations carry the cover.

I am grateful beyond words to Mary Berg, my local editor who read draft after draft and tenaciously re-worded, argued, polished and generally brought to bear on the text her deft knowledge of the English language, her incisive intelligence and her experience. She devoted herself to finishing this project and proved time after time that in the Between all is possible and that our interests can never be fully separated.

And finally, I thank my husband and partner, Adam David Miller for his unquestioning support of my ideas and ability, for his critical eye and ear through the many phases of this project, and for his loving patience.

The Emperor Has A Body
and We Know 'Cuz He's Naked:
A Fairytale for Our Times

More than once upon a time, and in places all over the world, there were women. One remarkable woman called Brazen bore a son whom she groomed to become a powerful man. This son took all of her sage advice and at a very early age became emperor of all the land. He got so high and mighty that he believed he was divine. And when he looked in the mirror, he saw reflected an image so young and handsome that for years he convinced himself he was indeed a god.

One day when he was approaching mid-life, the emperor looked in the mirror and saw a balding head, some wrinkles and a fat belly. He realized with shock that his body was starting to age. The idea that he would grow old and die had not occurred to him before—after all, gods are immortal.

Panic-stricken, he called in his four advisors: his wise mother, Brazen, Dr. Marcus Healess, Rev. Reinhold Sinbad, and The Right Honorable Immanuel Abstracticus.

Dr. Healess said, "You know, we can do some transplanting here and there, maybe some liposuction. You'll be as good as new. Why with modern plastic surgery…"

Rev. Sinbad interrupted, "No, no, no. That will never do. You must spend no time at all on your body. It's evil. Abolish the mirrors in the empire and concentrate solely on your soul!"

"That, my dear man of the cloth," said Abstracticus, "is a good start. Transcendence of body is critical. Perfect the Mind unsoiled by the body and you shall have within your grasp eternal and unchanging Truth."

Brazen could remain silent no longer. She exclaimed, "Oh, rot! If you haven't got a body, then what kept me in labor for three interminable days? Can't you see yourself? Her voice dropped to a whisper, "I understand your fear, Dear One, but if you build your life on fear, you'll **never** find truth."

"I fear nothing, fool woman!" roared the emperor, jumping up from his throne. "How dare you suggest it. Get out—out of my castle now and forever. If you weren't my mother, I'd have your head!"

Brazen gathered her magnificent fleshy body from her chair as if to fly and said, "Fine, I'll go—gladly—somewhere I'm respected—where I can speak without threats. I warn **you**, though—one day you'll regret sending me away like this." And she glided out of the chambers, out of the castle and into the empire where she began to foment change.

Meanwhile, the emperor decided to follow the advice of the doctor and the philosopher and find ways to cut himself off from his body. He spent his time contemplating the higher things in life, making wise pronouncements and producing universal systems of ethics, science, and religion that were taught in the universities to those who could afford the cultivation of their minds. The path to success, most people reasoned, was to emulate the emperor and concentrate on matters of the mind.

And as for the emperor's bodily functions, he appointed many "mothers" to take care of his body as his own mother had done when he was young. These women fed him, bathed him, dressed him, removed the wastes of his body and tended to his sickness.

To take care of the image problem, the emperor required his subjects to make for him divine clothes of the finest silks, satins and furs with colors and styles that rivaled nature's beauty. He would wear them only once so that the colors never faded. Everyone helped even though they had few clothes themselves and little to eat. But they dreamed that someday they, too, would rise above their bodies to the emperor's level.

Some gathered plants for dyes, tended the crops to make the finest fabrics, bred silk worms or mink, or stripped the earth looking for gold, silver and precious stones to decorate the emperor; and some tended to his physical needs: carried his books and papers, transported him from place to place so that he never had to walk. Doctors were at his service to give him drugs if he got anxious, could not sleep, or his bowels refused to move.

Now the image he saw in the mirror was as close to divinity as was humanly possible. And when he saw himself or anyone who looked like him, he saw the Universal and smiled comfortably. If, however, when he looked at a person, he noted difference from himself, then he saw bodies or "special interests" and he was suspicious. These "others" could not be fully trusted.

Since sex was strongly associated with his body, the emperor attempted to repress his sexual feelings. His wife, Soma, tried to rekindle their romance the only ways she knew how—with candlelit dinners and fancy new hairdos. Eventually, the emperor succumbed to his sexual feelings; but then the guilt began.

Again he called in his advisors, asking this time about sex. Rev. Sinbad spoke up and said, "Don't indulge in it. Resist!"

The emperor looked ashamed at the thought of his weakness. So Dr. Healess said, "Well, I say go ahead and do it but don't speak about it." And the emperor brightened a little.

Then the venerable Abstracticus said, "We do need to carry on the race and you being so wise, must procreate." The emperor cracked a smile. "However," Abstracticus continued, "sex does contaminate your higher calling. I suggest treating your wife as you treat your body—that is, as a necessary evil, knowing you are lord and master, fully in control."

And so it began that the emperor treated his wife as he did his body. After a while, the emperor could no longer look at any woman without thinking of body. Women, in some sense, were the emperor's body. They became so attuned to him that it was as if he were again a small child in the arms of his mother. But, these replacement mothers reminded him of Brazen and evoked feelings he would rather not have so he made sure the women were kept under the tightest control.

Many years and many plastic surgeries later, the emperor could no longer bear to look in the mirror because he had been unable to stem the tide of time— his face was puckered and scarred from all those plastic surgeries and his eyes were dull. Now out of desperation he banished mirrors from the empire.

It was then that women became his mirrors. He demanded that the women around him be young so that when he looked into their eyes he could believe he, too, was young. Women who could afford it covered their bodies with clothes like the emperor's. However, their bodies did not fit the clothes unless they dieted and wore restrainers on their breasts and girdles on their hips and waists. Even if they got into the clothes, the fit was most uncomfortable. But the emperor rewarded women who could control their bodies and restrain their appetites because it reflected well on him. If they were lean enough he could almost pretend they were bodiless, too.

Women throughout the empire became more and more powerless and miserable but were unsure what to do. They tried everything: some strove to become more attractive; some asserted their power over those who were lower in status; some tried to be the best wives and mothers possible; and some tried to be just like men.

Soma, a "good" wife, had followed the emperor's example and tried to control her own body. But finally, after using every method known to stay young and beautiful, Soma could not cover up her age. Seeing her, the emperor could not seek higher truths.

One day the emperor said to Soma, "You are old and fat, woman. I can't stand to look at you. Out of my sight!"

Soma was thrown out of the castle and onto her wits, which hadn't been exercised for some time. She sought out Brazen who took her under her wing as a daughter. At first Soma insisted on defending the emperor's writings to one and all. But Brazen took her along to women's gatherings where her ideas began to shift.

At one such gathering a woman called Airia said, "No matter how well I master the emperor's teachings and ways, no one listens to what I have to say."

"Well, what'd you expect?" asked Alma de Agua. "In the emperor's scheme, we women are just lowly bodies taking care of lowly things. A lot of the men believe that too."

"The emperor thinks he's better than us," said Eartherine, "because he thinks he stands nowhere and therefore everywhere at once. And according to him, all we do is stand—in the mud and the blood, I might add."

Soma began to see the problem. "Yes," she said excitedly, "but, hey, I know he's got a body—I saw it just last month. Just like you or me—ah, well, with minor differences, I mean."

"Oh, he's just a sham," said Brazen. "He only gets away with it 'cuz we believe in him. I was the first who did. Now I've given up doing what he wants. Only among friends can I be who I want to be. And as for that son of mine—I'm too old to teach sleeping dogs."

However, though the women grew and grew in spite of the emperor, their freedom could not be complete while he remained in power. Many who did not fit the emperor's criteria of "universal" were organizing into groups to try to change things. Brazen and Soma joined with other women, men and children to form the Truth Weavers. Their goals were to expose the emperor's f(ph)allacy and to create their own world where the web of life was sacred and respect for difference ruled. The Truth Weavers' ideas spread throughout the land.

Meanwhile, from high in the castle tower, the emperor continued to issue proclamations of Truth, Justice and the Emperor's Way. And though he had all the power and material things he wanted, he missed Brazen and Soma and something else that he couldn't name.

So when two Truth Weavers, Alma de Agua and Eartherine came to him with a story that a spirit had appeared and ordered them to produce their cloth for the emperor, he listened intently.

"What exactly did the spirit say?" he asked.

"That the fabric would reveal Truth and only people capable of seeing the Truth would be able to see this splendiferous outfit for what it was," replied Eartherine.

"Of course, we didn't understand and were scared, so we came directly here," said Alma de Agua, looking at her shoes.

The emperor was thrilled. Surely the fabric had been sent from the gods to assist him in becoming bodiless. The emperor reasoned that if, while wearing the fabric, only the Truth would show, then the fabric must have the power to make his body disappear altogether. And the timing couldn't be better since the Annual Procession of the Grand Emperor was just a month away.

He pressed the weavers into action. For weeks the two women worked up in an old warehouse, pretending to be weaving and sewing an outfit, when in reality there was no fabric. Everyone could see how busy they were as they pretended to take the cloth from the loom and cut the air with their scissors.

As the day of the Grand Procession drew near, the emperor became anxious about how the weavers were doing. He sent Dr. Healess over to check on the progress and report back to him.

Alma de Agua said to the doctor, "This outfit will make the emperor immortally beautiful—don't you think? Imagine, only those capable of grasping beautiful universal truths will see it and appreciate its qualities."

Dr. Healess looked at the looms and saw absolutely nothing but said, "Oh, yes, you're doing a magnificent job. Couldn't do it better myself," and he left quickly so they wouldn't detect that such a learned man was unable to recognize Truth.

The next day the emperor sent over Rev. Sinbad. But he, too, saw nothing and became concerned about the condition of his own soul. So he oohed and aahed over the progress and asked when it would be done. Eartherine replied, "if we work day and night, it should be done for the Grand Procession on Saturday."

Rev. Sinbad returned to the emperor and said, "What spiritual weavers they are! The fabric is divine—so delicate! You'll look heavenly."

A few days later Abstracticus checked on the work and reported, "The outfit is purely transcendental!" The emperor hadn't been this excited in years.

Meanwhile, the Truth Weavers, uninterested in the emperor's parade this year, had planned their own celebration in the forest at the same time as and near the Grand Procession. They would have live music, body painting, delicious food and lots of dancing.

Saturday arrived, a bright, sunny day with perfect visibility. At last Eartherine and Alma de Agua announced, "The emperor's new clothes are ready!" The emperor went excitedly to the warehouse with his servants who were members of the Truth Weavers.

Eartherine and Alma de Agua lifted their arms as if they were holding something precious and said, "This is the robe. Here is the train. These are the pants. They are as light as a feather and will make your Majesty feel as if he does not even have a body. That is their special virtue. Would your Imperial Highness care to take off his clothes," they said, "and try on the new ones in front of the mirror?"

The emperor did as he was asked. His servants dressed him, pretending all the while that they could see the cloth. They buttoned pretend buttons and smoothed over pretend wrinkles, making sure not to tickle the emperor. Then he stood in front of the mirror, trying to admire the garments he couldn't see and harboring many doubts. Even his advisors and servants were able to see it, he *thought, why not me? He reassured himself that when he wore the outfit, he would reach pure transcendence and that would be reward enough. Stalling for time, the emperor asked to be re-fitted several times.*

Outside, all sorts of music from reggae to mariachi to jazz could be heard from the huge Weavers' party already in full swing. More and more people waiting for the Grand Procession heard the music and abandoned that route to join the other party, until only a few loyal subjects remained awaiting the emperor.

Finally, to strains of All Hail the Chief, the royal entourage emerged on a float decorated with colorful balloons. The emperor, however, was decorated only in the Truth.

At first, no spectator wanted to admit that they couldn't recognize Truth when they saw it, so they praised his outfit. But because so few people turned out, the praise was faint. The emperor angrily imagined suitable punishments for those who didn't show up for his Grand Procession.

He was so preoccupied with torturous thoughts that he almost passed Brazen without seeing her. With a sharpened pencil she popped one of his balloons to get his attention. She stretched up and said, "Look at yourself—can you still not see? Our eyes no longer watch you."

Hearing this the emperor froze momentarily. Then he guided his float toward the forest as if to crash the Weavers' party. When the Weavers got a look at him, they began to chant, "The emperor has a bod, he is no god; the emperor has a bod, he is no god!"

All of a sudden a blue wool sweater was airborne, and then a red turtleneck, and then a shoe and a sock until the air was full of the people's clothing. The drumming, singing and dancing continued.

The emperor gazed at the naked dancing bodies of all colors, shapes, sizes, abilities, genders and ages. There in the crowd of ecstatic people, the emperor witnessed a Soma he had never seen before, so free and happy as she danced with her friends. A pang of longing overtook him.

Then he peeked at his own derelict body which he hadn't seen in years. He glanced over at his fully clothed advisors who were trying not to look directly at anyone, especially not the emperor. "But," he thought, "they fool no one, pretending not to see us!"

Looking out over the crowd who stood naked with him among the trees, he felt a warmth spread over his body. And his toe began to wiggle in time with the music.

Preface

"If the shoe fits, wear it," people always say—but they never tell you what to do if it doesn't. In my own case, the shoe rarely does fit. I have an inherited disability affecting the neuro-muscular functioning of my extremities and causing deformity in my feet. I tell friends that if they ever hear of a mad bomber of women's shoe stores, it will be me.

When I was in the seventh grade, our family moved to a new small town in Ohio. At the end of the year I found myself in the balcony at the awards assembly. I wore my fancy new yellow shoes (it was the 60's, after all). Though they did not fit well, they certainly weren't the "old lady shoes" I was accustomed to wearing. Unexpectedly, my name was called and I began the journey from my seat over several classmates to the aisle, down the stairs, along the middle aisle, across the front of the auditorium, and up ten steps and to the stage. Everyone waited. Halfway down the middle aisle my left shoe fell off. Time yawned as I retrieved the shoe and jammed it back on; it seemed an eternity before I finally reached the stage, red-faced and unworthy.

This story illustrates some of my history with the mind/body split. Because of my disability, I have spent a large portion of my life trying to forget that I have a body, concentrating on perfecting my mind. If it were not for a few inconveniences like the one described above, I might have been able to get away with it. I even went so far as to get a Masters degree in philosophy, about the most disembodied thing a person can do (short of getting a Ph.D. in philosophy, of course).

But there were a few other realities. Not the smallest of which was that I was a girl; and as a girl I was required to worry about how I looked. Getting good grades meant nothing if I wore the wrong clothes. One bought shoes to fit the image in one's mind of how a girl ought to look, not to fit an actual foot.

For many years, then, my goal was to transcend my body—I would work on my mind instead. I sent the blood in my body to my brain and away from my increasingly blue, cold and rigid feet. I got a lot of support for this strategy. I won awards in school; I was excused from gym;

I moved only to transport my brain from place to place. I did not look in the mirror and I never, never touched my feet unless it was absolutely necessary.

Whether I acknowledged it or not, my body stayed with me. I was off balance, falling on my perpetually skinned knees. Schoolmates did not see my brain—they saw a tottering, awkward person to tease.

I only wanted to be like everyone else. I blamed my body for my problems and it is true that therein lay my difference. People of color who longed to be the same as white kids; girls who wanted to be boys; people with disabilities—all report similar stories of dissociation from their bodies, the source of the difference. We were never advised about what to do if the shoe did not fit; but the message seemed to be that we should change, mold, mutilate and otherwise control our pain as we jammed ourselves into ill-fitting shoes.

What has taken me years to realize is that being deaf to messages from my body, ignoring the signs that I needed to change something, denying the importance of body, did not allow me to transcend it; I simply lost touch with body knowledge. Because I feared falling, I became rigid in my movements. That rigidity itself kept me off balance. I became more rigid. An unending cycle.

As humans we try to downplay our difference because it seems to keep us from being accepted and loved by others. The irony is that when we deny our difference, we cancel out the particularity and uniqueness that forms the basis for love. Our self-esteem suffers because we hide what we see as shameful parts of ourselves.

Each of us has an embodied position from which we see the world. Either we acknowledge this or we continue to delude ourselves into believing that our viewpoint is the universal and somehow better one. Viewpoints are created equal—they are simply the ground on which we stand, our experiences, our bodies. Power determines whose viewpoint is "correct"; it is the one that can be forced on the rest of the world as universally true. The validity of our particularities is denied, creating a barrier to understanding each other and the world.

To get at truth—to get close to anything universal—would take a dialogue among us all. Failing that, our knowledge is flawed. Embodying our viewpoints, claiming, sharing and valuing our uniqueness moves us toward greater understanding. Universalizing, denying difference, claiming sameness of Mind only, relying strictly on Rationality moves us in the direction of ignorance, hatred and delusion.

Approaching equal rights issues with an attitude of "we are all the same under the skin" misses the point entirely since we are always undeniably in our skin; we cannot abstract ourselves from our skin. We must refuse to jam ourselves into a standard that does not fit us and must instead change societal attitudes toward skin and disability and gender and sexual preference and poverty and religion and size and shape and age. The standard viewpoint touted as fitting all fits few, if any.

In Junior High I wrote a poem entitled "If everyone in the world were blind" about a way to get rid of prejudice and bigotry by making us blind to difference. Since then I have come full circle to an imperative that we *must* see each other and ourselves, not as whom we are passing for under the blindness test but who we are in our skins.

This is no easy task. How do we get from where we are, from our almost obsessive fear of difference to where we need to be? We have been taught to fear difference, to avoid it, to suspect it. We do that within as well as outside ourselves. We fear our own difference from the standard. For good reason, we avoid our own desire to break free from the standard—after all, we have been rewarded for our "fit" and punished where we cannot or will not fit.

Most of us discover ways to "pass" for something we are not, ways to appear "standard." We give the standard its power; we give it our power. And we fear people we perceive as different from us and from the standard because they threaten to blow our own cover by calling attention to difference.

The direction our society is taking threatens our survival on this planet. The idea that we can escape our bodies, our particularities, escape pain and death, escape our physical surroundings and support is illusory. We must awaken from this dream, and smell the flowers, hug the trees, hear the birds sing, taste the strawberries. The mind without a body, men without women, rational beings without our habitat are dead. Denying our bodies, freeing ourselves of earthly things, trying to be alike, trying to control everything, does not move us closer to "Truth." Quite the contrary, we just become more at ease with illusion and we settle for less. Our knowledge can be scientific and rational but we still will not have a clue to a real understanding of ourselves or our world.

I wish all we had to do to become whole was to add body, women, and color—add particularity to what we already have. We have left out an ingredient so let us simply add it back. This remedy is not possible, however, since we are not merely missing an ingredient, we are using the wrong recipe. The recipe is for domination and control of mind over body, men over women, white folk over people of color and humans over the earth. It is a recipe for war that we have used repeatedly without learning. We should be ready for new recipes, new tastes, new experiences.

We need to realize that the goal is not the most important thing but rather how we get there. I am talking about a way of living that acknowledges all of the ingredients from the start, and that does not try to bleach the flour or sweeten it beyond recognition but allows for many different goals, many different ingredients. Homogenized food is bland and boring. We may think our food is good because it is familiar, under control and predictable. But does it taste good; do we even bother to taste it anymore? We do not even know where it comes from. And with so few approved ingredients, it can hardly be healthy or delicious. Let us go to the kitchen and begin again.

There is no one way that is true for all times in all places. What we have at hand in the United States are many spices, many ingredients. What we need is a willingness to taste. All of us on this earth are needed in these recipes for life and creativity. No one is expendable.

That, in short, is what this book is about. It is about making our society fit all of us and not making us fit a standard made by one group in power. It is about reclaiming our bodies; reclaiming women; reclaiming the viewpoints of all those on this planet including the animals and the trees; learning to think, act and relate to each other as whole beings; it is about democracy in action, not through denial of difference but through demand for it. Admittedly, it is a lot to bite off and admittedly it is only a beginning.

Introduction

Having lived in the United States all of my life and been immersed in Western philosophy, religion, and culture, I have until recently accepted the belief that reality consists of two different and separable entities called mind and body. Institutionalized in our thinking and culture* is a deep split between what we view as body and what we view as mind. Mind has been seen as the essence of human-ness, that which separates us from the animals and makes us rational. What has been named body has been given a bad reputation in almost every field from religion to science and medicine. Bodies are seen as objects we must try to control and overcome. Our bodies mislead us, our senses trick us and our passions lead us astray. In myriad ways, we have been taught that the body is an obstacle to our well-being and salvation.

With this book I will attempt to move us toward a philosophy of the whole where there is no split between mind and body, where they are recognized as interconnected and inseparable one from the other. This philosophy of the whole reaches far beyond the confines of philosophy into all aspects of our lives and requires changes not only in our thinking and in our institutions but also in our relations to ourselves, to others and to the habitat in which we live.

When I first told my mother about this book, she said, "So you deal with mind and body, but where's the spirit?" I knew the answer then but had not yet written it into the book. My answer is that the spirit is in our

---

* In this book I am going to use the word "culture" to mean the "power-over culture"[1] when I refer to the prevailing views and values in the U.S. I am calling it the power-over culture to reinforce the idea that it is an ideology that covers over other cultures, and also that it is a culture in which hierarchical thinking is the norm. The power-over culture is not limited to white middle class America. In fact, the ideas and cultures of a variety of peoples do influence and change the power-over culture through time, though their contribution is not often acknowledged. Similarly, the hallmarks of the power-over culture—such as our television, advertising, school systems, marketplace, politics, social service agencies, churches, Constitution, workplaces, medicine—are absorbed by people once they have become a part of the United States (either by being born here or by immigration), so that we all become united in mind/body split thinking.

connections. It is between you and me, us and our habitat, our minds and our bodies. So in a sense this book is also about spirituality.

Although I am critical of the direction the field of philosophy has taken, I call what I attempt in this book "philosophy." Philosophy simply means the love of knowledge; and if we broaden what is included in the term "knowledge" beyond what is proven "scientifically" or what the mind "knows," then this book is philosophy. I believe I am practicing a love of knowledge by suggesting a new, more humane and at the same time more realistic way to live in the world.

But why write a philosophy book if the aim is political, social and individual change? The answer I would give is that we need a way to approach the underneath side, the assumptions that sustain our systems of thought. Political scientists write analyses of capitalism and socialism and the abstractions of power; social scientists conduct studies about how humans react to various situations and how we are socialized to behave; psychologists look for answers in the individual psyches of their patients; historians report, as best they can, factual information about what happened in the past, both to individuals and to societies; anthropologists write about cultures which differ from their own and explore other ways of life, their similarities and differences; the so-called hard sciences try to study only what is there, what can be verified and repeated.

However, in each of these fields we find a faulty framework. It is the rose (or is it rust?) colored lens through which we see the world. Until we acknowledge that something is wrong with the framework itself, not just with the theories and analyses we derive from it, we will continue to begin with assumptions that are misleading and wrong. And we will end up with avoidable flaws in the systems we construct.

This project is not undertaken as an academic exercise. Is it academic that even as we speak and write, our lifestyles, our politics, our economics, our science, our religions, our philosophies draw us closer to the annihilation of many of the occupants of planet earth, including our own species? We may think our fields are mind fields but the bodies they affect are real—our own and those of all the other creatures on earth as well as the earth's ecosystems.

Nor is this book a comprehensive critique or survey of all of the various disciplines mentioned above; it does not attempt to look exhaustively at the literature already generated in academia; this task would be gargantuan. Rather, this book examines how ingrained our assumptions are about the mind/body and male/female splits in various disciplines. I present a patchwork quilt of examples from different disciplines precisely because a claim to examine it all would be ludicrous; I am, after all, talking about the history of Western culture since slightly before Plato. It is up to the readers to take this critique and extrapolate from it ways to dismantle and then re-construct the pieces of their own experience into a more fitting whole. I hope to present enough breadth to make that application feasible.

The theory I present is simple; its application and ramifications, however, demand fundamental change. I follow some of those ramifications through various fields, social movements and current issues, giving examples to illustrate the theory's application in everyday life.

Theory and practice, as I see them, cannot be separated. A theory which asserts universality or bodilessness makes no sense in the world of embodied individuals. To speak of "justice" or "truth" and not take into account race and gender (which are associated with body) leads one neither to justice nor truth. Likewise, when a practice is not examined for its fit within the larger picture, practices that are destructive and perilous are endlessly repeated without a way to check them. How many times have you heard, "But we have always done it this way" as a justification for a practice? We need to develop theory that enables us to challenge the ways we have always done things and to find better ways of doing them.

I will talk a lot about the unreality of separating and categorizing the world. Our original separation of mind and body, male and female, rational and emotional, abstract and concrete, led us to believe that we humans were different from and superior to all other forms of beings on this planet. Only by letting go of the need to separate and unnecessarily bifurcate reality can we begin to heal.

For examples I will use my own concrete and embodied experience. Where possible I try not to universalize my statements and abstract from them history, context, perspective and body. I am critiquing the very tendency to universalize, to strip away the particularity of personal experience, to attempt to "purify" knowledge in order to reach the height of Absolute Truth. One of my goals is to expose that kind of "objectivity" as a fallacy. Rather, I recognize that what we call objectivity is simply another viewpoint or perspective located in time, space and power relations. It is the viewpoint that has been given the greatest power because it pawns itself off as universal and therefore "truer" and more "valid" than the knowledge each of us gains from where we stand.

I want to strip the emperor down to expose the pale, startled man trying to project omnipotence, wisdom and bodilessness onto the world.

By understanding this façade as the smoke-and-mirrors trick that it is, we can get on to the business of better understanding our world, each other and ourselves without the self-deception that there is a great emperor who has the answers.

Because we have been taught to think of mind as "I" and body as "it," that is, of mind as subject and body as object, we have the idea that we can and should control and manipulate our bodies to suit the image in our minds. We treat our bodies and our habitat as other than ourselves, apart from us, alien. This kind of thinking is at the root of our individual illnesses, our faulty relationships with others and our troubled political systems. When we think of our habitat and our bodies as objects to be controlled, as machines that have use value but no inherent value, we feel no compunction to listen to them as sources of knowledge and wisdom. Rather we feel justified in enslaving them and making them do "our" (our minds') bidding.

Western philosophy has coined a term to refer to the perceived split between mind and body and that is "the mind/body split." You will find philosophers since the seventeenth century preoccupied with this concept as a puzzle. If mind and body are separate and are made of different substances, then how do they communicate with each other at all? How do we explain their obvious effect on one another? After all, when the mind thinks, "I will move this hand," the hand moves. And a fever will make a person's mind delirious and so on. Yet many philosophers over the centuries have wanted (or needed) to assume a qualitative difference between mind and body.

Mind-only has been claimed by "emperors" in many disciplines over the centuries. One of our tasks in healing the mind/body split is to show where the body of the speaker or writer is lurking in their texts even when such texts claim that there is no body.

How simple to declare in the abstract that we will start giving more attention to the body and not think of mind and body as two separate and unconnected things; however, body cannot merely be added like salt to a soup. The problem is not that there is none but that there is and has always been a body that was deliberately denied and hidden. Furthermore, that body has historically been declared a poison and carries with it a taboo ingrained in all of us.

At the end of the emperor's tale, we can finally see and speak the fact that the emperor has a body and has had one all along. Exposure and honesty are required. To expose the body of the emperor is to make room for the other bodies that must enter the power structure if we are to heal the critical splits of our time. That the emperor continues to get away with his claim of bodilessness, when his sex and gender are hanging out there for anyone who cares to look, is dangerously absurd. We as a society can no longer afford to look the other way to appease him or to save him embarrassment. The mind/body split is maintained by an unwillingness to recognize that to be "mind-only" is impossible.

References to mind and body in the English language lack clarity. To be able to articulate the ideas in this book I have had to take a few liberties with language. For instance, there is no word that means body and mind interconnected and inextricable one from the other. For the purposes of this book I use the term "body-mind" to represent that concept. "Body" is placed first to value what has traditionally been so devalued and the hyphen shows connection (as opposed to the slash, which implies a split with mind valued over body).

When I speak of our body-minds I mean neither just biology separate from culture nor only the way culture has shaped us. It is not possible to discover what is purely biology or purely culture since I believe they are inextricably enmeshed. There is a fact of the matter, i.e., there are the raw materials making up our habitat and our bodies, but we cannot know about them except in the context of our language and culture. Similarly, culture has so much to do with shaping our desires and behaviors that it is impossible to determine what is animal instinct, if you will, and what is simply learned behavior.

Some philosophers (mostly deconstructionists) assert that there is no Earth or Body, that everything is simply a construct of culture. However, I believe that in deconstructing, that is, exposing the myth of "One Truth," we must stop at the point of an acknowledgment of both raw materials (body) and culture (mind), and their inseparable connections. We cannot definitively declare which is which, nor do we need to. Hence the coining of the phrase "body-mind" as a way to speak of both at once.

Additionally, dichotomies such as mind/body require concrete definitions of the terms involved which are mutually exclusive and most often have inherent in them a valuing of one term over the other. The words "body" and "mind" are not useless phrases; but to use them thoughtfully they must be reconceptualized so as to include in "body" the acknowledgment that at least part of it is infused with mind and to include in "mind" the awareness that it is part of body.

Take for instance my disability, which is genetic, meaning that my raw materials ended up different from most other people's. To get much more specific than that, however, is almost impossible. Looking at how

I walk, my balance or the shape of my foot will not identify what came
from biology and what came from the way I relate to my feet and to my
body in general. The development of my feet and my walk are thoroughly mixed up with the way I think and feel about my condition.
What effect, for instance, has my refusal to pay attention to my feet had
on their health and well-being? How much has the fear of being different influenced the shape of my feet, the speed at which the nerve
impulses flow and my balance? The effects of mind and those of body
are not clear-cut and separable.

The term "earth" is also problematic, since it is unclear what is included in its meaning: is it the land, the environment, the animals, the
planet? Instead of "earth," I am going to use the term "habitat"[2] which
means "the region or environment where a plant or animal is normally
found" and "the place where a person or thing normally resides or is
found" (Funk & Wagnalls, *Standard College Dictionary*). The habitat
includes humans and all that is in their surroundings. The use of this
word is an attempt to locate humans in a context that is inseparable
from humans themselves because it is where they are found. Humans
are never found in the abstract, without their habitat.

In exploring the mind/body split I am struck by its parallel with the
dichotomy of male/female. This parallel is hardly accidental but rather
works to keep both body and women in their place in the bottom half of
the dichotomy. Over the centuries, as the mind was increasingly conceived of as separate from and better than body, men were associated
with mind and women with body. Women were seen as being unable to
transcend their bodies because of their menstrual cycles and their role
in reproduction. Body and care of the body were projected onto women
by men so that men could think of themselves as purely mind, as immortal. Death was something men and minds could transcend.

I spoke earlier of the way we tend to think of body as object and
mind as subject; and we identify with the subject as ourselves. As a
society we do this same kind of splitting of men and women from each
other; we put women in the category of object, whereas men are the
assumed subjects, the "I" or "we" named in discourse. We can see this
assumption everywhere in our language, our institutions, and the media.

Take language as an example.[3] The exclusion of women from language has been brought to our attention time and time again in recent
years but seldom is the pervasiveness of this problem addressed. Men as
actors and women as the "other" or object permeates our culture. The
so-called universal "he" pretends to speak for all but can be dismantled

in case after case and shown to be referring to the male of the species and not to the female. "The citizen, he," certainly was not universal when the right to vote came up. That "he" had to be specifically expanded to include women and men other than white, propertied men.

Of course, the male/female split is as delusional as the mind/body split. Certainly there are biological differences between men and women that play a crucial role in the reproduction of our species; however, we are more alike in our biologies than we are different. There is a lot of overlap and similarity between men and women. When the genders are dichotomized, men and women are conceptualized as opposites with their definitions mutually exclusive. There is no connection, no shared ground. It is this forced division between men and women which is dangerous both to women who are stuck in the object category and to men who are also stuck, frozen in the rigid and equally unrealistic definitions of manhood required in the dichotomous mindset.

In theoretical terms this splitting off manifests itself in a denial of the importance of the unique desires arising from the female body. Most of the scientific studies involving sexuality are written from a male point of view, extrapolated to include the female. We will explore what sexuality would look like if imagined from the point of view of women instead of men, or at least from the point of view of men and women equally. We get a glimpse of what a world could be if it included a balance of men's and women's desires.

I will examine the societal and personal implications of a widespread misconception that woman = body = object. Because of the traditional association of women with body, a major source of women's power has perforce resided in the manipulation of their bodies. The goal of this effort is not for women to fulfill their own potentials as subjects, but to become the best object possible that will attract a powerful man through whom a woman can feel powerful herself. But the rest of women's selves— their subjectivity, expression of desires and direct power—is often repressed and controlled. A woman is forced to choose between success as a body only (by being as thin, white, blond and young as she can appear or by becoming a mother object) or success through divorcing herself from her body by giving up her own particular subjectivity and imitating men's attempt to become abstract and bodiless.

For women, identity is defined through object status but for humans (actually for men), identity is defined through being a subject in one's own right. In practical terms the split between men as subject and women as object often manifests itself in what has been labeled mental illness, neurosis or addictions. For instance, for sufferers of eating disorders such as anorexia, all body fat must go; in fact, it would be best if the body itself would disappear.[4]

A phenomenon more common than anorexia is that women are constantly trying to lose weight, thinking that if only they weighed such and such they would be happy. In *The Beauty Myth* (1991) Naomi Wolf stated that in the late 1980's, "thirty-three thousand American women told researchers that they would rather lose ten to fifteen pounds than achieve any other goal" (10). Weight loss rated higher than success in their field, travel, time off, having a meaningful relationship. This preoccupation with weight is a manifestation of something much more profound than losing a few pounds. I will argue that this impulse is directly linked to the mind/body split and to the assignment of object status to both women and body.

The other option for women in forming their identities is to take on the role of mother. The way mother is conceived in this culture falls once again under the auspices of women as object. A mother is a selfless being dedicated to the socialization of her children. This characterization, which leaves no room for woman as subject, mars the face of nurturance and love in the family unit.

At the same time that mothers take on the role of nurturer and connector, we as a society devalue not only connection but women and bodies. Mothers are in the most contradictory of all roles as guardian of the next generation and at the same time, as mindless bodies tending to the "menial" tasks of meeting the physical needs of men's children and men themselves. I do not think it accidental that there is currently an upsurge of writings by, about, in response to, blaming, obsessing on, mothers. Instead of looking to blame or praise mothers, I am more concerned with uncovering the double bind in which mothers and women in general find themselves and which makes it almost impossible to do it "right."

As we narrow down what it is that is missing in our world, namely, the acknowledgment of our connections, we look to the place we felt them first, with our mothers and what went wrong. Either we look back nostalgically to the times when we were in our mothers' wombs or before we were fully separated, or we blame her for our inevitable disconnection from her. The fault lies not with mothers *per se*, but with a society that devalues and dismisses the connections we ought to continue to make and to value after we separate from our mothers. Instead, we as a society encourage autonomy, isolation and independence as end goals.

All of this disconnection cries out for a new whole and connected way of thinking. Though many theorists have railed against dichotomies and pointed out their weaknesses, they have not put forward a workable model to replace them. A critique of one dichotomy is often made with yet another dichotomy. We struggle but do not know how to change the pattern.

I suggest a more accurate, inclusive worldview—the Between model—which reclaims the fluid and fertile space that has been deliberately denied to us in bids for power-over and domination. I propose creative techniques to tear down old structures and build replacements. We become the mirrors for the emperor, the pranksters playing with language, and the weavers of "new clothes" fit for us all.

There are many ways to begin to make a difference in how this society operates. We do not have to wait for a revolution; we do not have to wait for others; we do not have to quit our jobs or make other drastic choices in order to begin the change. In many ways we can begin at once to see and feel ourselves as connected to and in relationship with our habitat (including other animals, the food we eat, other humans, etc.), and our own body-minds.

Larger change, of course, is also necessary to save our lives and the lives of other species in our habitat; however, the personal changes we make are no less important. As we reclaim our own power, we will find it less and less necessary to claim power-over and will find it easier to make those larger changes.

As a woman and as a philosopher I refuse the limitations of the old patterns. I have set out in this book not only to expose the fallacies of dichotomization and the destructive nature of power-over, but also to create ways to heal the wounding splits. We must work toward a society in which we can be free and, in fact, encouraged to choose many lifestyles and ways of being in the world. In the chapters that follow I will show that much of our predicament is "man-made" and as such can be remade. We need an analysis of how we got to this point so that we may begin to move toward change.

I invite you to join with me and others in this shift of consciousness that will make the world a more inhabitable, joyous, loving place in which to live, a place where each of us in all our diversity will feel at home and welcome to express ourselves, listen to each other, to our habitat and to our fellow creatures.

i.

The Cut and Dried of Western Thought

1
Dichotomies:
Never the Twain Shall Meet

"You may have all growth or nothing growth, just as you may have all mechanism or nothing mechanism, all chance or nothing chance, but you must not mix them. Having settled this, you must at once proceed to mix them." (Butler, *Selections from the Note-Books* 149)

What is a Dichotomy and How Does it Work?

The word "dichotomy" means a splitting into two what is in reality a connected whole. The earliest records of dichotomous thinking go back to the 4th Century BC when the Pythagoreans developed a chart of qualities and included the following:

light—dark
good—bad
unity—plurality
male—female

The assumption underlying this chart is that we can divide the world into half and that any given thing must be either on one side or the other. Take as an example a 24-hour period of time. When we dichotomize a 24-hour period, we create two separate entities, day and night. This act of splitting leads us to believe that we have two completely separate qualities in the world called night and day instead of a continuum that has been divided into two. A given time is either day or night—no in between. This categorization discounts and negates the times which are neither day nor night but a little of both. It does not allow for nuance and mixture.

But even more dangerously, dichotomous thinking sets up one side as good and the other side as bad. The Pythagoreans never meant for the table of opposites to be free of value judgment. They conceptualized these opposites with the forces of good on the left side and the forces of evil on the right.

A way of looking at reality, then, is that it is divided into two opposing parts and arranged in a hierarchical manner. If the table of opposites were an artifact of ancient history, we would not have to be concerned about it today. But these divisions have remained in our thinking over time and have become institutionalized in the power-over culture. They make up the foundation of much of our world today.

This kind of thinking has been called either/or or dualistic thinking. Using this mindset, it is possible for the whole world to be divided into either positive or negative characteristics; any quality can be inspected and then put into the positive or negative column. Recently this kind of thinking has been criticized by many philosophers, feminists and deconstructionists especially, for valuing one side over the other without justification, and also for leaving out the middle, the possibilities that are mixed in some way, e.g., not only good or not only bad.

Dichotomization is a strategy for maintaining the status quo of power relations. Generally, those in power when the division is made are able to assign a higher value to their own qualities or to those qualities that will keep them in power. Unlike in our fairy tale, this assignment does not happen in one instant, and the decisions are not made by one person or group; rather, we can trace its evolution over time.

To help visualize dichotomous thinking, please take a look at the images below:

FIGURE 1   FIGURE 2

In this book I am defining what you see in Figure 1 as the way the world exists before we dichotomize it. The color white represents one of the qualities that has been falsely dichotomized and the color black represents that quality's "opposite." In Figure 1 there is a continuum of colors in which qualities are mixed together and joined; there is no one place in which a split can be decisively drawn without doing damage to our description of reality. If we must draw a straight line through the diagram to get only those things that are "purely" one quality, we err on the side of leaving out possibilities that have some of the quality we want. If we think again of the 24-hour cycle, we can see that Figure 1 is a more accurate description than Figure 2. Assigning each time of day as either day or night, for example, does not recognize the times which are a mingling of light and dark.

I have had occasion to do some of my writing in a cabin up in the woods of northern California. There is no electricity there and when I am there, I find myself becoming acutely aware of the slightest change in the light coming in the windows. I have experienced darkness profoundly in that cabin far from the city glow of street lights. And there is a time especially when there is a no moon and when clouds cover the stars when I can say, "Yes, this is night."

But sometimes in the middle of the day the fog rolls in or the clouds cover the sun and it seems more like night. Or I find myself confused by the light at twilight when the light becomes too dim to see what I am writing and yet the mountains and trees outside seem to be sharply illuminated. I do not know whether to consider it day and keep working or give up the day and light the kerosene lamp which brings on the night, eclipsing what is left of the day. My focus shifts outward from my papers until finally I can let go of the light and turn back inward and light the kerosene lamp.

There seems to be an urge for mastery in our assignment of dualities to the world, a desire to impose a precision that we feel is lacking in what we see around us. Twilight, as the name implies, is that light which exists between day and night. We can usually avoid thinking about that amorphous time by simply switching on a light. We then feel as though we are in control of the cycles of time. Unilaterally, we let twilight go by unnoticed as we switch on the light and declare it to be night. The world itself is the same no matter what we do about turning on the light. The twilight is still there with its magic and its mystery, as the light waxes and wanes in mini-cycles. French feminist philosopher and linguist Luce

Irigaray asks, "And why should night and day be so radically divided?" (*Elemental Passions* 34).

Think about another way that we make sure that night does not infiltrate into day—as a culture we leave no time for sharing our dreams and incorporating them into our days. Our dreams are "just dreams," unworthy of being brought with us into the light of the day. We put them aside as if they could have no possible connection to our waking life.

Refer to Figure 2. When we divide reality into two parts, the middle is eliminated and a gaping hole is left where empty space and distance are created. Additionally, the two sides of the dichotomy have moved into a hierarchical relationship with one on top of the other. In our example, where there was a continuous spectrum, darkness moves to the bottom and lightness is put above and distant from darkness.

In fact, the entity on top becomes the valued term and is therefore defined while the one on the bottom becomes its antithesis. It no longer has its own identity. Figure 2 reflects this by showing that all shades but black and white in Figure 1 have been eliminated. White is the valued color in the hierarchy, and black is its opposite. Darkness does not have its own shape, its own definition.

Because white women and all people of color have been historically located on the power-under side of the dichotomy, critiques of dichotomies are frequent in feminist and third world liberationist writings. Obviously, that power-under place puts one in a no-win situation. One's identity is wrapped up in being not-something. And the *something* is the entity that has power. I will explore this issue in detail later in the book.

However, as we will see, no matter which side of the dichotomy one ends up on, one is damaged. Even those in the power-over position are forced to cut off the parts of themselves that do not fit into the positive, top half of the dichotomy. The emperor forced Brazen and Soma out of his life and gave up his relationship with his body; he then felt dissatisfied with his life but did not know why. All of us are confused by what actually goes on in the world since so much of it overflows our categorization and characterization of reality. We are particularly confused because we continue to believe that *all* dichotomies are True, even those that actually distort reality. We struggle to find happiness within that structure, whereas it is the structure itself that is at core false and destructive.

For illustration here, I will use the emperor's fairy tale. Let us say we add this dichotomy to our table of dichotomies: emperor's fancy clothes wearers on the left and all others on the right. This action in itself looks harmless. We have just divided up a whole, all people who wear clothing, into two categories. If the categories were simply used for convenience and were not seen as having any particular power, they might, in fact, be harmless (there are such harmless cases in which qualities are legitimately opposites, e.g., the qualities of acidity and alkalinity).

Let us look now at our empire to see how our division plays out. I will show that the dichotomy is not a neutral tool; that one of the two oppositional qualities becomes the standard by which others are measured; that the elevated term, when associated with certain people, gives those people a superior place in society; and that the dichotomy, when linked with other dichotomies already in place, becomes even more insidious.

The Loaded Dichotomy

When we add terms to the table of dichotomies, we are required to place one of the terms in the positive column and the other in the negative column. In her book *Feminism and Philosophy* (1991), Australian philosopher Moira Gatens states: "The claim here is *not* that dichotomous thought is bad or oppressive *per se*, but rather that it can covertly promote social and political values by presenting a conceptual division as if it were a factual or natural division" (92).

The emperor in our story managed to split himself and people like himself off from the rest of the empire. At the same time he attempted to sever his mind from his body. These splits were not "natural" or arising from a biological or cultural essential reality; rather, they were imposed on the world by an attitude that the emperor adopted to "help" him deal with the world. And he had the power to make that worldview predominant, at least for a while.

Although there are some dichotomies that are neutral, they frequently do not remain so. Even the most innocent looking pairs of opposites when put on the list with the other dichotomies become loaded with value judgments. Take, for example, "up and down" or "right and left" which may seem at first glance to be simply descriptive. Even those pairs of opposites have often been infused with value judgments. "Up" has to do with godliness and "down" with the devil; "up" with happiness, "down" with depression. "Right" and "left" have roots that clearly favor right as "upright, righteous, straight" and associate left with evil (sinister) and weakness. Certainly some of the values are context dependent, for instance, "old and new," or "tall and short" or "big and small." But when value judgments are added to the dichotomies, they can no longer remain a neutral tool used to evaluate the world. Rather, those in power, like the emperor in our example, make the decision about what is best and they choose based on their own values.

If we are relying on dichotomies in our thinking, we should be aware of those divisions and how they affect our conclusions. We may think we are being completely objective in discovering what is "out there" in the world, when instead we are merely imposing our own values on "reality" through the use of dichotomies.

Going back to our story of the emperor, we saw that a value judgment was made about people who wore certain clothes but was not identified as such. Upon closer inspection in our hypothetical empire, we found that only certain people wore clothing like the emperor's. This seemingly innocuous division of the emperor's clothes from all others became insidious when the quality of "fancy dressing" was placed on the dichotomy table, and people who wore fancy clothing became associated with the desirable qualities on the left hand side of the dichotomy table—those of good, light, unity, and male.

Fancy-dressers took on special characteristics that were seen as better than the characteristics held by other members of society. Fancy-dressers were placed in positions of power. Their point of view became the one to which everyone deferred—it was institutionalized in universities, political documents, business and science. After a while the viewpoint of fancy-dressers (which was, of course, simply the viewpoint of those in power), became the universal, objective view. Not-fancy-dressers tried to anticipate how the fancy-dressers would answer questions or come to conclusions.

Not-fancy-dressers also tried to locate clothing that looked fancy. Some saved their money and bought clothes that look as close as possible to those of the emperor. Some managed to save out some cloth after they sent most of it off to the emperor. Still, they had to have bodies that fit the imperial style of clothes or they had to squeeze into them as best they could. The closer one was to passing for emperor class, the more power one was likely to have. Some, when among strangers, were able to pass for fancy-dressers; others could not.

Knowing that the fancy-dressers were superior gave the emperor instant clarity. He did not have to take time to investigate and then come to some kind of understanding or acknowledge more than one point of view. All he needed to do was to identify the fancy-dressers and he found knowledge.

One Term as Standard

As we have seen, when we dichotomize a continuum and value one part over the other, one of the terms of the dichotomy becomes the standard by which the other is defined.

This phenomenon is at times easy to pinpoint simply by looking at the terms used. Think of terms like "non-white." Clearly in that case "white" is the standard. It is a negative definition; what you do *not* have is more important than what you *do* have. In our hypothetical society it is easy to identify the power-over definitions at work since fancy-dressers are the standard. After a while, we no longer see cottons or wools; we see only "not-fancy" clothing.

Sometimes, however, it is not clear just from the terms used that we are dealing with a standard; and we have to look closer to see what is going on. Take, for instance, the male/female split as it applies to sexuality. If we look at Freud's ideas, which are still prevalent in Western thinking, we see that women's sexuality is always defined in relation to men's. For Freud, women were defined primarily by their lack of a penis. It was what women lacked that defined them. Even when he did acknowledge that women had genitals and was willing to discuss them, he did so only as they were in relation to the penis. For instance, he saw the vagina as an envelope for the penis to slip into, or he saw the clitoris as a small penis. In *This Sex Which is Not One* (1977) Luce Irigaray points out that, "All Freud's statements describing female sexuality overlook the fact that the female sex might possibly have its own 'specificity'" (69).

Defining things in this manner is so pervasive in our culture that our language itself reflects it. When we speak of difference, we are almost always assuming a standard from which something else deviates or is "other." Some scholars who are bothered by this terminology have begun using alternative words. (I almost said "different" words!) The word "alternative" more nearly gives equal status to all alternatives. It is that root from which comes the word "*alterity*," a word I will use in place of "difference" or "other."

In her book *Sexual Subversions: Three French Feminists* (1989), Australian philosopher Elizabeth Grosz defines *alterity* to mean: "A form of otherness irreducible to and unable to be modeled on any form of projection of or identification with the subject. The term refers to a notion of the other outside the binary opposition between self and other, an independent and autonomous other with its own qualities and attributes" (xiv). An entity represented by a term has a definition of its own without being defined by its relationship to a standard. This does not mean that we can necessarily define one term as completely independent of the other. But what it does mean is that there are positive qualities which are unique to what we define that are not dependent on the "standard" term. For instance, in the case of clothing, wool has its own unique qualities and is much more than, say, "not-silk." Wool has alterity.

For the French philosopher Luce Irigaray, the concept of alterity can be illustrated by looking at the elements of earth, water, air and fire. We have unique definitions that apply to these four elements, yet they are not completely separate and they are certainly not opposites of one another. We know that air is required for something to burn and that the soil has water and air in it, etc. Each one of these terms has alterity that we have not destroyed by dichotomizing them. For example, we do not try to reduce air to "not water." What if we did the same with the things that we *have* dichotomized, like men and women or mind and body?

Now looking again at Freud's definition of women's sexual difference, we see the effects of assuming a male standard to which the female must be compared. The alterity of the power-under term is damaged by the arrangement and so is anyone who does not fit the standard exactly. When we encounter examples of this standard we should ask ourselves, "What is woman's alterity?" and "What is the alterity of the other individuals not fitting the standard? Who are they when we are not comparing them to anything? Who are they in their own right?"

In speaking of women's sexuality, we might wonder what pleasures, erotic zones and organs women have that are completely and uniquely their own, without a male referent for comparison. And when we see the term "non-white" we must ask about the alterity of the people referred to. What is it that people of color have that whites do not have, and which is uniquely their own? Which particularities are shared among whites, blacks, Latinos, Asians, etc. and which are not? Even that kind of questioning does not go far enough because we have to take into account the particularities of each individual, which of course, will differ from others within the group.

Nonetheless, these kinds of questions get our body-minds out of the assumptions of dichotomous thinking and onto the recognition of alterity, acknowledging both our *similarities* that have been dichotomized and our *alterities* that have been all but obliterated.

You're Either For Me or Against Me

In this section we examine more closely what happens to those things which were in the middle when the qualities they possess are dichotomized. When a whole is dichotomized, the two parts become mutually exclusive but also mutually exhaustive. In our day/night example, the whole 24-hour cycle must be distributed to either the category of day or night. Moreover, there is no time that exceeds the category of night or day; that is, the terms night or day must suffice for all possibilities.

If we are still holding onto the continuum idea, we may be tempted to mix a little day into the night to arrive at, say, twilight. We may be inclined to assert that a moment can be dark and light at the same time. Or that it may be contingent upon whether you are indoors or outdoors. Looking at our table of opposites, we might think that the division is extreme and desire some cross-over. But this is where Western logic steps in and enforces the divisions.

One of Western logic's basic tenets, called the Law of the Excluded Middle, is that something is either A *or* not-A. There can be no overlap, no middle ground. Any nuance that might have escaped complete dichotomization is whacked again to make sure there is absolutely no middle, no connection. It therefore becomes impossible to describe twilight accurately. It cannot be defined as light, but has been put in the camp opposite light and must be defined as not-light. Irigaray states, "What poses problems in reality turns out to be justified by a logic that has already ordered reality as such. Nothing escapes the circularity of this law" (*This Sex* 88).

I recently encountered a neighbor who used this kind of logic. She was upset about certain kinds of noise in the neighborhood and was gathering signatures on a petition to demand that noisy neighbors leave the neighborhood. In asking me to sign it, she said, "If you are a good neighbor, you will sign this and if you don't, you are a bad neighbor and are against me." I said I thought there was room for middle ground and would be happy to support her efforts to deal with the situation short of asking the neighbors to leave; but I did not think the situation was such that they had to move in order to resolve the problem. She could not hear me and continued to see it in either/or terms only.

Since we have been trained to see the world as A and not-A, we are predisposed to using this formula for analyzing many situations and for accepting the validity of the results. However, intuitively, we often have a hard time thinking this way and resist relying on it exclusively in our dealings in the world; it seems to leave out so much of our experiences as body-minds. The structure of logic, at least this particular law, can be seen as benign, as rational without value judgments. Maybe it is, as long as we are dealing with abstractions, with A's and not-A's. However, when it is applied to the real world—and that means also to language—logic is used to make sure the dichotomies remain untouched and the power stays in the thing represented by the term in the left hand column of the table.

Also, when the process of dichotomization is employed in a political and social context, the consequences go far beyond simple inaccuracy; dichotomization becomes a tool of oppression. Take for example how we divide up the world, the continuum of skin colors, into "black" and "white" races. One cannot be both black and white even if one's parents were black and white. One must be either black *or* white. The "one drop" rule existed to make sure that the line demarcating white from black was enforced. Conveniently, during times of slavery and widespread rape of black women by white slaveholders, it was possible to create more slaves by using the "one drop of black blood" rule.

This dichotomy is codified by the Law of the Excluded Middle. Anyone crossing it is liable to be injured, locked up, or imprisoned. This oppressive thinking is inescapable when we accept dichotomization of the contents of the world, and the Law of the Excluded Middle as the form in which it appears. That combination creates a trap which reinforces power-over.

Where ethnicities such as Latinos or Asians fit into this schema is unclear. They may be lumped into a "people of color" category which shares the fact of oppression but not a common history. The differences among the people so categorized are then minimalized and perhaps trivialized, despite the fact that they are very real. This monolithic treatment ignores the alterity of individuals in the groups, giving rise to impediments and tensions among people of dissimilar ethnicity.

"White" and "non-white" categorization thus does violence to the complicated combinations of human relationships. The Law of the Excluded Middle may be a useful tool when it is applied to entities which are indeed separable and opposite; however, if its form is applied to people and skin color, we can see how the combination of false dichotomization and the Law of the Excluded Middle mandates that the power structure remain in its current configuration.

It is the whole process of dichotomization that we must deconstruct. If we simply give better treatment to not-fancy-dressers, we miss the essential structural problem. With dichotomization, the not-fancy-dressers will always be lesser than the standard. We can institute affirmative action; we can require that the emperor judge based not on clothing but on the basis of how well the job is done. But if, in the end, we still hold onto the dichotomization along with its false divisions, its standardization of one side and its mutually exclusive and exhaustive nature, we have not begun to solve the root problem. Rules we make will be ignored or sidestepped and members of the dominant class will always feel as though favors are being given out unfairly to the side that has been devalued. Meanwhile those who have been devalued feel as oppressed as ever and find that these "Band-Aid" approaches—while helpful on one level—leave them still outside, still less than those who fit the standard. The problem lies in using the model of sides at all. The dichotomy itself must be dismantled.

The Domino Effect: Linking of Dichotomies

Whichever side of the dichotomy table a term is on, it becomes linked with other dichotomized terms that are on the same side, and is automatically thought of as the opposite of all the terms on the other side. At this point, hundreds of years after the table was initiated, the columns of opposites are quite long. And each time a new quality is added, that quality is now in very good or very bad company and lots of it.

For instance, political philosophers such as the Frenchman Jean-Jacques Rousseau, writing in the 18th century, divided the world into public and private spheres. The private sphere involved what happened at home and the public involved what happened out in the world of business and politics. This public/private dichotomy became linked in Rousseau's philosophy with the dichotomy of culture/nature, so that he could assert that the private sphere was more natural than the public sphere, which was created by "men." Those same splits, in turn, became linked with the male/female split. Then, without philosophical support other than that of the assumed dichotomies, it seemed logical that women should be "naturally" confined to the private sphere, i.e. the home.[5] In *Feminism and Philosophy* Moira Gatens in analyzing Rousseau states, "By privatizing familial concerns and making them the special province of women, Rousseau leaves men free to move between the private world— where 'natural' relations between the sexes and between fathers and children are conducted—and the public world of culture, citizenship and politico-ethical relations with other men. These two self-contained spheres allow him to split his own, possibly inconsistent, needs and desires into two domains" (95).

This thinking—like all thinking that relies on mind-only—has no bearing on what is factual or natural. For instance, there is nothing in the logical construct of the above example which can possibly establish that a hierarchical family structure with a man at the top is "natural." It is a product of culture and laws that, for instance, humans are required to be monogamous and that fathers lay claim to children even though mothers do the work of raising children and taking care of the emotional and bodily needs of men. It is not possible to separate culture from nature in any simple way; thus, when this distinction is used as an organizing tool in philosophy, it is suspect. Often the linkage of dichotomies, with its substitution of concept for fact, masks a rationalization for the continued power and privilege of a particular group.

Let us take the mind/body split as an example. Earlier I stated that this dichotomy links up with the male/female dichotomy. I will spend several chapters looking at this phenomenon. For our purposes here I will say simply that this association of mind/body and male/female is detrimental to every one of the four terms involved. Body and women are on the bottom of the dichotomy and are devalued and seen as less than male and mind. However, mind and men also suffer. When mind is seen as male, it cannot draw on its female elements for balance; instead it must remain purified of the female and of the body. When the male is seen as mind alone, his body is neglected and denied a legitimate place in his existence and in the pursuit of knowledge.

Despite evidence to the contrary, the underlying assumption in the dichotomous world view is that mind and body are opposites and one is better than the other. Mind has historically been associated with men and body with women. Since we know that men have bodies and women have minds, we can see that the construction of such dichotomies leads us to conclusions that will never accurately describe reality.

Thus, not only are the gradations within a particular continuum destroyed; the associations and assumptions between dichotomies reinforce already faulty data. When people are divided into the categories of men and women, it also seems that they are divided into active/passive, dominant/submissive, willful/obedient, rational/emotive, etc. The two groups, men and women, then become opposites on a whole range of traits that have nothing to do with having different genitalia.

Think for a moment about the arena of sexual attraction. Here we can identify a situation in which dichotomization of men and women has caused people whose desires do not fit into a dichotomized view of the world to become the targets of violence. Since men and women are considered to be opposites and there are no men who are women or women who are men, women in our dichotomized world should be sexually attracted to men and only to men and vice versa. The area of nuance, of a woman's attraction to another woman, or a man's to a man, or a man's attraction to women without many of the traits usually associated in this society with women, and the myriad of other possible combinations that have appeared throughout history, is unexplainable. We do not have the words to describe these different attractions because we have destroyed the continuum of our experience by continually jamming everything into two opposing camps.

Our ignorance causes many to conclude that homosexuality is deviant. However, what is actually a deviation from reality is the false absolute categorization of "men" and "women" that we have relied on for centuries. We see that there exists in reality a whole range of attractions among a whole range of different people who cannot readily be divided into two distinct categories. This simply affirms that such categories are false and that relationships between people exist on a continuum which is more fluid than rigid.

We have to remember that men and women are much more than gender. When we view people simply as men or women we tend to lose the broader classification of human and begin concentrating on differences that reduce these entities to mere parts of themselves. We see a linking of dichotomies from two sets of genitalia to two sets of desires, two sets of attractions, two sets of behaviors, two sets of qualities, two sets of norms. And we must keep in mind that the two sets are not equal in nature; rather, one set is the standard and the other is defined as the absence or lack of that standard.

Our language encourages this splitting up of people by its demand that we make two camps, the "he" and the "she," before we can even refer to a person whose name we do not know. If we are not sure of the sex we traditionally use the male pronoun. Many assumptions go along with our assignment of the pronoun. The use of "he" is by no means gender neutral. We imagine a male subject since it is not possible for us to image a person of no gender. The "he" as subject and the "her" as object is the placement we are most comfortable with. "He" often refers to things that act of themselves, such as an animal (the squirrel, he), and "she" when referring to things acted upon, such as "fill her up" at the gas station, or to refer to ships or cars or other owned objects. I'll give one example from the newspaper, though readers are encouraged to find other examples that occur daily in newspapers and magazines. In 1972, the *New York Times Magazine* quoted psychoanalyst Erich Fromm as describing "man's vital interests" as "life, food, access to females, etc." (February 27, 1972). The subject is "man" and is assumed to be male and the list of "ownable" objects includes females.

It is more than coincidence that our language works this way. These dichotomies are deeply entrenched in our thinking. Because this linkage of one dichotomy to another exists throughout philosophy, we find such assumptions going unchallenged, allowing the dichotomy to "solve" the problems of complexity in the world.

How could the hierarchy be maintained if we could not tell what category to place a person in? Power relations begin to shift when we reveal ambiguity. I will address the issue of power relations in the next section.

Dichotomies and Power-Over: The Chicken and the Egg

A number of authors have commented recently on the drive in the over-culture to attain a particular kind of power, a power that could be called *power-over*. I am thinking in particular of the work of Starhawk, Riane Eisler and Evelyn Fox Keller. Starhawk uses the distinction between power-over and *immanent* power. Immanent power is our own personal power to understand ourselves and the world and has nothing to do with dominating others or exploiting the resources of the world. Power-over, on the other hand, is that power which dominates and controls others and the habitat. Power-over involves the repression of some part of ourselves or our society so that another part can dominate.

Power-over is precisely what our society is run on: power-over our habitat and power-over other people. The hierarchies we set up in families, business, politics, schools, government, sports, etc., are examples of the prevalence of power-over. To get ahead, we learn that we must step on others. To be the boss, to have money, to possess material things— these are our goals. Our superiority over someone or something else must be constantly demonstrated and maintained.

The range of power-over goes beyond dominating others. There is also a major power struggle occurring internally, the power-over of mind versus body. We align ourselves with mind and attempt to exert control over our bodies. The body is, according to this point of view, malleable, and takes its direction from the mind. We are taught to "control" our bodies from our weight to our sexual desires to the shape of our various body parts. In my own case, the messages I received when growing up were that I had to keep my feet in line or else. My mind was supposed to be able to make my disability go away by insisting on careful control of those feet—for example, I had to concentrate on pointing my toes out so that I did not trip. It was really my mind's failure when these things did not work—I did not concentrate hard enough or constantly enough.

Without separation, that is, without dichotomous thinking, we could not choose a power-over mode of behavior. If we saw ourselves as part of a whole, connected to others in essential ways, then the power attained by the suppression or oppression of others would be seen as self-destructive rather than expedient and efficient. If we believe ourselves to be disconnected, however, we can continue the illusion that we act upon others without affecting ourselves, without thought of how our actions might injure ourselves through our injuries to others.

Refer back to the two diagrams on page 14. It is no wonder that we are confused about what is in our best interests when our picture of the world looks like Figure 2 but the real world looks like Figure 1. Of course, we can see in Figure 1 that if the whole represents you and me, I can never act with disregard toward you because an essential part of myself is part of you and I cannot unhook that. But the paradigm depicted in Figure 2 creates the illusion that, I can, in fact, disregard you, my environment, my body, other individuals, other races and other genders as if they were not a part of me. The result is that our behavior belies reality and we are encouraged to act in destructive ways.

Our relationship with food is a good example of an area where we disregard connections. What would eating look like in a connected world? We could not just go into McDonald's and order up a hamburger without knowing the answers to some questions such as: "Where did the animal who was killed for this meat come from? How many trees were cut down to make a place for that animal to graze? How much water and land was used to grow food for that animal? What was the quality of that animal's life? What did the animal eat and were there any chemicals added to its diet to make it resist infections or get fat quicker? How much are the workers in the restaurant paid and do they have benefits? Where is the money I spend at this chain restaurant going when it leaves my community, as it certainly will? Do I have the right to kill a sentient being and eat its flesh?"

We do not have to ask questions like that if we do not believe we are connected to our habitat, to the other animals here, even to the other

humans here. Our pretended separation allows us to continue to operate in total disregard for others. But what most of us do not realize is
that whether those questions are asked or not, our interest lies in asking
them and in living in a way that respects others. We are in reality connected to them and as they go, so go we, both literally and figuratively. If
we eat the hamburger, the effects of not asking the questions or looking
at the whole are taken into our bodies. And where our bodies go, so go
our minds. We are linked together until death.

Because of the shackles of the English language, there is no straightforward way of distinguishing between others and ourselves without
dichotomizing the relation. We need a word to mean "different yet a
part of." The term "alterity" can perhaps help again. Remember that
alterity means that something has a definition of its own, without dependence on a standard. It is a positive definition, determined not by
what is lacking but rather by the assertion of the particular essence of
something. For instance, if we recognize that habitat has an alterity which
includes humans but which also originates from outside of humans and
in which humans are only one of many parts, we might be able to better
understand our role in our habitat.

If that tree outside my window did not rely on my definition of it to
be a tree, then I might not feel as free to cut it down on a whim. I would
need a way to develop some reciprocity, some appreciation of its experience of life. I do not mean that I would never cut a tree down, but that I
would never do so without careful consideration of the consequences,
such as resulting erosion, depletion of oxygen and the elimination of
habitats for diverse members of our ecosystem. These consequences must
be examined not only from my point of view, but as much as possible
from the point of view of the tree and its co-habitants. That, of course,
may sound farfetched to some readers. But it would not seem outrageous if instead of cutting ourselves off from every other creature and
thing in our habitat, we had found ways to communicate with the non-
verbal entities around us. One does not have to be a mystic to believe
that something one does not know about or understand is going on with
the trees, the rocks and the mountains. I do not have to be able to define
it; it has alterity and if I listen openly and with respect, it will let me
know what that is.

To retrace our steps a bit, then, power-over is fostered by dividing
the world into dichotomies where in reality an interactive continuum
exists. This division is not only false but also hierarchical, in that it

values and defines that which is represented by one term of the dichotomy over the other. When power-over is then added to the split, the distortion of reality is multiplied. When the power is lodged in the entity represented by the upper term, we lose the alterity of both the powerless entity and the powerful entity, which is altered and forced into rigidly ill-fitting behaviors.

With respect to the male/female dichotomy, we find every human affected. If the female part of the dichotomy is devalued and treated as the "other" of the male, all those people who are born female are affected adversely. In the power-over scheme, they are the powerless. Their alterity is not intact because they must fit into a world built for men and based on the desires of men.

Girls are taught to be "feminine"; yet when they exhibit these so-called feminine traits, they supply additional rationale for their oppression. Boys, on the other hand, are taught to repress those parts of themselves that are considered feminine. Instead, they learn to be aggressive, ego-centric, unfeeling, competitive, independent, and active. And boys are taught that they are the ones in power, on top. Their needs and desires must be recognized and catered to so long as they follow the rules about who men are.

This splitting up into "masculine" and "feminine" is so harmful because these traits are actually on a continuum and are not located strictly in men or women but are in both men and women. In order to "fit," we all have to deny many of our qualities. But, of course, none of these artificial splits tells the whole story. Since we are each in actuality made up of traits that cross boundaries between masculine and feminine, those traits sometimes assert themselves in spite of our training and in spite of the "privileges" we have been assigned. Some of us are thoroughly unable or unwilling to pretend to fit.

What power-over does to all of the players in the mind/body, male/female split—women, men, mind, body—is to eliminate immanent power in all four of those elements. We are forced to seek ways to dominate parts of ourselves, others and our habitat so that we can feel some semblance of power. But that is exactly what we find, a *semblance* of power. We seek to force everyone to agree on one point of view, be it through religion, philosophy, politics, or science. But what happens to our own voice, our own authentic point of view that comes from our biology, our heritage and our experiences? These differences become something to be transcended in order to fit into the point of view of the emperor. We spend our lives trying to figure out how to think and dress more like the emperor. Meanwhile, our own alterity is sacrificed to the blade of power-over.

The power-over mode works by breaking connections, and like splitting atoms, it gives us power. But when power is found by severing connections instead of through the connections themselves, we find ourselves splitting up the world: people are split from each other and bodies are split from minds, humans are split from their habitat. The power-over model has us in a stranglehold. It splits us through our well of being—our centers—where mind and body, men and women, Us and Them are stirred together. When we deny those connected parts of ourselves, we can find no state of wholeness. No one wins; no one is happy.

Power-over as a source of power is a chain reaction, like nuclear fission. The splitting cannot merely happen once but must occur over and over until we do not even realize we are doing it, until we can no longer experience something as whole. Rather, our presumed starting point is located after the split, as if the split were in our nature.

This split is neither in our nature nor a reflection of reality. We need illustrations of how deeply power-over thinking has permeated our lives so that we can devise modes of behavior that are more in line with reality. In the next chapters I will look specifically at how the mind/body split combined with power-over thinking has affected us in many areas of our lives including philosophy, religion, science, medicine, economics and politics. I will illustrate some of the sources and ramifications of this thinking, though of necessity these chapters are not meant to be exhaustive. I seek to give the reader a feeling of how pervasive dichotomized thinking is in our institutions and ideologies.

2

The Emperor is a White Man
and We Know 'Cuz He's Naked

How does the mind/body split insinuate itself into our thinking? We can thank the emperor for this. By the emperor I mean those in power in our culture, politics and/or economics. (Keep in mind that although the vast majority of emperors in western culture have been and still are white males, not all white men are emperors. Still, being either the same gender and/or the same race as the emperor gives one certain advantages, privileges, and power-over those of the other gender and/or other races.) The emperor pretends to mouth the universal point of view, that of mind only. He thinks his ideas have no body; for instance, the philosophies he writes are mind only and no bodies need apply; the religions he creates are man-centered and god has no race or sex because "he" (the universal "he") has no body; the history he writes is supposed to be the way it really happened, just the facts, ma'am; the laws he writes are supposed to apply to everyone no matter what race or gender.

The emperor glorifies an ideal, the mind free of body. Perhaps he calls that ideal the soul or knowledge but the goal is to purify mind of body, men of women, and deal only with abstractions such as justice, truth, freedom, God. What he associates with body, with particularity, he considers bad and divisive and he tries to transcend—such things as diversity, mortality, love, emotion, change, sex, and, of course, women.

But all the while, as the emperor walks around pretending he has no body, we know different. We can see his sex and his race hanging out all over the place because he is naked but also, for women, because they birthed him, fed him, sexed him, cleaned him up, gave him emotional support, dressed him and raised his children.

The result of trying to disembody our world and our ideas is that our knowledge, our understanding, can be neither true nor universal. Objective truth is an oxymoron—objective means uninfluenced by emotion (read body) and truth means an accurate picture of reality. If objectivity expressly leaves out part of reality (i.e. body—emotions, gender and color), how will we ever get an accurate picture of reality? If our philosophies, religions, sciences, economic systems, politics, histories, etc. rest on this kind of falsehood while they claim truth, how can it be possible to reach an accurate understanding of our world such that we can live in harmony with it and each other rather than destroying it and each other?

The following sections explore these questions in various disciplines showing how the mind/body split, the emperor, has ruled historically and continues to rule today.

Philosophy and Religion

Throughout history, Western philosophers and religious thinkers have blamed the senses, and thus the body, for error and sin. They sought ways to rise above the ordinary day-to-day world and to reach for the unchanging solidity of eternal truth. Humans seem to yearn for answers that once discovered will be true forever. It is easy to understand an attraction to a world with fixed rules, where universals and Truths exist if only we are disciplined enough to search them out.

Philosophers have often fallen prey to this desire for eternal truth and their advice to others has often been that they become as dissociated from their fallible mortal bodies as possible while they still live within them. For centuries many philosophers, priests and scientists have spent their lifetimes developing methods for getting outside and above the body and its mortality and cycles.

One effective technique for transcending the body (at least for men), has been to project body onto women. Women are separated out as different in kind from men, and then undesirable parts of men, namely things associated with the body, are attributed to women. Men's needs for clothing, food, reproduction, nurturance, and aesthetically pleasing surroundings have been chores delegated to the women, freeing the men to pursue "higher" (read mind) goals. It was believed that by assigning the chores connected with the body to women, men could dissociate themselves from death and the life cycle.

In order to purge themselves of mortality and change, philosophers found ways to purge men of women. Robin May Schott in her book *Cognition and Eros: A Critique of the Kantian Paradigm* (1988) stated, "By conversion to the way of truth, the philosophical soul can escape the mortal fate of being born of woman" (41). Women, after all, are the ones who bring this mortal body onto this earth and therefore can be condemned as complicit in the crime of entrapping the souls of men. Women have been blamed for human mortality as if by giving birth, women also cause the inevitability of death.

We can see some of the origins of this thinking in the philosophy of Plato. For Plato the senses were not to be trusted to reveal knowledge of anything Real. Our senses could tell us only of the world of appearances, the changing, aging world of mortal bodies. He wanted something fixed and unchanging, something universal; he devised a world "outside" the visible world to give him that eternal and unchanging solidity. For him there existed a real world of Forms which though not accessible through our senses could be intuited through the rational mind purified of body. In that unchanging world of forms, there is no such thing as death, or birth for that matter; everything stays the same in perfection.

When our souls were born through woman into a body, Plato felt that our universal and unchanging souls became contaminated; after we were thus defiled, we were doomed to spend our lives trying to purify ourselves again.

In certain writings of Plato (as in the *Phaedo*), an extreme suspicion of the body is evident. Plato stated, "While we live, we shall be closest to knowledge if we refrain as much as possible from association with the body or join with it more than we must, if we are not infected by its nature but purify ourselves from it until the god himself frees us" (*Phaedo*, 15). The thrust of this argument is that the seeker of knowledge should free the mind from influences and deceptions put in its way by the body mostly to distract it from true knowledge. Plato thought that the body should be controlled by the rational mind lest the passions and appetites rule, resulting in anarchy and the failure to attain knowledge.

True knowledge for Plato was knowledge of "universals," the essence of things as they existed in the unchanging perfect world of the Forms. Plato's push is toward "universals," toward the discovery of the One Truth that is free of particulars, free of the body. In keeping with that idea, in The Republic Plato hypothesizes an ideal state in which women and men alike could become philosopher kings, the highest possible occupation. What is required of a philosopher king is a transcendence of and control over the body by the mind. Since the mind has no sex, Plato would say that both men and women could be philosopher kings.

Some have actually called Plato the first feminist philosopher for that seemingly egalitarian statement. However, while his idea that the mind has no sex may sound good in theory, in reality—in our habitat on planet earth—women and men have no way of ever leaving their bodies behind and becoming mind-only. In setting up a hypothetical republic here on earth, Plato merely paid lip service to the bodies of even the most valuable philosopher kings. Plato talks about such things as food, housing and reproduction. And because he does, he is forced to have a body in mind when he theorizes; the body he falls back on is always the male body.

The impossibility of existing as mind-only becomes particularly apparent when one reads The Republic from the point of view of a woman. If we assume that a particular philosopher king is a woman and then read each section, universality quickly crumbles. In Book 5 Plato speaks of women being held in common and mated with a partner who deserves a special reward because of bravery or whose genes must be continued. Are we then to picture women as well as men getting these same rewards? It is almost as if the women who are to be philosophers or guardians must literally be *without* bodies; because to think of them *with* bodies would mean that at least some men would have to be held in common for the women or else women would be given other women to mate with for reward in battle, an idea which is almost certainly not what Plato had in mind.

Though he emphasizes the importance to the philosopher kings of exercise, which both men and women would be required to do, he still does not deal with differences inherent in the female body. As long as the female body is the same as the male body and can perform the universal exercises, the body can be dealt with like a machine, a necessary adjunct to the universal mind. However, he makes no provisions for the possibilities that women philosopher "kings" might get pregnant, menstruate or lactate. The association of such things with his heroes, the philosopher kings, makes one blush for Plato. Difference or particularity cannot fit into his Republic; women can be philosopher kings only if they exist in the abstract, as minds-only or with bodies that act exactly the same as men's.

We can see from the problems that Plato runs into on this issue that though he thinks he is talking about universals, when the ideas are envisioned in scenario form, it is apparent that the whole model is based on a male body and not a universal body or on no body at all. He, like so many of us doing philosophy, universalizes from his own perspective, his own point of view and his own body.

Western philosophers beginning with Plato seek a place of immortality as far from women and from bodies as possible. The advice they give is that while we are still in our bodies, in this world, we must attempt to free ourselves from the body's influences until we are freed from it by death. Death is the only way we can be totally purified and the only way we can approach understanding "universal" truths. But since there is no such thing as a universal Mind devoid of body, what we notice throughout the history of philosophy is instead a universalization of the standard body of white male intellectualism and privilege.

By not directly addressing the problem of Plato's mind/body, male/female split, our philosophical foundations are weakened and fundamentally flawed. Philosophers do not recognize that to generalize from Plato's theories by describing "universals" as if they applied to all humans compounds the fallacies inherent in them.

Though Plato himself was not considered to have been particularly religious, his thought was taken up in some of the Christian theology that appeared in later centuries. Because of the close connection during the medieval and modern periods of the church and the university, it is important that we look at what some of the religious thinkers during these periods were writing.

I will look first at the writings of St. Augustine, who was born in 354 AD and greatly influenced the course of Christianity. Augustine considered the body to be suspect because it was a center of pleasure; for the good of the spirit, the body must be controlled by the will. In his work it is primarily the woman's body that is incapable of reflecting the superior element of the soul. Women's bodies go through menstruation and pregnancy and no matter how much will women assert, they cannot control their bodies. Augustine thought that a woman could be loved for her rationality but not her physicality. Feminist theologian Rosemary Radford Ruether in her piece called "Misogynism and Virginal Feminism in the Fathers of the Church," printed in a collection of essays entitled *Religion and Sexism* (1974), quoted St. Augustine as saying, "A good Christian is found in one and the same woman to love the creature of God whom he desires to be transformed and renewed, but to hate in her the corruptible and moral conjugal connection, sexual intercourse and all that pertains to her as wife" (Ruether 161). Augustine used women's bodies against them in support of his sexual hierarchy in which men must control both their own pursuit of pleasure and women who are the sources of their physical and spiritual temptation. Bodies, and in particular women's bodies, were mandated to be controlled by the will.

St. Augustine also linked death and sexuality. He felt that God's punishment for original sin and fall from grace was to put out of men's reach the control of their bodies' sexuality and death. He argued that other parts of the human body such as muscles and mouth and lungs can be controlled by the will and if man had not sinned, he could control his sexuality and mortality in the same way. Philosopher Robin May Schott states it this way: "Instead, his loss of control over his body, manifest in sexual desire and death, is man's punishment for his disobedience to God" (47). As the object of man's desire and as the perpetuator of birth and therefore death, women, in St. Augustine's view, are guilty by association with body. As the representatives of physicality, women must be kept subordinate to men, much as the passions of the body had to be subordinated to the will.

Writing in the 13th century, Thomas Aquinas adopted an approach toward the body that was more rationalized and scientific. Instead of looking to the will to control the passions, Aquinas expected reason to play that role. In his *Supplement to the Summa Theologica*, Aquinas stated, "Now there is a loss of reason incidental to the union of man and woman, both because the reason is carried away entirely on account of the vehemence of the pleasure, so that it is unable to understand anything at the same time..." (question 49, article 1). The passions were not bad in and of themselves if they were directed at something that reason chose as appropriate to pursue. But men must keep rational control over their desires. Philosopher Schott explains it this way; "Moreover, by positing the mastery of reason over the passions, as a necessary condition for knowledge, and by sustaining the ascetic view that women are less capable of rationality than men, Aquinas implicitly endorses the hierarchical relations between the sexes as a precondition for the flourishing of reason" (Schott 71). Reason was set off in opposition to the body and to women. To Aquinas, the only purpose of the creation of women was to reproduce the species, a purely biological role.

Around the same time in history, scientists were beginning to define man as distinguished from animals precisely because of his ability to reason—notice the so-called universal "man" and "he" here. One has to wonder if women were really meant to be included in that universal being that philosophers spoke of and to, or were women in reality thought to be closer to the animal realm? In the thinking of Aquinas, at least, the dichotomy between men and women is severe, with women rating somewhere between animals and men in the hierarchy.

The Reformation overturned the belief that chastity should be required to achieve true spirituality; however, instead of simply freeing the priests from their chastity, the Protestants encouraged all people to control their sexuality within strict confines. There was an admission that the body was necessary to the maintenance of the species but procreation was relegated to the lowest aspect of human life. Schott states, "Women are denigrated because they are identified exclusively with their function in sustaining the existence of the flesh, which is a subordinate aspect of human life" (Schott 79). The body could not be ignored, however, but had to be cured somehow of the diseases that it harbored. The body was not seen as a source of sensual pleasure but rather as an evil to be overcome and controlled.

A new science of the body was developed at the peak of ascetic Protestantism. This scientific interest in the body could be seen as a secularized version of the religious causes of purity and salvation of the soul. The religious view was that the body was a site of corruption and therefore required strict religious regulations to keep it in line. For science, also, the body was seen as an object that tended toward impurity and corruption and required science to treat it and cure it of its ills.

Writing in the 17th century, Rene Descartes had the precarious job of trying to reconcile religious and scientific thought. He thought he could separate the two realms so that one did not interfere with the other. In that way science could progress without constant interference from the Church and the Church would have its own realm. Central to Descartes' thinking was that mind and body were two separate substances. The body was a source of suspicion while the mind was considered to be more knowable and, in fact, the source of certain knowledge. Descartes stated in his Sixth Meditation regarding perceptions of things located outside of us, "For knowledge of the truth about such things belongs to the mind alone, not to the combination of mind and body" (Descartes 57). We could know bodies only through the use of the mind, and with the help of mathematics and geometry. What did not fit into those disciplines, such as the data we receive through our senses, could be neither trusted as objective nor known with the same kind of reliability as quantitative data.

Where Plato tried, though often unsuccessfully, to include the body in his scheme, Descartes succeeded in his analysis to split the body off into another realm completely. Descartes began his Meditations from a place of isolation from other people and from his senses. As a starting point for his philosophy, Descartes secluded himself in a room by a fireplace, closed his eyes and looked into his Mind. What he came up with as a foundation for philosophy, then, was the *cogito*: "I think, therefore I am." He felt he could conceive of mind without body; the only thing he could not conceive of was thinking without mind. Descartes could doubt everything except his mind. He had his starting point for philosophy: if one thought, then one existed—the mind was the necessary and sufficient condition to qualify as existence.

Because for so long we have assumed that mind and thinking were superior to body and feeling, we might acquiesce to the notion that "to think" could somehow be separated from "to feel"; and not only separated but conceived of as the essential characteristic of existence. Many a philosophy student has felt the "truth" of those ideas. Intuitively the ideas seem true, but then one could argue that intuitions rely on our comfort with dichotomies in general. Of course we are comfortable with the mind/body split—all of our institutions including language assume it.

However, if we were to conceptualize thinking and feeling, mind and body as an integrated whole, it would be absurd to say, "I think; therefore I am." How about "I smell the coffee burning, therefore I am?" Or questions like "How could I be thinking unless I had been born onto this earth through woman's body and had a physical brain to think with?" or "How could I be speaking or writing this language without being part of a community in which language arose?" These are questions which were not considered by Descartes but which would surely arise if we did not split ourselves from others and from our bodies. His attempt to build a philosophy free of any assumptions fails immediately, resting as it does on a series of assumptions about himself and hence about women, body and community.

Descartes practiced the art of reduction—everything, even living things could be reduced to the sum of their parts. The mind plus the body equaled a human. Each of those parts could be separately analyzed and then added together to understand the working of the whole. He used dichotomous thinking based on a model like that of Figure 2 in Chapter 1. According to that model, where mind and body are separated by a gap, there should be no reason why one could not be studied in separation from the other. In studying the body aspect of the human being, Descartes used the analogy to the human body of a machine which could be taken apart and studied piece by piece to figure out how it worked. Noted physicist Fritjof Capra writes in *The Turning Point* (1983), "Clockmaking in particular had achieved a high degree of perfection by Descartes' time, and the clock was thus a privileged model for other automatic machines. Descartes compared animals to a 'clock… composed…of wheels and springs,' and he extended this comparison to the human body: 'I consider the human body as a machine…My thought…compares a sick man and an ill-made clock with my idea of a healthy man and a well-made clock'" (62).

Further reducing the human body to that which was mathematical, Descartes distrusted sensory data and feelings as secondary sources. If it could not be laid out mathematically or geometrically, it was not reliable information. Descartes' distrust of the body itself as a primary source of wisdom and knowledge became an issue that had far-reaching ethical implications for science. With the removal of emotions such as anger, passion and love from the objective physical world, the objects of science—bodies—became simply amalgams of moving particles that could be explained mathematically but which could never be a source of intellectual or moral authority. Somatics professor and author Don Hanlon Johnson in his book *Body* (1983) discusses how those qualities which could not be quantified were placed in the arena of the subjective, private self and were not part of knowledge shareable among community members. Those "values" were alienated from knowledge and from importance in community (23).

In analyzing the material world, Descartes wanted to rely on qualities that could be measured. For instance, in studying an ear of corn, Descartes would deal mainly with the size and shape of the corn. Such things as texture, taste, or smell were not considered to be objective and were thereby deemed unreliable and ultimately unknowable. Similarly, in analyzing the body, Descartes relied on quantitative, measurable parts as if the body were a simple machine. One problem with applying the machine analogy is the assumption of a power-over mode in which the body simply does what it is told to do by the machine-maker or the mind. The body does not initiate action but only responds to directions issued to it. Ruth Berman, a noted philosopher of science stated, "Natural processes are abstracted, distanced from nature, made perfect, and converted into immutable laws. The *particular* characteristics and dynamics of each individual situation are blurred, lost in statistical summations" (*Gender/Body/Knowledge*, 240). Applying the machine analogy to body tends to simplify its workings and make them reducible to predictable causes and effects. It also assumes a sameness generalizable from one body to the next as if we were all made from uniform parts ordered from the factory.

The philosophy of Descartes represented a big step in the development of science and of the movement of humans away from feeling totally governed by mysterious forces. It is a shame that philosophers who followed Descartes, instead of noticing the fallacies that existed in his philosophy, relied more and more on those very theories that perpetuate the mind/body split.

I do not have the space or time here to explore all of the philosophers who followed Plato and Descartes. Suffice it to say that much of Western philosophy that follows Descartes continues to assume the split; we see it in the writings of the positivists, the existentialists and the deconstructionists. Even though philosophers disagree with one another regarding how much of the world we can know through our senses, knowledge is defined as something that happens exclusively in the mind. The fields of cognitive science and philosophy of mind use artificial intelligence and computer science as their primary models for study, which are, of course, inherently bodiless.

In addition, the split between men and women in philosophical thought has been almost completely ignored until the recent advent of feminist philosophy.

Religious thought, like philosophical thought, has evolved and changed over the centuries. Though many religions have come a long way from the early days of the Reformation in regard to integrating the body into beliefs, we can still see a fundamental split that many religions rest upon—that split between the body and the soul, with the soul occupying the dominant position in the dichotomy.

Many religions encourage us to strive for control of our bodies and our passions by our minds and our souls and often urge us to hope for true happiness only after our bodies have died. Many people believe that bodies are impure and unclean and should be viewed as a necessary evil that we must live with while we are on this earth. In certain religions, sexuality is not seen as a source of pleasure but rather as a tool of reproduction to be used for that purpose only. Sexuality and the embodiment of it (women) must be kept under control at all times lest man sin against God.

As long as the mind/body split remains intact in religious institutions, women's status cannot be on a par with that of men. Although there are movements within some churches to place women into positions of power, dichotomies continue to be central to much theology. In most of the religions practiced in the power-over culture the centrality of a transcendent God, the father, is claimed. There is no place of honor and status for either body or women in this scheme. These are things which must be overcome or left behind. As long as divinity and power rest only within the male domain, through the worship of God the father, women will remain representatives of body to be saved only by transcending their bodies and their femaleness to identify with a "bodiless" male deity. The mind/body, male/female split is not then healed but rather assumed and reinforced at the base of most Judeo-Christian religions.

Science and Medicine

In the field of science, the goal has traditionally been to achieve objectivity, repeatability and verifiability. The tool developed to reach that goal was a particular dichotomy, the subject/object dichotomy. A subject (the scientist) examines and tries to understand an object—one which can then be predicted and controlled. Refer to the dichotomy model (Figure 2 on page 14). The scientist sees him/herself represented in the top part of the figure while the object of study is in the bottom half. It is thought that if scientists remove themselves from the object of study and simply observe and document, they will discover what really exists in the external world.

The roots of this thinking—that the object can be separated from the subject—go back to the time of Descartes and the beginnings of modern science. Fritjof Capra stated that the notion that nature was different from "us" and was, in fact, a machine, a clock which we could control and dominate for our own purposes, became increasingly important around the time of Descartes (60-61). When we see a separation of us and them, we should recognize that a dichotomy is at work.

In her book *Reflections on Gender and Science* (1985), Evelyn Fox Keller makes a critique of modern science for its male bias, for the assumptions about "man's" relationship to nature, for the distance created between scientist and object of study and for the push to dominate in our habitat. The dichotomy, the separation, is used to justify and encourage the exertion of power-over. Keep in mind that even in science the dichotomy is a false, imposed one, while in the real world subjects and objects exist as described in Figure 1. We have a scientific method that documents what is taking place in the severed, down side of the dichotomy, the object side, and we learn nothing about our connections, about the part that is both subject and object at the same time. This is a built-in limitation of the use of this kind of science.

Experiments can be controlled only in an environment that has been severely and artificially "contained." The pre-condition to "good" science is the use of the scientific method and the creation of distance and power-over between the subject and the object in the name of objectivity. Experiments take place in the arena of a dichotomy that is artificially cut away and boundaried. The scientist artificially sets those boundaries so that s/he can get a clear and solid answer with no ambiguity.

Before the scientific method was firmly entrenched, when healers, particularly women, tried to work with the body-mind to prevent illness or to utilize age-old methods of treating illness, they were branded as unscientific, and, during certain periods in history, accused of being witches, tortured and killed.[6] I do not advocate eliminating the scientific method but I do urge us to find ways to understand the rest of the world, the part that we have conveniently left out in order to do "science."

Part of the notion of objectivity is the idea that humans can successfully observe their objects of study without adding any value judgments or becoming emotionally involved. For instance, the scientists at Los Alamos, New Mexico who worked on developing and manufacturing the atomic bomb were encouraged to put aside reservations their body-minds may have had about what their study could lead to. Instead they devoted themselves to a "higher" calling, Science itself. The split of the scientists from their own values and their own emotions and particularities enabled them to create a bomb that killed or maimed millions of people.

When we think we are promoting the study of Science, we often find ourselves actually promoting a certain kind of science which serves certain embodied interests that are not mentioned at the risk of sullying the "pure" study of science. While the case of the atomic bomb is an extreme one, I would argue that the day-to-day practice of science is adversely affected by the mind/body split in many more mundane ways as well. Our choices of what to study, the projects that are given grant money, the framework in which scientists work, are all affected by that split.

The practice of traditional science limits itself to the areas to which splitting and power-over lend themselves. Advanced technologies, weapons production, certain kinds of surgical techniques and medicines, pest control, farming methods, hunting and livestock production, flood control, transportation systems, etc. lend themselves to power-over techniques developed by scientists. Thomas Berry writes, "...human cunning has mastered the deep mysteries of the earth at a level far beyond the capacities of earlier peoples. We can break the mountains apart; we can drain the rivers and flood the valleys. We can turn the most luxuriant forests into throwaway paper products. We can tear apart the great grass cover of the western plains and pour toxic chemicals into the soil and pesticides onto the fields until the soil is dead and blows away in the wind" (*The Dream of the Earth* 7). We have practically perfected that kind of knowledge and technology.

Because this society emphasizes power-over rather than cooperation with the whole, we limit ourselves and our "solutions." For instance, technologies such as wind and solar power have often been overlooked as ways to meet our energy needs while we sink big money into nuclear power. If our priority were to work with our habitat instead of exercising power-over it, we would be less inclined to opt for high technology solutions that can be and are controlled by those with money. "Free" enterprise will always opt for developing the technologies that can be controlled by humans and sold to other humans.

In Northern California where I have spent time working on this book, some people produce electricity for their homes from the creek running through the land. They built and maintain the system themselves. But because there is little money in it for anyone, there are few relatively maintenance-free systems available for small users. If people are not mechanically inclined or if they have no access to alternative forms of power, they become captives of the monopolies that provide electrical service from large, often nuclear, power plants. Those power plants use the most dichotomous thinking yet—that of splitting atoms and in the process creating extremely toxic and long-lived waste products. A different system built on the tenets of Figure 1 would encourage rather than discourage ways of working with our habitat that rely on cooperation and not power-over.

Some branches of science, like physics, have come up against the impossibility of an absolute mind/body split, and of absolute objectivity. Werner Heisenberg, a physicist, discovered that impossibility in doing experiments with quantum theory. He coined the phrase, "the uncertainty principle," to explain his discovery that if an observer measures the position of a sub-atomic particle, the momentum of the particle will be altered by the act of observation; and if the momentum is measured, the position will likewise be altered. The act of measurement by an "observer" changes what is going on subatomically and makes certainty impossible. The subject and the object are not separate but are affecting each other even as the experiment is in motion.

Bertrand Russell described this paradox as the set of all sets which do not contain themselves, and thus does not contain itself, so cannot contain all sets.[7] There is no way to get outside of what we are studying. There is no point of absolute objectivity.

We must come to terms then with the idea that we cannot stand outside the world to measure it; we are a part of it and therefore influence its measurements. This idea becomes more difficult to grasp when we leave the field of subatomics and enter the macro level, but the same problems exist. For instance, in studies of the body, aberrant data that is unexplainable is simply thrown out and the remainder—however incomplete—provides the desired uniformity which enables the formulation of a law or principle.

When the conventional ways of doing scientific research are applied to the human body, more direct effects of the mind/body split are evident—first in the approach and then in the result. Following Descartes, the notion that body could be controlled scientifically like any other object in the world became an unquestioned assumption in much of science. In her book *The Death of Nature* (1980) Carolyn Merchant explains that the body was thought to be composed of inert particles moved by external forces rather than forces inherent in it (193). We, as humans, with our rationality could manipulate and control these inert objects just as we control the machines we create to do our bidding.

The split between mind and body made humans vulnerable to all sorts of problems. Since we became more and more removed from our own bodies, we had increasingly less intimate knowledge of them; we began to look to experts to fill that created void. These experts supposedly knew about the sorts of objects our bodies were and could deal with them professionally. They worked to find ways to break the body down into its parts, find out how it worked and then intervene to "cure" problems. Medicine, which had previously been the purview of midwives and other healers who aided people in understanding their own bodies, became the domain of scientists and doctors who had exclusive control of that knowledge.

An emphasis on control and "cure" has forced doctors to look at the body only where it behaves predictably, instead of acknowledging differences between bodies and complexities within bodies. By splitting the body from the mind, doctors and scientists treat the body as an object undeserving of respect, patience and care. They treat it as "other" than us and attempt to cure it.

Take, for instance, pregnancy. Before doctors inserted themselves into the process, pregnancy was considered a natural phenomenon, a part of the miracle of life. Women's body-minds knew what to do. A pregnant woman needed only some assistance in understanding what was happening to her and how better to work with and be aware of her own body.

The imposed medical model treats pregnancy as an illness that is to be cured by giving birth. The thrust of medical procedures is to maintain power-over the body of the woman so that her condition can be remedied. In this model, pregnancy is not about cooperating with the body but it is about controlling it. It is not about a woman understanding her own body but about the doctor predicting and controlling what happens to the body of the patient and her baby. The doctor works primarily on the body as object, and actually, works with an isolated part of the woman's body, the enlarged womb.

When I think of what medical science does by dwelling only on the controllable parts of our bodies, I am reminded of a Sufi story. A neighbor of Nazrudin loses a coin and comes to Nazrudin for help in finding it. Nazrudin begins looking for the coin over by a lantern and the neighbor asks him why he looks there, since the coin was lost over in a darker area. Nazrudin replies that he is looking under the lantern because the light is better there. Sometimes in order to find what we are looking for, we must move out of the well-lit, predictable area into arenas in which we are less sure of ourselves and where our methods are not foolproof. Just because the results are clearer and repeatable there in the well-lit area does not mean we have exhausted our search.

When Western medicine treats the body without the mind we see the other side of the coin from the universality we discussed earlier; instead of all minds being seen as essentially the same without the particularity of the body, here we see all bodies treated the same without reference to their own particularity, as they are being lived at the moment. All we need to do is diagnose the disease and we can look it up in a book or on a computer to see how to treat it. Often doctors do not bother to find out how this particular illness may be different in this body-mind than it was in the last one they treated. That would require time and interest—getting to know the person, not just the disease.

In my own case, as I mentioned earlier, my feet are oddly shaped because certain nerves function properly and the muscles they serve are strong; other nerves do not function well and the muscles they serves are weak. The unequal pulls on the bones of the feet by the muscles caused my feet to take a unique shape early in my life, a high arch and curved toes. I have gone the route of consulting Western doctors for this disorder. The consensus among podiatrists and orthopedic surgeons is that I should have surgery to break bones and cut muscles and, in short, rearrange my feet so that they are shaped like everyone else's feet. The surgery could do nothing for the cause of the problem, that is, for the weak nerves or muscles, but would "cure" the side-effects of the nerve damage—the shape of my feet. In fact, cutting my feet would probably do further damage to the already diminished nerves and would render some of the muscles useless. Though cosmetically my feet would look more "normal" after the operation, the presenting problem of weak muscles and diminished nerve functioning would be exacerbated. The surgeons I visited did not investigate other ways of improving my condition; in fact, what they identified as my "condition" was not what I identified as my "condition."

It was as if the surgeons felt they could simply take the feet off, fix them, and then put them back on and I would be cured. Since the problem is neuro-muscular and not originally skeletal, I had grave doubts that breaking bones and cutting muscles would "cure" me. I have, after much searching, found medical doctors who are more inclined to work with the body (instead of against it); they themselves work closely with physical therapists and people who make orthodic devices which support the weak muscles while allowing others to stretch to their maximum. I am much more comfortable with stretching and support than with breaking and cutting, and I think in the long run these methods will be more effective.

I must admit that it is not always the doctors who are at fault in urging unnecessary surgery to solve problems. Some doctors try to convince patients to follow a plan that is primarily in their own hands and often patients have dropped the ball. Most of us are trained to go to the doctor to fix what is wrong (that is, if we can afford it); we have a great resistance to doing the things necessary to help ourselves. With a method like surgery, we can remain passive while the doctor controls the outcome.

Another example of that kind of thinking is in the area of the use and abuse of antibiotics. Patients often come to see doctors already knowing that what they need is an antibiotic. As authors Schmidt, Smith and Sehnert state in Beyond Antibiotics (1993), over-prescription of antibiotics in this country has led to a myriad of side-effects, such as the recent emergence of drug-resistant strains of tuberculosis. Yet patients may insist that *something* be done. "These patients often place significant demands on their doctors to prescribe. They will often go elsewhere if the doctor does not comply with their wishes" (Schmidt et al 44). It is not just doctors, then, who need to be educated about body-minds and about prevention and healing, but all of us. We are all to some extent complicit in perpetuating a seemingly endless cycle of illness and "cures" rather than prevention and healing.

In addition to reducing humans to a part of themselves, i.e. the foot or the stomach, often medicine does its work on what can be thought of as the inert and quantifiable body. Quantity of life replaces quality of life as the goal of medicine. What is important is what can be measured, such as the number of years lived or white blood cell counts, etc. The ill person's feelings and values are not necessarily acknowledged or given weight but are often secondary to the medical goal of keeping the body alive. Medicine and rationality (mind) impose their will on the body of the patient.

Family and friends of ill people, too, are encouraged to base their hope on keeping the body alive. When I was a court investigator, I inter-acted with people who had or were about to have conservators appointed to take care of their affairs. I remember a case in which a young woman had been shot by a stray bullet and though her body was alive with the help of machines, she was brain-dead and had been for ten years at the time I first saw her. Her mother could not let go of her, could not face the fact that her body-mind was already dead but insisted that as long as the body was alive so was her daughter. When the daughter got pneu-monia, a way for the body to escape and die, the mother insisted that she be treated aggressively to cure her of the illness and keep her alive. There was no forum for discussion with the mother about the fact that the body-mind of her daughter had been effectively dead for some time. She may still be "living" in that state as I write this book.

When we encourage the split of mind from body, and concentrate on "curing" the body, we enable ourselves to ignore the difficult but necessary discussions about what life is. We forget that an ill person is still a body-mind and we go into gear treating a body without thought of the mind.

The lesson learned by those around a person artificially kept alive is often not compassion but a deadening of what it means to be human. Our legitimate feelings that a loved one is already dead are discounted because the object of traditional medicine, the body, can still be legally defined to be alive. The separation of mind and body is so thoroughly ingrained in Western medicine that concerns about quality of life do not have official standing but must be informally or surreptitiously broached by a health care provider, family member or friend.

The life/death dichotomy is at work here. Because we split these two parts of a whole, we cannot understand the relationship of life and death. We keep quiet about death while we are healthy as if by not speaking about it we avoid its inevitability. When a person becomes ill, we are often inclined to hand over the decision-making to doctors who, as we discussed earlier, often treat the body as inert and unconnected to a particular person living a particular life. Doctors have no specialized knowledge about their patient's life or how they would want to die. We would delegate such important decisions at no other time in our lives. We would not have a midwife decide if we should have a baby or a lawyer that we need a divorce. But when it comes to illness of the body, we leave decisions to technicians who are experts on bodies but not experts on our particular body-minds, our lives, or our deaths.

The discussion of quality of life is a long way from occurring in the halls of hospitals. Of course, an interesting battle that is being fought there now is between two forms of power-over, money and keeping the body alive. Since these two goals often conflict now that medical costs are so exorbitant, we can see what strategies will be resorted to. All of a sudden quality of life is brought up as an issue when the real question is, "Who is going to pay for this?" The question is asked, "Do you really want your aunt so and so to suffer needlessly?" as if that were suddenly a prime concern of medicine.

When the mind and body are dichotomized, boundaries can be drawn around each so that we can treat "just body" and we can believe we are acting out of "just mind," out of objectivity. Science devoid of the ac-knowledgment of its own subjective position lures us into thinking that it is objective; medicine's body, devoid of mind, lures us into thinking that the goal of medicine is the treatment of bodies devoid of mind and of habitat.

A huge area that is missed because of the perceived split of humans from their habitat is the link between environmental decay and disease. So often an individual cure is sought when the treatment called for should not be on person A, B, C, D, etc. but on the habitat itself and on stopping the dumping of toxins into the air and water. But because we do not look for long term connections, but for quick and easily measurable explana-tions in our search for cures, we fail to take the appropriate steps to keep ourselves healthy. This issue will be discussed in detail in Chapter 12.

In the next section we shall look at some economic and socio-political effects of top-down dichotomization.

Economic and Socio-Political Systems

In this section I will look at how the mind/body split plays out in components of the monopoly capitalism of the late 20th century and at evidence of the split in our political systems.

One of the crucial tools that keeps the economic system functioning is the public school system. Sociologist Harry Braverman writing in 1974 stated, "The minimum requirements for 'functioning' in a modern urban environment—both as workers and as consumers—are imparted to children in an institutional setting rather than in the family or the community. At the same time, what the child must learn is no longer adaptation to the slow round of seasonal labor in an immediately natural environment, but rather adaptation to a speedy and intricate social machinery which is not adjusted to social humanity in general, let alone to the individual, but dictates the rounds of production, consumption, survival, and amusement" (*Labor and Monopoly Capital* 287). A large part of what children "learn" in school has less to do with content and more to do with learning the routines they will later be asked to perform as adults.

From the time we were children most of us were forced to sit at identical desks and complete our work sitting in the same positions. We got into trouble if we left our seats or wiggled too much. The needs, desires and particularities of the body are expendable for the cause of the greater good, improvement of the mind. We are trained to cut ourselves off from our bodily experience.

Don Johnson, a well-known writer in the field of somatics stated in his book *Body* (1983), "Educational theorists such as Rudolf Steiner, Maria Montessori, and John Dewey have argued for decades that a sound education must be grounded in the development of a child's sensibilities through bodily expression and the arts.... Despite these numerous voices calling for reform, schools have changed little in their policies toward the bodies of students (Preschools, some private schools and alternative schools are the exception)" (190). As a child I could go along with that systematic exclusion of the body from school programs. I was happy to ignore my body as much as possible and do the things I was good at like math and history. Once in the third grade I had a perfect attendance record—never absent. But I got the flu and refused to pay attention to my illness until my body took over and I threw up in the middle of the class and had to have my mother come and take me home. Sometimes the messages the body sends have to be unmistakable to overcome our lack of attentiveness to it.

Another side of cutting off from the body in schools is that we do not place importance on what our bodies have to teach us or what we can teach our bodies. Two categories of study having to do with the body get short shrift under budget cuts: 1) subjects whose content includes learning about the body, like health, nutrition, gymnastics and sex education; and 2) the courses that have to do with non-verbal, often non-linear expressions of feelings that originate in the body and can not be analyzed in the same way as math or science—subjects such as dance, art and music. The subjects in both of these categories are thought of as adjuncts, or indulgences, not necessary for the education of the mind or the body politic. Gymnastics has often been used as a way to wear out the body so that students can concentrate on their "serious" studies.

A common tendency even when gymnastics is taught is to once again treat bodies as machines. If only mind were in control and told body what to do, the person would excel and win. Those who cannot excel at these competition-based activities often experience trauma and exclusion. All bodies are not the same, not simply because one person is motivated while another is not; there are genuine differences in abilities. In my schools the choice for me was either to attend gym and suffer total humiliation or get a doctor's excuse not to go. I chose the latter as soon as I could get a doctor to agree to write an excuse, because I could not tolerate the humiliation. The excused-from-gym route, while it relieved me greatly, was not at all helpful in my development as a person. I simply became more adept at separating from my body and less able to feel integrated.

It would be far superior to teach gym teachers how to deal with differing abilities. Competitive models are not the answer, sometimes not even if they proclaim that people compete only with themselves. I can do that, too, but what I am often doing is forcing my body to do something my mind requires of it and if it fails, once again my body is despised. Is it not possible to teach a body-mind to learn the limits of one's abilities and to find ways to make those limits acceptable both to oneself and to others? If gym teachers were creative in finding ways to accomplish this goal, gym could be an excellent opportunity to teach students to relate positively to students who are differently-abled than themselves. Instead we end up teaching that it is all right to divide into camps of "we" and "they" and legitimize discrimination.

To some school officials, having only the mind attend classes would be preferable to having the body and mind come together. In fact, future trends may have children remaining at home and learning via the computer, and schools will not have to deal with the bodies of children at all. Now, body is dealt with as a necessary evil, as something to be tightly controlled so as not to distract the student. What happens, however, is that the body is not easily repressed and tends to express itself in ways that get the student into trouble. Unless students can learn to control and repress their bodies, they find it difficult to succeed in school.

We have all heard the adage that a student who comes to school with an empty stomach cannot learn. Even with the use of computers, there is no way to successfully send only our minds to school. And that is good. When we deal with the inseparability of mind and body, we are forced to look at poverty, class, race, ethnicity and gender. Mind-only study gives us an out, a way to, under the guise of the universal mind, conveniently forget about very real inequities in our systems of education, economics and politics. Our bodies have needs we cannot ignore. Our schools should be a place to explore connection and integration so that we can learn skills for living healthy lives.

A better approach, of course, would be if there were not "mind" studies and "body" studies but rather a recognition of the necessary connections between them. A more interdisciplinary approach would encourage, for instance, while learning the history of a particular area (please, not just Europe and the United States), the students could also explore the culture of that time period: sports, dances, music; the kind of medicine that was practiced; people's relationship to their habitat and what they ate; and their family and community structures. What were the experiences and expressions of people at that time in history? What was it like to live as a body-mind then?

Now think about the way workers' bodies were treated beginning with the Industrial Revolution, and we can once again see the invasion of the mind/body split into our thinking and institutions. With the introduction of the factory and mechanization, workers' bodies and their labor became just one more commodity to be bought and sold by factory owners. Decisions were based not on an individual's needs but on how much work could be squeezed out to increase profits. Managers (mind) decided how often a worker on the assembly line could take a break or go to the bathroom; workers were treated as machines and all bodies were expected to be the same.

Workers could sell or rent their bodies to an employer. The body was seen as a passive machine which took orders and could be controlled and standardized like any other machine. If workers did not fit those contrived standards—for instance, if they had health problems or idiosyncrasies like being too short or too tall, or if they had any special needs at all—they could be fired and replaced by others who did fit. Injuries on the job did not alert owners to the need to change the factory but were often blamed on the workers themselves, who did not live up to the standards.

These ideas have not died, especially in non-union workplaces. When I worked as a cook at a summer camp not too many years ago, I was not as fast at chopping onions as some of the other workers. Even though I put in the extra hours it took to get the work done (without extra pay), I was not asked to return the next summer. The faster and more efficient workers were asked to return. I had done the work but I did not meet the standards. In a system where people are treated not as body-minds but as machines, there is no tolerance for differences in abilities.

Ideal workers have someone else to take care of their bodies and their family needs because the workers cannot get time off for such things. In fact, the closer to robot a worker can be, without bodily needs or family relationships, the better. If there are bodily needs or relationships, they are expected to be subservient to the needs of the workplace. For example, although single women receiving public assistance are now being required to work outside the home, the law looks at single mothers as if they had no children and therefore makes no provision for child care.

Additionally, feelings of any kind: anger at speed-ups, concern for other workers or for the environment, alienation from the decision-making or product, or feelings of exploitation do not belong to an image of the ideal worker (machine) who is there to serve the owners of capital.

The standard varies from job to job, but it hurts everyone including white males because it allows no room for variation, no room for bodily differences. And bodies *are* different and their performance fluctuates from day to day. Workers are forced to exert power-over their bodies and then to expand that to power-over other people. They jockey for positions above those who can not adjust as well to the structure of the workplace.

Our bodies are forced to conform to standards of nine to five work, of shoes that are uncomfortable, ties that choke us, seats that are bad for our backs, and schedules that do not allow for our individual differences. Illustrations of how these standards make people's lives miserable abound. One that comes to mind is my friend who has worked at the same job for the past 15 years and who is now in her mid-fifties. She is having problems with her back and is not able to walk as much as she once could. Her job includes some responsibilities that are in the office and some that are out in the field. If responsibilities were shifted a bit among the workers, she could conceivably be allowed to work only in the office. But there is no mechanism for treating anyone differently so that even though a feasible plan could be developed to meet her needs, it is not likely to happen.

One requirement for success in this system is to rise above and sever our connections with others. This individualism pushed by our society pits one worker against the other. Don Johnson writes, "Instead of capitalizing on the harmonious aspects of biological reality, our social forms are built on, and enhance, our deepest fears. We are habituated by those forms to think of each other as separate egos, pitted against each other in a struggle for food, land, friends, wealth and sex. Fragmentations permeate our entire society, enhancing divisions among races, classes, neighborhoods, and professions" (178). We form a hierarchy based on how well our bodies fit the standard and then we deny that a standard exists.

We need to recognize the differences in bodies, in abilities and in responses to environmental factors. To expect each body to work at the same speed, to run the same number of laps, to start work at the same time, to be the same each day of the year, to be constantly under control, is to ask for a societal sickness that is even harder to diagnose than individual illness. The closer we can come to the standard body the "better" we are and the more we "succeed." But the more we ignore and betray our own bodies, the less able we are to live whole, healthy lives, and is not that what true success is all about?

Success continues to be tied to how much money we can make and in a very real way can mean the difference between surviving and not surviving. Consider how wages are determined in our economic system. We utilize a so-called "universal" pay scale that is supposed to be based on a neutral tool, the market. This scale ostensibly has nothing to do with particular bodies but rather with competency. What we find, however, is that one's position on the pay scale is very much determined by the kind of body one has, whether it is male or female, white or of color.

1996 Bureau of Labor statistics show the median weekly earnings for full time and salary workers by race and gender. In 1995, the median weekly salary for white men was $565; for white women $415; for black men $411; for black women $355; for Hispanic men $350; and for

Hispanic women $305 (U.S. Department of Commerce 426, chart 663).
If we average those numbers together in groups of men, women, white,
black and Hispanic, we come up with the following:

White	$490
Men	$442
Black	$383
Women	$358
Hispanic	$328

It is not a personal failure on the part of women and men of color
that they are not able to make the highest wages or garner top positions;
rather, a closer look at the so-called objective, value-free pay schedule,
reveals an unwritten code—that a white male body is almost always
necessary to climb to the highest rungs of success. Thus, the problem is
not what we originally thought, that the "universal" standard is being
applied unfairly, but rather, that the standard is not universal at all but is
a white male standard which, no matter how it is applied, will always
favor white males.

Women and men of color have been led to believe that they could fit
this standard if only they worked hard enough. They bought into the
idea that a standard was all right so long as it was applied fairly; after all,
they wanted to believe that they could do it just as well as a white male.
What is that elusive "it?" The best "non-standards" can do is to try to
transcend their own bodies, their own particularities and their connections with others and strive to be more like the "It," the white male
standard. Of course, not even all white males can meet this standard
because it is an idealized norm that does not allow for individual differences. The enabling factor in the continuance of that norm is that we
accept the mind/body split and believe that mind-only is acceptable and
even possible.

The effects of the societal denial of connections and of bodies are
everywhere we look. As we find that power-over and demand for conformity control the workplace, we also see that attitude reflected in our
streets. Hate crimes are on the rise. Those who deviate from the white,
middle class heterosexual male norm are fair game to have it pointed
out and used against them. Our whole economic system is built on it—
how can we claim that we discourage it? Laws and censorship are limited in what they can accomplish when the actual societal messages
we give people daily in how we socialize them contradicts any laws or
codes of ethics we may create. We must look beyond the mere words

about equality and see the reality and the practice, not just in the laws but in our institutions, our language, and our imaginations.

The consumer side of capitalism is also served by the mind/body split. We buy clothes, accessories, cosmetics, hairstyles, simply to fit the "image." We divorce ourselves from our own tastes and comfort and our sense of what our bodies need. The mind tells the body that it must look good and conform to the standards of our society and so we put on high heels and ties. The mind separate from the body is prone to accepting all kinds of masochistic practices. Without the body as a source of wisdom and a check and balance against the mind, we can cram ourselves into all kinds of shapes simply to appear as we wish ourselves to appear.

Particularly for women, this control of the body is mandatory. Since women are strongly associated with the body and judged by how they look, it becomes their duty to make their bodies fit an ideal standard. Of course, models who sell women's clothes do not look like 99 percent of women in the country. The image of a 12 year old anorectic model wearing adult clothing aimed at adult women sells only because it appeals to an image in the mind, put there by advertising. It has little to do with the actual shape or needs of the body. I will go into much more detail about this issue in Chapter 6, entitled "Shamed if She Does, Shamed if She Doesn't."

For capitalism and the creation of ever more "needs," the mind/body split is a great boon. For the satisfaction of actual needs, it has far-reaching and negative side-effects. The manufacture and sale of unnecessary products wastes our natural resources, creates waste products, often toxic, that must be dealt with, and requires painful testing on animals. A mind-only without the grounding of a body will accept ever more ridiculous styles and requirements with the excuse that these things are necessary for acceptance and success.

If fur coats are "in" this season, I do not have to wonder how that fur got to the store, what animals were killed to make it, or even if I am going to sweat like crazy in it. I can buy the coat thinking only of the impression I will make on others, how it will set me ahead of so many others who cannot afford to buy such a coat. Minds-only, people severed from their habitat, competing people separate from each other—all of these play into the hands of a system that wants us to buy more things.

Our bodies' actual needs are not reflected in the economic system in this country either from the point of view of the laborer or the consumer.

Next I will turn to the political system for evidence of the mind/body split at work. Looking at the U. S. Constitution and the Bill of Rights, we can see that the emphasis is on rights of minds split from bodies and not on protection of bodies at all. We find a belief in freedom of speech, freedom of assembly and the freedom to own property and the like, but when we talk of freedom from hunger, from homelessness, from the cold, we are no longer in an arena of guarantees at all. Those body concerns are not deemed important enough to be protected in the Constitution.

In fact, the only rights that were given originally were to citizens who fit the standard body type: white, male and propertied. How would this kind of division have been possible without a strong mind/body dichotomy? With such a split it was possible to speak of freedom of speech and assembly and the other mind rights guaranteed in the founding documents. But from the start there is an implicit (and sometimes explicit) exclusion of certain people who could be cast as body and not mind, i.e., black men, all women and those without property. Thus, the "universal" term "all men" or the pronoun "he" could be used in those documents without being problematic. The "he" referred to white men of a certain class.

To include body in the Constitution would, in essence, have meant including particularity. Jean-Jacques Rousseau, whose ideas were used as a basis for the U.S. Constitution, was vehement about excluding concrete particularity. In his writings, the foundation for the elimination of particularity was the dichotomy between public and private. The private sphere was basically the family, where he granted that people could be differentiated and unique and could have feelings toward one another. The private sphere was considered to be a "natural" state ruled by "natural" laws that predated civil society. The public or civil sphere, on the other hand, required conventions or agreements to put aside certain particular interests to work for an ordered political life. The public sphere had to be devoid of the concrete particularities and emotions that thrived in the private sphere. Political philosopher Carole Pateman states, "In civil life individuals transcend, or leave behind, the particular and ascribed characteristics which distinguish them in the private sphere and appear as unrelated equals. They enter the sphere of individualism— which is also universalism—as bearer of rights (liberties), as owners of property and as citizens" (*The Disorder of Women* 20). In the public sphere the mind is split from particularity and therefore from the body and emotion and from every other citizen.

That public/private split (which as we saw earlier has been inextricably linked to the male/female split) brings with it problems that are reflected in the power-over culture. In entering the public sphere, we

are told to leave behind our particular interests and make our only interest that of universality and justice. As Moira Gatens says, "The metaphor of the body politic has functioned in the history of Western societies
to restrict the political vocabulary to one voice only: a voice that speaks
of only *one* body, *one* reason, and *one* ethic. If these 'other' beings attempt to speak to that body, their speech is not recognized" (*Feminism
and Philosophy* 125). As we have seen before, universality is a false notion disguising the interests of a very embodied class of white males.
When the white male unpropertied class, white women and African
Americans were granted exceptions to the rule by amendment to the
Constitution, they were granted citizenship and the chance to leave their
particularity at the public doorstep, to accede to being a bodiless part of
the universal. However, there was still no change in the mind/body, pub-
lic/private split. The only way non-standard body types were ever included in the protections was when an exception to the rule was created.

To this day when there is a conflict between a particularity and the
"universal," the pejorative epithet of "special interest group" is invoked.
Rousseau would say that these special interest groups are not keeping
up their end of the bargain but are dragging their particularities into
public with them. Many of the people in "different" bodies (although
still not gays and lesbians in many places) have finally been allowed in,
after much struggle, but only if they pay homage to the universal and
leave their particular needs out of consideration. Still when white women
or African American men or women speak, unless they find a way to
distance themselves from their gender and/or race, they are seen as breaking the rules that require leaving the body out of the discussion.

A good example is the debates that generally arise over appoint-
ments to the Supreme Court. In 1994, when President Clinton was deciding on a possible candidate, discussions in the media implied that
since the last appointment by Clinton had been a woman, Ruth Bader
Ginsberg, he was now safe to select a person without regard to body
type. But what that translated into was not a lack of consideration of
body type but rather quite the opposite—an assumption that he was free
to pick a white male judge. Since the body he picked was a standard one,
in essence the default position, the issue did not have to be discussed as
it would have been if he had picked a "non-standard" type. In that instance he picked Stephan Breyer, a white man.

Because we as a society have a fall-back position of white male as
"universal," we overlook the obvious—we go along with the idea that
this time Clinton is not having to pay homage to a special interest group—

but if we look closer, what we see is that he is paying homage to the special interest that has received favor in this country since Western ways began to dominate here: the white male.

The abstraction from body allows us to pay lip service to the ideal that we are all equal; however, the embodied reality is that the power-over model is firmly in place. In the end, those in power in this country—in Congress, on the Supreme Court and in the Presidency—not to mention the heads of corporations and the military—are still members of the privileged class, ethnicity and gender. No matter how well those who have "different" bodies from the standard espouse views which downplay body and difference and which accept the universal (read: the white male privileged) standard, they are still, for the most part, excluded at the highest levels.

There are some notable exceptions to this rule, but they are still very much anomalies. An example in the Senate was the election of Carol Mosley Braun from Illinois. She calls attention to the assumption that she ought to "fit in" and become indistinguishable from Jesse Helms or Orrin Hatch. Instead, at least after she was first elected, she refused to play along. She proceeded to call attention loudly to the fact that her ancestors were slaves and therefore she has not pretended to be white or to have no body at all. That kind of action is the most threatening to the white male structure of any I have witnessed. When someone can strip away the façade and refuse to be disembodied, they threaten the very foundation upon which this country is based.

The tension between the "universal" and the embodied particular is clearly illustrated in the threats to affirmative action in this country. Some argue that if only we would stop seeing a person's skin color when hiring or admitting to schools, then we would truly have an egalitarian society. What assumptions underlie the request that we "overlook" something like skin color or class or gender? As long as those who oppose affirmative action use such terminology as "overlook," "transcend," "get beyond" to refer to the bodies of people who have historically been mistreated in this country, we will know we are still dealing with a "universal" white male standard. The denial that such a standard is white and male becomes fiercely stated just when it appears that there may be room made for "others" in places of privilege. However, treatment cannot possibly be fair when one group, the one in power, promises to overlook the embodied reality of other groups.

Many in oppressed groups participate in the desire to have their bodies "overlooked." They, too, want to forget that they are black, brown, women, disabled, etc. The lure of universality is great in a society that continuously touts the state of mind-only. Those of us who have been discriminated against because of factors connected to our bodies would often just as soon "forget" that we have them. We try that route and then wonder why we feel invisible and unheard. The goal of getting beyond body is at the same time self-annihilating and impossible. Impossible because once we deny our experience, our color, our gender, our disabilities, there is still no place for us at the "mind-only" table peopled by white, heterosexual, able-bodied men who were not asked to check their bodies at the door.

We hear phrases like "qualified," "best person for the job," "best fit," "highest test scores," "deserving" and "meritorious" to justify the hiring of certain people for jobs. When we realize that inherent in the definitions of these phrases lurks a white male standard, the words lose all sense of fairness that we may have associated with them.

Exposing that emperor's body in the terms we use, in our discussions of hiring or admissions policies would, if nothing else, at least show us what we are *actually* doing and not what we are *ideally* doing. Pete Wilson in his bid for the presidency referred to the results of affirmative action as going back to "tribalism." According to *Webster's New World Dictionary*, tribe means "a group of persons or clans descended from a common ancestor and living under a leader or chief" (638). Privileged white males are the most tribal persons I know of. They even have a president and their tribal council meets every summer in the Bohemian Grove in California.[8] Their tribal customs are the official language and laws tolerated and given power in this country.

Tribal is the opposite of "universal" because when we talk of ancestors and descendants, we have introduced body and birth into the discussion. Wilson wants to distance himself from the idea of tribe but at the same time he is asking that those of his own tribe continue to be given preferences.

At least the white supremacist groups admit they are basing their beliefs on tribalism (even if they do not use that word). However, most of the anti-affirmative action tribe will not admit to being a tribe because to represent the universal is much more persuasive. And that is where they must be exposed. They argue that race and gender are irrelevant; I argue that exposing the race and gender of the emperor is key to creating an egalitarian, inclusive and democratic society.

Abstract mind principles are generally the ones we fight over, which of course indirectly affect bodies, but only through an ineffective trickle-down system. For instance, the right not to be discriminated against because we (our minds) believe we (our minds) are all created equal. Translation in body language: those in power will do their best to overlook your skin color or gender if it is different from the standard white male. The translation shows that we are not talking about equality but about permission given by the group in power to others that, at least for the time being, their bodies are "close enough to pass." This grant is, of course, better than nothing and has certainly changed many circumstances for the better. But the root problems remain.

Embodiment of the rights debate quickly shows that these are not inalienable rights about which we speak—they are privileged class-given (or sold) rights and therefore can be taken away as quickly as they were granted. But rights are supposed to be something with which each individual is born, not something that is contingent on the whims of the class in power. For fundamental change the white male standard itself must be exposed and eliminated.

The societal sickness is deeper than an operation or two can cure. We must go to the roots of the sickness, the mind/body split, individualism and idealized white male standards, competition and capitalism to see how to heal it, not just fix it for a fleeting moment and on a case by case basis.

We have seen how pervasive the mind/body split is in our culture from our philosophies to our guaranteed rights. In the next chapters, I will look more closely at the effects of the mind/body split and the effects of the association of women with body and men with mind. Mind (knowledge), body (the personal body and the habitat), men, and women are each harmed in different ways by this dichotomization. I will analyze each component separately to show how it has been affected over time. As I have already explained, these four components are not in reality separable; however, for the sake of discussion and analysis of the way our society currently conducts itself, we will use the divisions artificially created by the power-over culture.

First we will look at what effect these splits have on what we consider to be knowledge and ethics. Perhaps if we can identify what is wrong with our current methods for understanding the world, we can move ourselves toward a different kind of world.

3
Groundless Knowledge and Severed Ethics

In this chapter we focus on the effects of dichotomous thinking upon what we call "knowledge." How do we know what we know and what qualifies as knowledge? Readers who have not taken classes in philosophy may ask, "What does knowledge have to do with anything?" The reasons requiring one to ask such a question are tied up in the mind/body split as well. Philosophy, which is supposed to be a discipline dedicated to the love of knowledge, has been a major culprit in defining knowledge as residing in the mind, separate from the body. This disposition asserts itself in concrete ways that I have mentioned earlier. One is that all knowledge is believed to be located in the mind; that is, it is through thinking, cognition, that we know what we know. Philosophy, and thus knowledge, have been equated with that which the mind alone can grasp.

The body's role in this pursuit of knowledge varies from philosopher to philosopher. Some philosophers place no importance on the senses and others place a great deal of importance on them; but in most cases, the key to philosophy is what the human (read man) can know in his mind, whether before or after making use of the senses. If philosophers locate knowledge in the mind only, then logically, a major goal of philosophical inquiry would be to isolate the mind, to purify it of the influences of the body and of particularity.

Is the philosopher's search for knowledge a goal that is relevant to our daily lives or is it just some abstract endeavor which is useful only theoretically? I once attended an introduction to philosophy class in which a student asked the professor if philosophy dealt with the issue of the meaning of life. The student had obviously been thinking of large questions and was looking for direction for his life. The professor replied in the negative and proceeded the rest of the term to prove it by making the ideas as abstract as possible. It seemed almost a contamination of the purity of the ideas to bog them down with actual content from the world and from students' lives.

Think of the emperor in the fairy tale. He came as close as one might in purifying himself from body and he propounded great philosophical Truths but his life remained a mess. The only idea that he tried to apply to the real world was not a part of the philosophy but was a precondition to it—the removal of body and any particularity that did not suit him.

I would like the answer to the student's question about philosophy to be that yes, in the most important of all ways, philosophy is crucial to the living of our lives. The way we philosophize should bring us closer to understanding the world, the world in its entirety, not that which has been artificially severed so that philosophy could remain pure.

As we have seen, dichotomizing our body-minds may initially seem to make us better able to predict and control our world, but it has not proven effectual in bringing us closer to real knowledge and understanding of how the world in all of its complexity functions and how we ought to function within it.

Another way of saying this is that the process of dividing the world into the objective and subjective in our struggle to find truth, precludes us from reaching the truth. We split the subjective from the objective (the mind from the body, males from females) as a precondition for knowledge. The precondition we set by requiring "objective" knowledge then actually becomes the biggest obstacle to achieving whole knowledge.

If, in our search for knowledge, we realized that subject and object were connected, that mind and body were connected, we would see that ethics and knowledge were also inextricably linked, that knowledge itself is always situated somewhere. The emperor's tower was still located in the empire and on the earth and his thoughts never reached divinity, though it was not for lack of trying. We do not "know" in a vacuum, as Descartes wanted to believe. Rather, we constantly make decisions about what we will study and how we will go about doing it, what subjects we will choose, what hypothesis, who will conduct the experiment, etc.

As we discussed in Chapter 2, if scientists believe they have successfully removed themselves from their experiments, they do not have to deal with ethics or values. Rather, they convince themselves that they are on a quest for "pure science." We have already discussed what effects this illusion of a "value-free" science and philosophy has had historically. In this chapter I want to speak about challenges to that value-free point of view in the pursuit of both knowledge and ethics.

Knowledge

N. Katherine Hayles, a scientist and literary critic who studied chaos theory, stated in her book *Chaos Bound* (1990) that traditional science cannot handle the paradox of Heisenberg's uncertainty principle because it threatens objectivity (11). Adding subjectivity in the form of perspective (body) introduces an entirely new dimension that is analogous to finding that we have many more numbers than we thought we did, and that they do not all follow the same rules. The difficulty cannot be resolved by merely adding "body" to our already existing scientific methods of studying the universe. The inclusion of body changes the nature of science, taking it out of the subject/object dichotomy.

Currently there are huge changes occurring in certain branches of science and mathematics, which are more consistent with the idea of integrating "body" into theory. Some of the major tenets of science, such as objectivity, provability and linear cause and effect, are being questioned. The dichotomy is being shown to be false.

An example of this breakdown can be seen with the emergence of chaos theory. Chaos theory involves the following key elements: non-linearity, that is, that what is observed does not follow strict lines of cause and effect; that systems are complex; that there is a super-sensitivity to initial conditions; that there are feedback mechanisms; and that the observer is part of the observed.

Saying that systems are complex does not imply that simply by adding more equations we will be capable of predicting events. Rather, the complexity is *qualitatively* different. One cannot string together several or even thousands of linear equations to get the solution to a problem; thus, even a super computer would not yield an answer. Whereas linear equations can be mapped as straight lines or planes and can indicate proportionality, non-linear equations "connote an often startling incongruity between cause and effect, so that a small cause can give rise to a large effect" (Hayles 11). When there is chaos in a system, the goal of predictability must be replaced by a mapping, a kind of dialogue, an attempt to simply understand.

This phenomenon was first observed by Edward Lorenz, a research meteorologist who coined the term "Butterfly Effect" (the more technical term is "sensitive dependence on initial conditions") to describe how something as small as the flutter of butterfly wings could multiply and have huge effects on the weather somewhere else. It is inescapable that events of a small scale will mingle with larger ones, making weather predictions beyond a few days unreliable. Scientist James Gleick in his popular book *Chaos* (1987) stated it this way: "To produce the rich repertoire of real earthly weather, the beautiful multiplicity of it, you could hardly wish for anything better than a Butterfly Effect" (23).

One of the most interesting parts of chaos theory is the observation of self-organizing systems that arise out of what seems to be chaotic, random activity. For instance, Gregoire Nicolis, a life scientist, described how amoebae, which are one-celled creatures that feed on bacteria and the like, have no observable means of communication and move about aimlessly. However, when the food supply runs out, they respond by joining together into a structured organism that has the added capacity to mobilize to an area where there is food. Then the organism's cells differentiate into a stem and a spore pod, and when conditions are right, reproduce amoebas (Nicolis 1990). Instead of moving further into dissipation, as the second law of thermodynamics, if applied mechanically, would suggest, these unicelled creatures are able to creatively make order out of chaos—"for only a world rich in dissipative processes would have been able to support self-organization" (Hayles 101). There is chaos and there is order; but neither of them exists in isolation from the other. Within order there lurks chaos and within chaos there lurks order.

When the reaction itself produces the catalyst for more reactions that produce more catalyst for more reactions, feedback loops are created. Each reaction thus relies on the product of prior reactions. In this non-linear system, small changes do not even out over time but instead are multiplied and exaggerated. Ilya Prigogine and Isabelle Stengers in their book *Order out of Chaos* (1984) state, "Although the effects of 'non-linear' reactions (the presence of the reaction product) have a feedback action on their 'cause' and are comparatively rare in the inorganic world, molecular biology has discovered that they are virtually the rule as far as living systems are concerned" (153). I am particularly interested here in the idea that in the human body, chaos is more the rule than the exception. If chaos theory is valid—and it certainly seems to be—our attempts to understand the world, and particularly the body, in a purely linear fashion are grossly inadequate.

In *Chaos Bound*, Hayles makes the point that often physics and phi-losophy of science classes study chaos theory at the very end of their semester, almost as an afterthought. Chaos is marginalized and studied as if it were an interesting sideline or anomaly. Because chaos theory requires major changes in the way systems are viewed, often teachers themselves have not become reconciled to its possibilities and feel threat-ened by the challenge to the traditional, well-established ways of con-ducting scientific inquiry. Linearity, a more familiar and comfortable way to see the world, is still considered the norm; non-linearity, the unfamil-iar and unpredictable, is seen as the exception.

Traditional science has been concerned solely with repeatability and proof, and has therefore confined itself to certain parts of the world that work predictably. If reality is closer to a model of interaction than of dichotomy, much of reality will be excluded from the traditional analysis.

When we invest scientific inquiry with the ability to give us knowledge and that inquiry is predicated on the severing of reality, we do not just sever ourselves from our objects of knowledge, but we also sever science from ethics and we use this model as a way to live our lives. We have thus enabled ourselves to create science and technology without reflecting on the possible effects it might have on our lives and without reflecting on who it is that all of this science and technology ultimately benefits.

Helena Norberg-Hodge lived with and studied the culture of Ladakh, a small village in India from the early 1960's to 1990.[9] When she first got there the people had had little contact with modern "development." They were a self-sufficient community even though they lived at extremely high altitudes with long, cold winters. They had none of the technologi-cal wonders that dominate lives in Western culture. And yet they were happy and wealthy in their own ways. They did not have a money economy and simply pitched in and helped each other out when needed, trading and sharing what they had.

Recently the Western world with its roads and cars and capitalism has invaded the place; and while it brings in money and imports, it also destroys the self-sufficiency the people had built there for centuries. No longer are many concerned with sustainability; now the goals have changed to consumerism. Now they compare themselves to the rest of the world, and they feel poor. They can see a whole different way of life that looks interesting and exciting on the television; they want it.

They now have many more technological innovations and with those innovations there should be more free time to enjoy life. However, as we in the Western world know, though technological advances are touted as time savers, one has to pay a high price for them and then constantly earn more and more money to pay for them. Additionally, devices like computers and fax machines, while they can save time, can also have the effect of making more work. We in the Western world are working more hours than ever before.

Technocrats rave about the computer networks and the information highways that are being set up under the auspices of making the world smaller and more inclusive. But we should be wary of these "advances." These exchanges are bodiless. If human-to-human contact is reduced to words or images on a screen, what becomes of the real people on the outside of the computer? We sacrifice eye contact and all of the other non-verbal communications that are often decisive in formulating accurate assessments of the people we are dealing with and the dynamics of the situations that confront us. We cannot expect computer networks to replace our whole way of knowing.

It may be that we will decide that we want to forgo those things in order to "progress"; however, not to consider these factors in making decisions about our technologies is to fall into the obvious well worn split between mind and body.

I could say that we have created a bunch of mindless technologies but I would rather say that these are bodiless technologies. They are creations of minds devoid of body, devoid of values and emotions and concrete perspectives. We easily let our minds have their fun with virtual reality, video games, television, and the like. Meanwhile, our connections to our bodies, to other people and to our habitat atrophy and do not have a voice in our decisions. These connections hold wisdom that we ignore as we move toward goals that have more to do with capital and consumerism than with quality of life.

When our science and technology and our pursuit for knowledge exclude the body, we have no brakes on a slippery slope toward splitting up all meaning. Technologies are created in the abstract, without concern for the possible effects both on our bodies and lives and on the life of the planet. But in fact these pursuits do not exist in the abstract and they can never be value-free. The values and perspectives are there. They can be seen in the actions of those who benefit in a power-over way from breaking down the fabric of our existence in the name of "science and technology." We have only to look at who continues to get rich and to have power and status in the world.

We might want to ask ourselves why the culmination of 20th Century scientific knowledge is the development of nuclear fission as epitomized

by the atom bomb, the ultimate in power-over. It seems the logical out-
growth of a body-politic bent on destruction of the connections binding
its most vital elements.

To fall back on the "universal," which is really a code word for rich
white male, abandons us to work toward goals that are not our own.
Who benefits from this splitting, disconnection and alienation? Who
benefited from the emperor's way of doing things? Even those in power
cannot see beyond power-over to the possibilities aching to be expressed.
In our fairy tale, we must feel sorry for the emperor as well, who thought
he was acting out of universals. That attempt nearly ruined his life.

Ethics

Where, in fact, many philosophers have connected ethics and knowledge,[10] it is often in an attempt to make ethics follow the same universal
rules as knowledge, rather than to attempt to apply ethics to the search
for knowledge.[11] I will go into some detail about the subject of ethics here
in order to show the connections and similarities between knowledge
and ethics and to shed light on the issues using a mind/body split critique.

One refrain we hear over and over is that we, as a society, have lost
our sense of ethics; that is why we hate each other and engage in war,
crime, racism, consumerism, promiscuity, pornography and greed. Ethics as a field of study has been claimed by philosophy and thus has been
frequently conceptualized as mind-only. What philosophers want to do—
that is, those philosophers who think that ethics is a part of philosophy
at all[12]—is to find a system of ethics that is universal, that establishes
rules which are both intuitively correct and rational. Many seek laws of
ethics, like laws of science, that are "true" for all times in all places.

Many philosophers who believe that ethics belongs in philosophy
will try to prove that it is indeed objective. Accepting the need for universals and for objectivity, they look for rules and formulas that will
define proper behavior. Other philosophers say that even though ethics
cannot be completely objective, there are ways to keep it from the accusations of being relativistic, dependent in some way on individual circumstance or personality or location in the world, considered to be the
kiss of death for a system of ethics.

Both of these routes to the formulation of a system of ethics are
attempts to transcend individuals and their particularity and discover
something larger, clearer and more pristine, uncontaminated by human
bodies and experience.

Let me give an example here from traditional ethics. A few years ago I attended a lecture on ethics at an American Philosophical Association conference. The discussion centered on a classic hypothetical situation in ethics, the lifeboat scenario: a group of people is in a lifeboat which is going to sink unless one of them is thrown overboard. Descriptions of those on board were given—one is old but brilliant, one is young but retarded, one has young children, etc., and participants were asked, "what should be done?" During the discussion period, a man in the audience said, "we've got to have rules of ethics so that when we're in a situation like the lifeboat, we can make a decision and not feel remorse."

That statement epitomizes the danger inherent in abstract, bodiless ethics. Our systems of ethics should not keep us from feeling remorse— of course the people on that boat would most likely feel remorse no matter what they chose to do, no matter which rule they followed. The object of ethics should not be to anesthetize—to numb our feelings— but to pay attention to those very feelings that traditional ethicists urge us to repress. What do our feelings as well as our rationality tell us to do? It is all right to feel remorse or pain or anger; we would be less than human if we did not feel. The drive to purge emotions from ethics may be thought of as a way to relieve us of those painful emotions; however, all the purge does is allow us to make decisions based on less information than is actually available to us.

If we define ethical behavior as I do—that is, as behavior which comes from integrated, whole beings who deny neither themselves, their bodies nor their connection with their habitat and with other people and peoples—our attempts to find an elevated, perspectiveless, bodiless place from which to judge right and wrong is immoral in itself. Severing ties and acting according to a universal rule or formula, as so many philosophers have advocated, is misguided.

Refer again to the dichotomy diagram. Traditional ethics asks us to draw clearer and clearer lines between ourselves and others, our minds and our bodies. Human beings are capable of feeling and being aware of what we share with one another. We are, in other words, capable of empathy. This empathy should not be purged from our systems of ethics but rather used to guide us.[13] When we try to reach objectivity in ethics, we simply move further back into our cove of subjectivity, severing ourselves from what we see as the "object" of our study.

I am going to look in some detail at certain studies that have been done regarding the development of morality in humans. The illustration used here can be generalized to evaluate other knowledge systems that make similar claims to universality and have at the heart of their analysis a disembodiment.

How do humans in Western culture learn what is considered ethical behavior? Lawrence Kohlberg, a famous psychologist who began publishing his work in the late 1950's, looked at how humans learn moral behavior. From his study of white upper middle and upper class adolescent boys, Kohlberg developed his theory regarding moral development in humans, which is still taught in colleges today as a great contribution to the field.

Kohlberg's work has been critiqued by Carol Gilligan in her book *In a Different Voice* (1982) which challenged the notion that such studies could be done using only boy subjects and then generalized to the way *all* humans develop morals. Gilligan conducted similar studies using both boys and girls as subjects. She discovered that the girls, for the most part, did not score above a level three (six being the highest and most abstract) on Kohlberg's scale. She then challenged the validity of Kohlberg's scale on the basis that his conclusions were drawn from exclusive and therefore insufficient data.

The "Heinz Dilemma" was the hypothetical situation that both Gilligan and Kohlberg used in their studies. Gilligan described the hypothetical as follows: "In this particular dilemma, a man named Heinz considers whether or not to steal a drug which he cannot afford to buy in order to save the life of his wife. In the standard format of Kohlberg's interviewing procedure, the description of the dilemma itself—Heinz's predicament, the wife's disease, the druggist's refusal to lower his price—is followed by the question, 'Should Heinz steal the drug?' The reasons for and against stealing are then explored through a series of questions that vary and extend the parameters of the dilemma in a way designed to reveal the underlying structure of moral thought" (Gilligan 25-26).

The question, "Should Heinz steal the drug?" highlights the bias of Kohlberg's study. He does not ask a general question that would allow room for many kinds of answers, for instance, "what should be done?" but rather he frames the issue so as to elicit a simple and unambiguous answer for Heinz. This framing encourages the subjects to answer as if Heinz were living in a dichotomized world where he is isolated from everyone else—including his wife, the pharmacist, the community, and his habitat—and can act alone. The subject in the study is to make a judgment as if s/he were Heinz; and the "right" answers, that is, the answers that rated the highest level of moral development according to

Kohlberg, would be those which abstracted Heinz from the situation and were answered according to "universal" rules.

Gilligan found that, in general, a different voice could be heard coming from the girls. This different voice was one that insisted on viewing the dilemma in context rather than in the abstract. The girls tended to want more information and refused to answer the questions directly. One subject, Amy, "envisions the wife's continuing need for her husband and the husband's continuing concern for his wife and seeks to respond to the druggist's need in a way that would sustain rather than sever connection" (Gilligan 28).

What Kohlberg might have been observing in boys, as we saw in the last chapter, was the way their own identities had been developed; and thus the way they see the world, in terms of difference from them. Nancy Chodorow in her book *The Reproduction of Mothering* (1978) discusses the formation of boys' identities in the section called "Mothering, Masculinity and Capitalism" (180-190). Boys are not-mother and not-female. When they look at a hypothetical situation, they base their answers not on connection but rather on drawing the boundaries clearly and decisively. They are encouraged to abstract information and to distance answers from their own realities. Also they are taught to identify with the subject, the decision-maker, and not necessarily with others whom the girls may have called on for help. Ignoring connections allows subjects to become "objective" and to use abstract principles rather than to contextualize their answers.

Amy's identity does not rely so strongly on severing connections. However, she is unsure of herself; she gets mixed up easily and does not excel in the system presented by Kohlberg. In fact, she leans toward making decisions only out of respect for the alterity of others at the expense sometimes of her own alterity.

For now I want to concentrate on a critique of that traditional way of looking at moral development where detachment is desirable. This way of looking at the world is a denial of perspective and thereby a claim to universality; it is a denial of the connections between the subject and the object of study; and it is a denial of the other's alterity. Let me take each one of these issues separately and illustrate them.

Denial of a Perspective and a Claim of Universality

This part of the dichotomy model is perhaps the most pervasive and dangerous. In order to claim universality, the subject denies her own perspective. The subject claims to have transcended her own particularity and to have found a place to stand that is outside any one viewpoint. Here one pretends it is possible to remove oneself from the other and to simply look into that "other" space and observe. This method in a sense "works" in that there is something there to be seen, recorded and analyzed. The problem is our assumption that data gathered in this way is a valid reflection of the whole, universal reality.

Actually, when using that method, we are denying our bodies and thereby denying that we must stand anywhere at all. We try to take only our minds over to that hypothetical spot outside of perspective, that place of universality, in order to simply "observe" reality. When we think we are separating our bodies and our minds, we are in reality attempting the impossible and instead skewing our "knowledge." It is Russell's paradox all over again: one cannot stand outside one's habitat and observe it without being part of it.[14]

As I stated earlier in this book, the easiest way to sustain this illusion is for one to have the "universal" body, a standard white male heterosexual body. If one's body is female, disabled, of color or gay or any combination thereof, it is much more difficult, if not impossible, to reach universality. Bodies that do not fit the standard are constant reminders of differences in experience and history. They threaten the exposure of the white male body lurking behind the false front of universality— because universality is not what it claims to be, but is simply another name for sameness, for fitting the standard body.

To use the Kohlberg example here, a typical boy's response to the "should Heinz steal the drug" question is "yes, he should steal it." In defense of that position the boy asserts the "universal" principle that life is more important than property and therefore it is all right for Heinz to steal the drug. Where did this principle come from and is it universal? Simply because a principle is abstracted from particular experience and context does not make it universal. Maybe it came from the boy's own experience in the world, in his time, and in his culture. Another culture might view the wife as property and therefore on a somewhat equal footing with the drug; and what's more, stealing may be a crime punishable by death. In such a culture Heinz would have to weigh his own possible death against that of his wife's. We see, then, that the decision the boy makes for Heinz in Kohlberg's studies is actually an embodied perspective. The decision the boy makes for Heinz is an embodied perspective, disguised to look bodiless and universal and thereby endowed with the power of a universal.

The ethical decision appears, then, to be determined by whichever agent has the power to ordain their view "universal." It is no more true than that. If the girl wants to be equal to the boy, she must leave her body behind (which is advocated by some theorists[15]) and thus pretend to become more like the "universal" which, in actuality, means jumping into the shoes of a privileged white male.

The irony is that the very thing we call universal in Western ethics has been limited to one particular brand of the white male; that which we cling to for justice and fairness and equality is in its very construction exclusive. Our attempt at inclusivity and fairness, when we see it as denial of body and of difference, is self-defeating.

Denial of Connections between Subject and Object

It is assumed in the search for objectivity that an observer can exist in pristine isolation from the object of study, unsullied by any relationship between them. I have already talked about the effect such thinking has not only on what is known, but also on what is considered to be *knowable* in science and medicine.

But think now about the effect this mindset has on ethics. If we see ethics from a dichotomized viewpoint, we see self and other as severed. We then try to deal with this arbitrary schism by trying to balance the two sides so that neither the self nor the other is treated "badly."

If we work from the dichotomized model, the ideal state is one of "impartiality," abstraction and linear predictability. The choices are very limited in the Heinz dilemma if Heinz is seen as an isolated individual not affected by the positions of the other participants in the story. An answer can then be given quickly and decisively without need of investigation and dialogue, i.e., "If I were Heinz, I would remove myself from the situation, be as objective as possible and decide 'rationally' what should be done." I, as Heinz, would not need to know myself, my feelings, my values, my relationships; I need only know principles of justice. Life over property wins—steal the drug.

The moral agent can simply use mind and "rationality" to decide how to act. One does not have to know how Heinz feels about his wife, what her quality of life would be like with the drug, how many animals were killed to create the drug, what were the environmental costs to produce the drug, or what his wife wants to do. In Kohlberg's analysis, all of these considerations are irrelevant; if you need to rely on them you will never reach the highest point of morality, which he called "justice."

Denial of the Alterity of the Other

The inclination when operating from the dichotomized worldview is to deny the alterity of one side of the dichotomy or the other. Respect for alterity in the Heinz dilemma would mean hearing from Heinz's wife. We do not even know her name (for my purpose I am going to name her Cornelia). Cornelia is completely objectified, devoid of feelings, desires, intelligence. When Heinz is the moral agent, our inclination as we dichotomize is to objectify Cornelia, to see her as voiceless and inert, and to rely on Heinz to think and act.

What happens when we switch roles to a situation where the sick person is not so easily objectified because it goes against the model of who is subject and who is object in this society? Pretend the patient is a man and the agent is a woman. Consider for a moment that Heinz is sick and ask yourself the question, "What should Heinz's wife do?"

We may feel compelled now to reverse the position of the moral agent and allow Heinz once again to assume that role; and Cornelia, though she must do the acting, will take direction from the sick bed of Heinz. How often might we get responses like, "Mrs. Heinz should ask her husband what he wants and follow his wishes"? Participants might answer this way because it is harder to deny the alterity of men than it is that of women.

This is all wild speculation, of course, since to my knowledge that experiment has never been done. This hypothetical experiment, however, points out assumptions in our traditional view of ethics and uncovers its bias. Suffice it to say that if we were not operating out of the dichotomized worldview, our answers would not depend on the gender of the patient in the sick bed; instead, we would consider the alterity of all of the participants in the scenario. We would be much more inclined to want to know about the relevant relationships of Heinz and Cornelia.

Heinz's location in space and relationship is the body part of this analysis. Only if we eliminate his body, his unique placement and perspective, can we come up with an abstract, mind-only answer like "steal the drug." All of a sudden when body is added, this dilemma becomes much more complex and messy. There appears not to be a single answer.

Knowledge and ethics that deal only with the artificially boundaried world, the predictable world, the dichotomized world are not enough. It is imperative that we see that understanding lies outside of those boundaries, outside of linear time and in a milieu of constant change, not in solid, rigid, once-and-for-all answers.

4

Life of the Body in a Dysbodied World

The Personal Body—Dysbodiment

For the purposes of this chapter I will be using the term "body" to mean the fraction we refer to as "body" after we dichotomize the whole being, the body-mind and make it a mind/body with "mind" as the upper term and "body" devalued and given a submissive role. We hear the phrases "beheaded" or "mindless"; but there is no parallel term for a cutting off of the body so it had to be invented. I use the word "dysbodied" to mean cut off from the body. An extreme case of dysbodiment was represented by the emperor's actions in the fairy tale.

In this chapter I want to look at what has in fact happened to the dichotomized body-mind. I will be speaking about both men and women; but keep in mind that for women the issues around body and body image hold a place of higher importance, because as we discussed in the last chapter, women and body are often equated.

Our training teaches us that bodies are "other" than ourselves. I will look at some of the factors that go into developing that model of dysbodiment. Then I will look at how Westerners behave in regard to three specific body-related issues: our health, the foods we eat, and sex.

Our narratives about body tell us repeatedly that "body" is not subject, not mind, not conscious and not important—that it is "other" than "us." And repetition of that mantra over time becomes a self-fulfilling prophecy—the more we treat our body as "other" and ignore its messages, the less fluent we are with its language. We become mono-lingual, speaking only that language that "mind" can articulate. Infants seem to understand and be in immediate touch with their bodies' needs and desires; but they cannot articulate them. However, as soon as an infant learns the language of the mind, its needs and desires must be tailored to fit only within that limited scheme of either/or dichotomous thinking. Repression of the body's unarticulated messages starts when language is learned. The feelings that overflow the boundaries of logic's A and not-A must be discarded, disbelieved or destroyed if we want to make sense to and communicate with those who have control over our bodies at those ages. And we must make sense to them for our own survival's sake. Verbal language does not grow to fit our needs as infants; rather, the infants must find a way to contain their feelings within the constraints of language.

We need a translator to tell us what we are feeling—first, when we are too young to speak for ourselves; and then secondly, when what we have to say will not fit neatly into the categories of language. Perhaps an infant cries: it is hungry for food or the feel of its mother. Since our language does not have simple ways of conceptualizing the latter, the mother assumes the former; so she gives it food. Thus, feelings of inchoate longing come to be understood as, "I'm hungry."

From these simple translations we move on to more and more complex kinds of extrapolations; and our understanding of how we feel and what we need becomes more and more the purview of outside authorities. It has been observed that at ages as early as two weeks old, children's emotions are being shaped by the child's parents. By viewing sloweddown video tape, psychologist Daniel Stern (*The First Relationship, Mother and Infant*, 1977) has documented that parents' body language molds infants' emotions to fit into the parents' ideas of good and bad emotional states. Adults' body language can be seen to be restraining an infant whose emotive expressions are "undesirable" and to be exaggerating and encouraging other emotions that are perceived as positive.

There is a vicious circle in effect here because the more we listen to outside authorities and internalize their messages about our bodies, the less able we are to hear our bodies' own needs, and the more we must turn to outside authorities for help. Our bodies are what ground us, what keep us connected to the earth; and yet we cut this information out from under us so that our grounding becomes tenuous, atrophied, and deadened of vitality.

In the midst of writing this book I got a bad case of poison oak. My inclination when I first began to be tormented by itching skin and oozing sores was to dysbody myself. I stopped everything connected to my body except those things necessary for survival. Rather than find out what my body needed and was trying to tell me, I opted out. I stopped all my routines like swimming, bicycling and walking. Instead of replacing these exercises with ones I could have done, I did nothing further with my body except to obsess over the oozing and itching.

This bout with poison oak reminds me of a bad marriage. When something goes wrong in a couple's life, instead of pulling together to get through their difficulties, the two people turn against each other; and one tries to control the other or tries to "win" the argument. If the relationship is not solid, when trouble comes along each person seems to want to be "right" or in control and they fly apart instead of pulling together to try to work it through. This poisoning alerted me to a problem in my own marriage of body and mind. I forgot to pool our resources, listen to my own messages and learn something.

I think that now I can better understand the inclination of people who are in chronic pain or who have serious illnesses to want to escape or transcend their bodies. It occurs to me that if I had had a closer relationship with my body—that is, if I had been closer to working as a body-mind instead of a mind/body, when something painful or gross happened to my body, I might have been better able to communicate with it. Otherwise, I fall back on the old pattern of domination of mind over what is going on with my body.

Because humans are taught from a very early age that our bodies are apart from us, a kind of inert appendage of our minds, we do not see the importance of listening to and validating our bodies' needs. We are drawn from paying attention to what hurts or feels good in our bodies to *what we are told* hurts or feels good. Our feelings become externalized and intellectualized. We are taught about pain and pleasure mind-to-mind. Outside authorities of one sort or another—parents, teachers, television, religious authorities, bosses, etc.—tell us when and what to eat and drink, when to go to the bathroom, when to sleep and for how long, what to wear, how long to sit in one place or exercise, when, how and with whom to have sex. Even in our most private moments, when no one else is present, these authorities stay with us in Cheshire cat style, because we have internalized their messages and the "authorities" have become our own minds. Our minds have exerted control over our bodies in so many ways that it is almost impossible now to find out what the body-mind as a whole needs or wants.

As you read this, keep in your awareness the dichotomy model of mind and body and the gap shown in that model between body and mind. Then remember that we were not born with this split condition; it is imposed on us by a culture that insists on the reality of dysbodiment. It is an authoritarian, power-over model in which we have no recognized need to listen to the body; the body is instead to do what it is told—to be seen and not heard.

We talk of mind over matter—in dieting, in exercise and in sex. The goal is not to work with one's own body but to regiment and discipline it into conforming to an externally imposed standard without regard for its alterity. Because of this imposed standard, we lose any sense of subjectivity in the body. We lose the ability to be aware of our bodies when something goes wrong or when we want pleasure. Instead we impose on ourselves an intellectualized version of what we are supposed to want. The body is relegated to the status of passive, malleable object whose use is to serve the mind.

When I was growing up, I walked about 5 or 6 blocks to school. I had a pattern of worrying that I would be late for school so I had to hurry to get there. Then, very often, I would fall down and skin my knees. The pain of the skinned knee according to dysbodied philosophy would not be sufficient to make me change my errant ways. No, outside authorities had to intervene to force a change. I was threatened with being sent to school with kneepads such as football players wear if I did not get control of my feet and legs. This was not my mother's special brand of torture; it is how we in this society are taught to treat our bodies.

I have only recently begun relating to my body differently, partly because willing my feet to do something and threatening my mind with ill-fated punishments has not worked. That technique only served to make me rigid and unbalanced and unable to find out how I could best support my body-mind.

When it comes to our own health, many of us are so cut off from the messages our bodies send that even when we receive a seemingly unmistakable message, we misconstrue it. One sort of message that the body sends across our created chasm is to malfunction, to stop working correctly and to give us pain. When we feel it and still ignore the pain, it has to get worse to be noticed.

We have so many remedies geared to shut up the body—aspirin, ibuprofen, antacids, laxatives, codeine, sleeping pills, caffeine, nicotine, diet medicines, valium, anti-histamines, alcohol, food, etc. I am sure you can add more. Anything to shut our bodies up. It is a paradox that in order to feel well quickly we block out the warning signals that might lead us to be well. We think we are well because we do not feel pain and meanwhile we may be developing cancer, heart disease or diabetes.

If we acknowledged that mind and body are interconnected and inseparable, a "cure" that merely turns off the warning signal would hardly be a victory. If we stop our investigation with the termination of the pain, we have not healed what ails our body-mind; we have merely attempted to sever the body from the rest of our lives and from our minds.

In our society this attitude of transcendence is something to be proud of; *we* have control of our bodies. However, in essence, what we do is to simply ignore communication from a body that is in pain and needs attention. We develop patterns of not listening to the body for clues as to what kinds of food we should be eating, how much rest we need, what kind of exercise is optimum, what kind of job best suits us and whether our air is breathable. Our training has closed us off from the daily communications that should be occurring because we have convinced ourselves that what is important is what society has taught our minds to want.

For instance, I used to think dairy products were good for me and consequently, I ate them a lot. My parents and I had been convinced by the dairy industry that dairy products were ideally nutritional. Not until a growing awareness of our inhumane treatment of animals convinced me to stop eating dairy products did I realize that what I had thought all these years were "sinus" headaches were actually caused by dairy products. When I cut down on the dairy in my diet, I no longer awoke to postnasal drip and a sinus headache. For years I had taken aspirin or some other pain reliever to get rid of the headache, never dreaming that the cause was something I was eating. Instead of looking for answers in myself by keeping track of what my body was doing, what I was eating and the effect that had on my health, I looked for easy answers to relieve the pain.

Because we often do not pay attention to our bodies when we are healthy, we lose the ability to notice something going wrong in its early stages. Instead of tuning in, we up the volume of our minds to rise above our bodies. We are then more vulnerable to whatever comes along and invades our bodies. And we find we must turn to doctors more frequently to find out what is wrong with us.

Sometimes the doctor is not to blame when the patient does not get the best medical advice; many patients are resistant to the very idea that they should take responsibility for their bodies. They go to the doctor in order to let someone else deal with it, tell them what to do, make their decisions. As we discussed earlier, sometimes those decisions are not medical at all but rather ethical or quality-of-life decisions which only the patient and her family and friends could adequately address. Giving up our own power and our own values by handing them over to a medical expert is a self-destructive habit that we need to change.

Our system is structured as if our bodies were machines on which our minds could simply set a dial to get the desired response. Because our training in this culture focuses only on how to set the dial, it seems self indulgent to pay attention to our bodies. Think about the notion of self-indulgence in this society—an assumed preoccupation with the pleasures of the body.

We are rewarded for being the opposite of self-indulgent, for being self-ignorant and for suppressing all signals from the body-mind and listening only to the mind. The mind will go on controlling the body in ignorance until the body becomes ill and demands attention. How many times have we heard praise for someone who never missed a day of work and who could work even with the worst head cold? They continue working even when they are sick, repeating the adage "mind over matter." Our *Will* will prevail (read "our mind will prevail"). How often have we admired such persons for their strong will instead of pitying them for their self-ignorance?

I have a friend whom I will call Karen, who pursued the socially acceptable tactic of mind over matter with dire consequences. She was working in the business world and daily she ignored feelings of stress, the signals that she was headed for collapse: the headaches, the muscle aches, the constipation, the stomach aches which got worse when she did something hurtful to herself or someone else. She willed herself to be objective, unemotional and "successful" in the corporation. In her case breast cancer caused her to stop what she was doing and listen to her body. She had the cancerous breast removed, quit her job and went back to school in nursing, a field that had always interested her. She finally heard a message from her body.

But this is not a one-time-only message; rather, the health of body-mind requires constant receptivity to one's own messages. Now that she is studying in a different field, is she once again going to ignore all messages from her body until again she is sick? She feels she was in a certain sense saved by the cancer; I wonder if she got the message not only that she was in the wrong field but also that she was not listening to her body on a consistent basis. Now she is in school and studying hard; but she is eating junk food, she is not exercising or paying any attention to anything which she conceives of as below the neck. Because her body is, after the mastectomy, "imperfect," she has more reasons for being disgusted by it. She has cut off her sexuality entirely and is bent once again on total dysbodiment. This pattern is self-fulfilling since the more she ignores her body, the worse she feels and the worse she looks and then the more justified she feels in her behavior.

I hope it will not take another dire message from her body to wake her up. I am not blaming her for her cancer; but I blame the mindset that we in this culture insist upon—that body can be ignored, is secondary, is controllable by our minds. It will take radical changes in our thinking and lifestyles to alter this ingrained relationship of mind and body. We need to support each other in finding ways to re-learn the language of the body so that we only need experts for their specialized and technical assistance to our already ongoing care of ourselves.

If medical advice were truly just that, advice, we would not be in such a predicament. But when we abdicate all responsibility for our own health and hand ourselves over to doctors who do not know us or the context we live in, we ask for trouble. When we go to the doctor, say, for a pain in the foot, the focus becomes just on the part of us that is in pain. Then we miss the larger implications of the pain.

I am reminded again of experiences I had in trying to treat my disability. When I was having some pain in my left foot, I went to numerous doctors who examined my feet. I consulted with them about how to proceed with recovery and healing. When the doctors saw me, they began theoretically reconstructing my feet. The only solutions they came up with were what I term "tinker toy" solutions—that is, they saw my feet as tinker.toys which they could take apart and put back together differently to make the feet "normal." I would begin to tell them my family history and their eyes would glaze over. They were simply not interested in anything except building new feet. My feet were isolated from the rest of my body and isolated from the rest of my life and family history. The doctors' goal was to make these funny looking feet go away and replace them with normal looking feet.

I, however, was not as concerned about how my feet looked as I was about how they functioned in relation to the rest of me. I can now say that I was concerned about my whole body-mind, though at the time I had no such idea. I knew intuitively that my feet were not tinker toys and that I did not want to hand over my feet to doctors who played a game in which I was neither a player nor a rule maker: and in which, as far as I could see, I could never be a winner. I walked, no, ran, away on my misshapen feet.

The mind/body split allows us to treat bodies as if they were all the same, objects that follow exactly the same rules, thus rendering the details of a person's experience irrelevant. We assume that the prescriptions and suggested actions for a certain diagnosis ought to be the same for everyone. But if one is thinking of the body-mind as an inseparable whole, how much sense would it make to treat each case the same way? Each body-mind is different because it has lived through a whole series of different events called a life.

I prefer to think that body-minds resemble regions of the earth. Some are humid rain forests, others are dry deserts, and some are moderate zones. I tend to be a humid person with a high body temperature, needing lots of water. Other people require very little water to maintain a balance. We do not all react in the same way to similar environments or circumstances. Thus, when I see standards set up for everyone such as "everyone must drink eight glasses of water a day," or minimum daily nutritional requirements, I am skeptical. We should be aware of our particular body's needs; and health professionals should not diagnose and treat a problem until they have found out about their lives of particular bodies, not just what the presenting symptoms and standard operating principles tell them.

I am reminded of a story a nurse-practitioner friend of mine tells about an 85 year old woman whom I will call Cary. Cary had been living with diabetes for many years and living mainly on cupcakes, fruit cocktail and chocolate. When my friend saw what Cary was eating, she was appalled. Though Cary seemed to be doing fine and her blood sugar counts were on target, my friend could not believe it could be true. She suggested to Cary better ways to go about controlling her disease that had been medically and scientifically proven to work. Cary would just look at my friend and say, "Girlie, I've lived with this body for 85 years and I guess I ought to know what keeps her going." My friend had to agree that this was true. That example is perhaps extreme, but it shows that our medical experts could perhaps learn from their patients as well as from their books before advising their patients.

In the past a doctor was often familiar with the families of each of her patients and would know something about their lives without having to ask. For the most part those days are gone, at least as long as we have the current health services system. That information may not have been codified and regimented but it was useful as an aid to making diagnoses and understanding health problems.

Cures in Western medicine are often focused on one part of the body as if it were not in relation to the rest of the body, the mind, the diet, the habitat and the life of the person who is sick. The medical establishment often creates "cures" that are part of the problem and not a part of a healing process. In her article, "From Healing Herbs to Deadly Drugs," ecofeminist Marti Kheel states, "Western medicine obstinately continues to deny the importance of environmental and lifestyle factors in the causation of disease. Even though it has been estimated that 80 percent or more of all cancers are attributable to environmental factors, medical research continues to pour billions of dollars into finding magic (chemical) cures for this and other diseases" (Kheel 103). The very idea of a personal cure, of ridding oneself of disease is problematic. Is that not just a way to make a body shut up? Get rid of the symptoms of the disease; often instead of helping the body back into ease where it has been dis-eased.

Part of the problem here is the focus on cures rather than prevention. A health system built on experts fixing our bodies does not translate easily into language of prevention. Prevention implies a change of lifestyle, habits and awarenesses. It requires each person to monitor her own health. Doctors do not have an automatic place in such a model. In *Beyond Antibiotics* (1993) authors Schmidt, Smith and Sehnert state, "Perhaps it is because our medical system is intent on studying *disease* rather than health. It is interested in spending money and resources on learning about pathology rather than wellness" (10). More holistic practices have emphasized health for centuries. In Eastern medicine, practitioners look at what might be out of balance with the body-mind and they look beyond the presenting symptom.

Western medicine is gradually being influenced by more holistic practices and by people demanding that health practitioners see them as whole people. Many books and television programs have been produced on this subject and it is not my intent to rehash what has already been well-documented. My intent is simply to show how the evolution of Western medicine is a part of the mind/body split phenomenon so prevalent in our culture.

Our self-ignorance makes us extremely vulnerable to being told by others how to fix ourselves and what products will "help" us. We have illnesses whose specific origin may not be directly accessible to us. We often have a kind of free-floating desire—originating with the inchoate hunger still unfed from childhood—that wells up endlessly and requires massive interventions to make us feel good. We know something is wrong in our lives but we cannot pinpoint it—perhaps there is a medicine, food or sexual pleasure that will provide us with just the thing we need.

Advertisers are quick to jump into that gap between mind and body and tell us what is wrong with us and how we can fix it. Advertisements appeal to a mind split-off from body: to quick, efficient ways to eat, short cuts, frozen foods, fast foods, foods high in fat and sugar. The dysbodied mind tells the body what it ought to want to eat; and that dysbodied mind is highly susceptible to advertising.

The mind/body split is an ideal set-up for the marketplace. When a television commercial advertising chocolate cake is followed by a diet advertisement, contradictory desires are promoted which cancel each other out and make us buy more of each product in a vicious circle. Advertising creates a desire to eat a lot of fattening foods and then makes us feel we must be thin to be attractive and have a decent sex life. Both products capitalize on our being out of touch with the needs of our bodies so that the seller can identify them for us. After we have eaten and dieted and eaten and dieted for years, it is almost impossible to ascertain when we are actually hungry and what it is we want to eat and what our ideal body weight might be.

When the dysbodied mind craves something, we must be suspicious because it is liable to crave a quick fix of mind-over-body power. We lack something which consumerism seeks to fill and fill and fill. The hole we create by dichotomizing body and mind can never be filled by more dichotomizing. It cannot be filled because it is not real; it is a creation of our minds. The more we dichotomize to fill it, the deeper it gets.

It seems paradoxical that our methods for filling the hole make it deeper. However, when we split something up, we get a shot of power and momentarily feel powerful. But that power is fleeting and the shot must be constantly repeated. Each time we split, we take away from our immanent power.

It might seem that if you ate what your mind wanted, you would eat the "right" foods. Maybe you think your body is to blame for craving hamburgers and French fries. But more likely what we like to eat is socially defined; we learn it from our families, from our friends, from advertising. We hear or see the advertisements and are pushed into wanting certain kinds of food. We then feel varying degrees of satisfaction from eating the wrong kinds of food, not because our bodies are pleased but because we have been manipulated into thinking that unhealthy food is pleasing. Our ignorance is a perfect set-up for authoritarian control of mind over body.

Eating foods that are bad for us is a way to feel we have defied any authority the body may have. It is a way of saying, "I will eat whatever I want, whatever fills my psychological needs at the moment." Sometimes that need is for comfort and is filled by eating a beloved food from childhood. We eat something that is bad for our bodies to demonstrate that mind is in control and unaffected by repercussions in the body.

I have finally realized that eating two doughnuts and drinking coffee first thing in the morning makes me feel absolutely horrible for hours afterwards. I do not have control of that effect on my body. The taste of doughnuts is not something that my body is craving but is something my mind has categorized as comfort food, as sinful but delicious, as an assertion of control of mind over body. The sin is not the sin of allowing my bodily impulses to come out, but is rather a joy I get from transcending my body and eating what I, separated from my body, want. It is once again the use of power-over mode. It is mind saying to body, "Take this and this. I'll show you who's boss." An antacid will convincingly stifle any cries of pain.

When we dysbody ourselves, there is not even an "other" whom we dominate to do our bidding. It is literally part of ourselves that we repress and devalue. It is distressing to think that a certain part of ourselves could suppress another part in order to feel in control and powerful. In the long run, of course, it is self-destructive because like it or not, rationalize it or not, when our bodies are sick, our minds are deeply affected. Over-consumption cannot make us whole; in fact, it takes us further and further away from reconciliation between mind and body.

Sometimes the push to consume certain things comes from what we think of as highly reliable sources. For instance, we have been told by nutritionists, teachers, parents, and, of course, the dairy and meat industry that we need a lot of protein to be strong—the more the better. Studies are now showing that too much protein is harmful and USers are overeating it. The over-consumption of meat and dairy products causes major health problems in the form of high cholesterol and risk of cancer. Additionally, John Robbins in *Diet for a New America* (1987) states that the more protein we have in our diet, the more calcium we lose, no matter how much calcium we take in; "The result is that high protein diets in general, and meat-based diets in particular, lead to a gradual but inexorable decrease in bone density, and produce the ongoing development of osteoporosis" (193). The dairy industry advocates drinking more milk to increase our supply of calcium when dairy products themselves add to the over-consumption of protein that causes our bodies to be unable to absorb calcium.

I recommend reading *Diet for a New America* because it elucidates the implications of what we eat. Without alternate sources of information intervening, we simply go on repeating patterns that are generally acceptable in this society. When we accept at face value that which has been taught to us as good, we remain ignorant about how these foods make our bodies feel, how the foods are grown and delivered to us, and whether the foods are healthy in the long run. It is crucial to body-mindfulness that we become aware of all of these factors. There is no way to eat apolitically. You are making a statement or voting, as it were, each time you eat.

The images of the ideal body that are so prevalent in our culture may give one the impression that we as a society are indeed concerned about body and not just mind. We are concerned about living longer, being in shape, and perfecting our bodies. Much time, attention and money are focused on these goals. This focus on body, however, often does not lead to a reintegration or healing of the mind/body split or require body-mindfulness. Rather, what is emphasized is a split-off body, a dichotomized body, a body *image*—not a body with recognized alterity that is interconnected with and inextricable from the mind.

The body images we see in magazines and on TV belonging to "successful" people compel many of us to force our bodies to emulate them, even when our bodies do not remotely resemble the image we see. When we cannot produce that image, we feel like failures and blame many of our problems on our appearance. Because women's identities are wrapped up with how closely they can mirror that image, they are especially susceptible to its tyrannical power.

Health and quality of life are not found in the prevailing cultural images because each one of us has our own individual healthy weight, diet and amount and type of exercise. By concentrating on body as object, we lose the integrated self that has knowledge and immanent power in itself, no matter what the cultural image holds out to us.

In the area of bodily pleasures, like sexuality, the cultural image undermines our immanent body-mind power. Sexuality is about power, not about pleasure. It has been culturally defined as a means of finding power through splitting what is powerful in connection. First the power-yielding split is made between men and women, subjects and objects and then the split is made of bodies from minds.

This constant splitting through which one part gains power and then dominates the other part is practically synonymous with sex in our society. The power in sado-masochism and in milder versions of domination-mode sex comes from that surge of power we experience in splitting ourselves apart. When Andrea Dworkin describes heterosexual sex as inherently rape, she may be referring to this phenomenon. As it is portrayed in this culture, the sex act becomes the splitting apart of the woman, a violent splitting or stabbing rather than merger or connection of people. The focus on genitalia and certain body parts indicates a further split that occurs within the body.

We have so trained our bodies to respond to certain stimuli that we can no longer experience other kinds of pleasure. Sensuality is practically synonymous with sexuality and is confined to the bedroom. The splitting off of sexuality from the rest of our lives and of men from women becomes a self-fulfilling prophecy. Our bodies are taught to respond sexually to these splits and then find it difficult to respond to anything else. In *Elemental Passions* (1992), Luce Irigaray asks a key question: "And how can we feel whole in this universe of sutures? This tracery of scars?" (101). Again the alterity of the body is not heard from and is difficult to find. I will deal with the subject of sexuality further in Chapter 12, "Fabricating the Between—What Threads are Missing?"

Our Habitat—The Environmental Body

From the power-over culture's roots in Judeo-Christianity comes the notion that humans are meant to have dominion over the earth, to control it, to reap its treasures, and to tame it for our purposes. What we do to our habitat parallels what we do to our bodies. Consumption is beyond what is needed to thrive and the wrong things are consumed. As with our own bodies, when we try to dominate our habitat, we split ourselves from it and every creature here. We do not see or feel our connections to our habitat; we pretend we are apart from it. Because we see ourselves as separate and better than our habitat, our lines of communication are severed. Then we have a hard time ascertaining what is "right" or "wrong" for our health or for our habitat.

This dichotomization has gotten us into a mire of environmental problems. We see our physical realities as objects to be controlled and dominated for the purposes of certain men (literally men's minds). We appear prepared to go so far as to entirely cut off our supply of oxygen and clean water and sicken and kill our bodies. Because the mind/body split paradigm is so comfortable for us, we do not witness the destruction of our own life support until it is almost gone and is affecting our very breath. We are at that point now. And still we look to a dichotomized world view to give us relief.

Jeremy Rifkin stated in his book *Algeny* (1983), "We adamantly maintain ourselves as subject and reduce everything else to object. Greater separation from nature makes it easier and easier to capture, maim and kill with impunity" (52). The more dichotomized and unconnected we are from other creatures in our habitat or the earth itself, the less we care. We have thoroughly convinced ourselves that whatever harm we do, we can fix with science and technology, with more power-over.

We exercise our control over the part of the world that fits the scientific model, that can be objectified while we ignore the rest. We attempt to control the "other," the object of traditional science, whether that is our habitat or our bodies. Traditional science tries to predict and then control every move of the universe; however, such a goal could only be achieved by actually making the world into a dichotomy, by destroying all of our connections and eliminating all the areas that cannot be predicted and controlled. Success would mean the end of our stay on earth; we would have so distanced ourselves so as to destroy our life support. Treating the world as if it exists as a dichotomy is destructive enough; but making that mindset a reality would drive a stake through our hearts.

For instance, when we perceive an energy shortage, our first inclination is to go from bad to worse. Fossil fuels create air pollution, acid rain, holes in the ozone; so we turn to nuclear power whose waste products are even more deadly. We have no place to store the waste and the threat of accidental release of radiation is real and has happened both in this country and in the former Soviet Union. Is it not possible to recognize the danger and decide to go a completely different way rather than to "fix" it with more of the same?

But if energy shortages are a warning from the earth about our lifestyles, we cannot hear them over the roar of more turbines. Fritjof Capra puts it well when he says, "Our ever increasing energy needs reflect the general expansion of our economic and technological systems; they are caused by the patterns of undifferentiated growth that deplete our natural resources and contribute significantly to our multiple symptoms of individual and social illness.... In our present, highly unbalanced state, more of it would not solve our problems but would make them worse" (239). More energy does not solve the larger contextualized problems of our damaged relationship to our habitat.

Thomas Lovejoy of the World Wildlife Fund states that nearly 17 percent of all plant and animal species remaining on earth will become extinct by the year 2000 (Eckholm 9). But instead of taking any large steps to change our behavior to halt the extinctions of more species, we try to further control species and our habitat. For example, we capture the last two falcons and breed them in captivity until we let them loose again. Saving that species to return to the same or a worse habitat does not do it, or us, any favors. Exercising power-over always seems to be our first choice, but it is seldom the best choice.

In Richmond, California in the summer of 1993, there was a chemical spill that created a cloud of toxic chemicals which blew over the area and sickened hundreds of people. When such a spill occurs, we do not ask if we really need to create such toxins to begin with. We instead focus on the negligence of the company that spilled the chemicals. We rely on those companies and the environmental protection agencies to keep us from harm and then we panic when that expectation is not met. But we are beyond any façade of protection since the protection agencies themselves cannot keep up with the new wastes that are produced everyday nor are they funded or adequately supported politically to do the kind of job it would take to make us safe. And some chemicals will never be safe.

We rely on these chemicals every day of our lives and yet at the same time they poison our air and water. Consumers buy ever more products that contain these chemicals. Many do not bother to find out how the products are made and what their side effects may be; instead we abdicate responsibility when we shop for products, as if their presence there on the shelves sanctions our use of them.

We poison ourselves, though if we embody that "we," it becomes clear that people of color and poor people (as in the Richmond incident cited above) are often disproportionately affected. Factories and toxic waste dumps are most often located in economically disadvantaged areas. However, with such phenomena as acid rain, borders are not respected and the poison cannot be controlled. Eventually, none of us, no matter how much money and power-over we have, can escape the pervasiveness of our lifestyle and attitude toward our habitat. We cannot contain our waste; it overtakes us.

Another example is water shortages in California. The first response when a shortage of water in one place is discovered is to pipe in water from someplace else. The water shortage is a warning issued from our physical surroundings that our current lifestyle requires too much water. But instead of dealing with that issue, responding to the warning itself, we bring in more water.

If our goals require us to dam a river or drain a lake, we hardly flinch. Lakes and rivers have no standing in and of themselves and there is no attempt to consider the implications of their destruction. Also not on the agenda for discussion is the huge waste of water by agriculture and the beef and dairy industries. Where is the discussion of what kinds of agriculture we should be doing in a state with a drought and whether or not we should even have cattle within our borders? Where is the discussion about our lifestyles, our consumption habits, our part in this equation? Those in the place of power-over seem to be exempt from participating in the blame or taking responsibility for our current situation. That they should continue to reap the benefits of doing whatever they like at the expense of our habitat does not seem to be questioned. The discussion could focus on how to use less water and work in cooperation with California's resources with all of our interests on the table. Rather, our first choice is to accept the assumption that we must continue to do everything we have always done. Thus, our focus is limited solely to *which* water to drain out of which ecosystems. When the chosen ecosystem shows signs of water depletion and destruction, we may then try the same thing on some other ecosystem.

Ecologist Thomas Berry states, "In its order of magnitude, this change in our relation to the earth is much greater than experienced when the first Neolithic civilizations came into being some twelve thousand years ago. Nothing since then, not even the great civilizational structures themselves, produced change on such a significant scale. Such change cannot be managed by partial accommodations or even by major adjustments within the civilizational contexts of the past. The context of survival is radically altered" (42-43). Just as we shut up our bodies' warning signals, so too, do we ignore signals warning us that the earth is sick. We proceed as if nothing were wrong. Or if we do finally get a message that something is wrong, rather than tend to the problem, we make the warning signal disappear.

The analogy with personal health is a strong one. For instance, we find out that dairy products are not good for humans, can create phlegm, and give us stomachaches, headaches, and high cholesterol. Instead of encouraging a reduction in intake of those products, we spend our resources creating a diet supplement that gets rid of the symptoms. If, instead of seeing the headache as the problem, we saw it as the warning that dairy products were not good for us, our solution would be to stop eating dairy products, not to find ways to override the signal. Similarly, if, when confronted with a water shortage, we examined our whole framework that begot the shortage in the first place, we might begin to work *with* our habitat to solve problems rather than forcing it to conform to our imagined needs.

The water shortage is not an isolated problem. If headaches can be a warning signal, then so too could the water shortage be a warning that we are polluting the air and causing global warming. More and more water is needed to do the same things we used to do with less. So trying to "cure" the water shortage is simply a diversionary tactic.

There are hundreds of examples of environmental problems that come from our disregard for our connections. These have been well documented elsewhere. One final example I will present because it is so indicative of our attitudes is the continued destruction of our habitat by the beef and dairy industries. The raising of cattle both here and abroad is rife with environmental problems.[16] To support the developed countries' addiction to beef, we have burned rain forests to make room for grazing; we have turned fertile plains into deserts; we have fed beef instead of humans; and we have aggravated the hole in the ozone layer.

From Jeremy Rifkin we learn that, "by the time a feedlot steer is ready for slaughter, it has consumed 2,700 pounds of grain and weighs approximately 1,050 pounds. Currently, in the United States, 157 million metric tons of cereal, legumes and vegetable protein suitable for human use is fed to livestock to produce 28 million metric tons of animal protein which humans consume annually" (*Beyond Beef* 161). When hunger is at epidemic proportions in the world, we go on promoting and consuming beef as if our consumption had no effect on others in the world. But those "others" are in the down-side of the dichotomy and we do not think of our relationship with them. It is as if there is no relationship; again this is a thought pattern derived from dichotomous, we/ they thinking.

Cattle production is a primary factor in causing land to turn to desert even here in the U.S. through over-grazing, over-cultivation, deforestation and improper irrigation techniques. In examining the human toll of this spreading desertification, Rifkin's projections indicate "tens of millions of dispossessed and displaced human beings wandering across eroded fields, parched deserts and denuded forest clearings, in search of a safe haven, finding only crowded urban slums, shanty towns, and sidewalk encampments at the end of their futile journeys" (*Beyond Beef* 201).

In addition to desertification, in California, as I stated earlier, we are concerned with droughts. When we eat beef Rifkin urges us to keep in mind that "nearly half the water consumed in the United States now goes to grow feed for cattle and other livestock" (*Beyond Beef* 219). These are the direct side effects of our consumption of beef. In order to practice body-mindfulness we must become educated on the effects our habits have on others. Eating is something most of us do every day and it is a place to start right now to put into effect a new consciousness of connectedness.

The problems we are creating for our habitat are not someone else's problems; they are our problems. Until we feel the truth of that, we will continue to look for ways to simply silence our habitat. As long as our minds shut up our bodies, certain humans shut up other humans and humans shut up our physical realities, how can we expect to understand the world we actually live in?

If separation, diagnosis, control, and domination were not the goals we as a society have espoused, we could acknowledge the relationship between mind and body, the relationships between people, the relationship between habitat and people and the interconnections of all of those levels. Our problems cannot be seen in isolation from each other; they should not be dichotomized into separate entities such as social problems, individual problems or environmental problems; all of these levels must be explored together. The health of each depends on the health of the other because we are all part of each other.

In the next two chapters we will look at the effect that dichotomization, men from women and whites from everyone else, has had on men's and women's realities.

5

Fissures of Men:
Are Men an Oppressed Group?

We have discussed some of the effects on women of being dichotomized from men and put in the category of "body." I want to discuss
now what effect this dichotomization has had on men. Men have been
placed in the dominant position in the dichotomy—over women, and
along with mind. They have been in this power-over position in relation
to women for centuries and have benefited greatly from that privileged
position.

From the perspective of the dichotomous world view, men are in an
enviable position compared to women; but, if viewed from the perspective of wholeness, men, though they have power-over, are denied access
to their immanent power by virtue of their split from their own bodies,
from women, and from each other. In fact, while men have benefited,
they, along with women, have had difficulty living whole and satisfying
lives and expressing their creativity and potential.

I want to briefly address issues of race and class that complicate an
analysis that deals primarily with the male/female split. There is never
simply one dichotomy functioning at any one point in time. To speak
about the privileges "men" have had or still have is difficult because
sometimes those privileges are granted only to white men, or straight
men, or able-bodied men and sometimes they are a privilege granted to
all men simply by virtue of being born male.

In certain contexts it appears that white women have more power
than black men, and in others, it does not. This discussion, if treated
with care, could be a book in itself. Here I will simply note that in every

example I use, if the race or class of the men and women are shifted around, we will see different mechanisms of coping with the dichotomy and the hierarchy.

A hierarchy is formed within the male power-over position that puts some men in power-under positions vis-à-vis each other even while they remain in the top part of the male/female dichotomy. This hierarchy is held in place by forcing certain men into positions closer to body than other men. The highest position is, of course, a place of transcendence of body, which actually means having a standard white, male hetero-sexual body that is not "necessary" in one's work. The possession of the "universal" body is the first step toward transcendence. The second step is having enough privilege not to have to use that body in one's work but to use only the mind and rationality. Putting a man in a category closer to the body is a way to put him down, to incline him toward the female half of the dichotomy. Working class men, including white men, are thought of as closer to body and therefore inferior to men in upper classes. Certain men are put as far down as possible within the male half of the dichotomy and are accused of being effeminate, ruled by their passions, closer to body, or lacking mind.

To the founding fathers of this country, male slaves were counted as 3/5 of a man—still in the category of male but not fully male. Racist policies since then have relied on the fallacy that black men are closer to body and therefore more animalistic and unable to control their pas-sions and their sexuality than their counterparts in white society. The easiest way to get power-over another man is to show how much closer to body he is. By referring to skin color, whites find something in the body of blacks that is different and can be pointed to and exploited for power-over.

For men of color, one way to move up in the hierarchy is to disavow their bodies, become non-threatening, asexual. They can attempt to show that they have risen above their roots in poverty and ethnicity. This move requires cutting their ties to those who are still caught up in the fight for justice for all humans regardless of skin color. They convince them-selves that they have transcended body and therefore, to them, skin color is no longer an issue. They urge others to go the same route. Clarence Thomas is a good example of this strategy (see discussion in Chapter 6). He tries to blend in, to take positions that conserve the status quo as if his interests lay in that direction and not in the direction of change.

Men of color, who are "othered" within the male side of the dichotomy, are caught in a double bind. They can achieve some power-over through their power over women, but many of the other power-over routes are closed to them. They have access to little power-over but they are still socialized that to be men, power-over is the power of choice. This phenomenon is perhaps why we see a kind of machismo exert itself in men of color and working class men that may not be as necessary with white men of privilege who are more freely given other forms of power-over. But all men are strongly socialized to get their power through power-over instead of through immanent power; the ways power-over manifests itself has to do with where the available power-over is.

For the remainder of this chapter I am going to speak primarily about the power men have in relation to women. Although I shall not continue to make a distinction between men of different backgrounds, these differences are, of course, always present and complicate overly general approaches. Therefore, keep in mind as you read this chapter that each man has developed his own unique way of handling his life and the society around him. No one individual is all of the things I will be describing; without being aware of it, we all slip around the dichotomies, which are, after all, merely human-made divisions.

By virtue of being male, men of all classes, ethnicities and religions have in common one kind of power-over, and that is power-over women, at the very least women of their own race; and in certain ways over all women. This power is one that men are raised with, a gift given them simply by being born male. They are the subject to women's object; they are the agents of power-over. What they traded for that power-over are the qualities and attributes that have been associated with women and body. The split and the subsequent enforcement of it requires that men be separate from anything having to do with women and femininity.

Within the very identity of men is the exclusion of those things that are female. Here I refer to Nancy Chodorow's work (*Reproduction of Mothering*, 1988) in which she asserts that in the development of the identities of males, a distinction has to be made between boys and their mothers. Boys have to become what is "not mother" or "not girl." Early in their lives they learn to dichotomize. The greatest insult that can be levied against a boy is that he is acting "like a girl."

Boys' narratives make them the heroes of the stories, the ones who do the dangerous things and who seek out and fulfill their desires. Boys in general are not supposed to care how they *look* but to value what they *do* in the world. Independence, aggression, competitiveness are all encouraged and linked to the development of boys' identities.

Early in childhood development, the male and female spheres are polarized and traits are situated either in one sphere or the other. In *Words and Women* (1991), Casey Miller and Kate Swift cite Ruth E. Hartley in her study "Sex-Role Pressures and the Socialization of the Male Child" published in 1959: "For many boys the scramble to escape femininity takes on all the aspects of 'panic, and the outward semblance of non-femininity is achieved at a tremendous cost of anxiety and self-alien-ation'" (Miller and Swift 67). Repressing, denying and fearing those parts of themselves that are defined by the culture as feminine, boys learn early to abandon their alterity and seek to fit a societal mold or risk ridicule and exclusion. Body and the "feminine" are in the denied cat-egory, as are the qualities that allegedly to go along with them, like ex-pressions of emotions, non-linearity, cyclic time, regeneration, compassion, life giving qualities, cooperation with others, and love of others without domination.

Our society as a whole devalues those qualities so that both women and men are in danger of pushing them underground. For men the prob-lem is even more acute. This phenomenon appears to be the opposite of what women face when the very construction of subjectivity conflicts with the development of a feminine identity. Here we have masculinity defined against so-called feminine qualities. So it is not that men do not have the qualities, but rather how can they develop and express them when to do so is contrary to their identities as men. Male identity is threatened each time a man ventures outside of the domain of the mind, rationality and maleness.

Men are in even more danger than women are of living split lives, split from their bodies and split from women. For a man to value and express his loving side, his artistic side (unless he can make a lot of money or gain status through it), his nurturing side, especially in the public sphere, is frowned upon and discouraged. If he wants to have those feelings, he must keep them to himself or express them only at home. Heaven forbid those qualities are brought into the workplace or into capitalism itself; business, which for the most part relies on their exclusion, would have to change drastically.

Men are trained that to succeed they must compete in a ruthless and uncaring way. Relationships in business are valued more for what some-one can do for you than how they make you feel or enhance the quality of your life or the life of the community. Men are encouraged to be selfish, to break connections, to compete in a way that shows they are in control, autonomous and independent.

When I worked in a law firm as a paralegal, I wondered why so many of the male attorneys had a problem asking for help or advice. Particularly the young associates or the law clerks could have saved themselves many hours of work and foolish mistakes if they had just consulted with the paralegals who had been doing the work for many years and had more practical training even if not the same level of academic training. But many of the law clerks would do anything rather than ask a paralegal a question. Mind you, they had no problem telling paralegals what to do in a power-over way. But when they needed advice or assistance in an assignment, they could not get up the courage to ask. They might have appeared weak or vulnerable. Better to spend the client's money wasting time or actually do the work incompetently than consult with someone who had not been to law school, someone who was in the lower half of the dichotomy, a non-lawyer (the lawyer/non-lawyer dichotomy is one unto itself!).

The primary value in large corporate settings is how much money a person can bring into the firm. Many qualities that are crucial to the administration of the place and the morale of the workers are invisible and given no recognition at all. In the firms where I have worked the burden often fell to the women to keep the emotional life of the firm intact. Men used women as emotional support and drained their time and energy, making it harder for women to clock the billable time required to be "successful." Men, on the other hand, are expected to deny those parts of themselves that are cooperative, vulnerable, in need of assistance, loving and helpful. Thus, not only do women get burned out from doing this unacknowledged work, but also men find that there are parts of themselves that have to remain unexpressed and unexplored.

To desire access to the devalued side of a dichotomy is to begin to value it and thus to undermine the weighted nature of the dichotomy and threaten its existence. The closest we get to that kind of undermining is in parts of the gay culture where men emulate the styles and content of what has traditionally been defined as female. This parody strikes at the heart of the dichotomy and therefore threatens its stability. These parts of gay men's culture which mimic or take on "female" traits are most often targeted for ridicule by the larger society. Homophobia toward gay men has its roots in misogyny. To *choose* to take on "feminine" qualities, to value those qualities, calls into question the original devaluation of those characteristics associated with the female.

In their family lives often men are expected to bring home a certain amount of money to keep the household running. A man can begin to feel like a workhorse, sent out each day and good only for the paycheck he brings home. If heterosexual men want to participate more in their home life, with children, friends and mates, with decorating the house, with cooking food, etc., they have to take care not to be labeled effeminate or seen as freaks. Dichotomizing and power-over force all of us into standards that we do not fit and which deny our wholeness as human beings.

Though more men are taking responsibility in the home, we are still a long, long way from anything close to equally shared responsibility for house, food and children. Arlie Hochschild, a sociologist and the author of *The Second Shift* (1989), interviewed families beginning in 1976 and following up in 1988 to see if men were taking on more responsibility for the household chores and childcare responsibilities, what she termed the "second shift." She found that little in practical terms had changed. Most women she interviewed in the late 1980's "do the lion's share of the work at home, do most of the daily chores and take responsibility for running the home. But something was different, too. More couples *wanted* to share and imagined that they did" (20). It seemed that the couples had new awareness that the responsibility *should* be shared but the reality did not reflect that new awareness. Instead, in order to keep peace, couples pretended that they shared more equally in the work at home. They collude in the illusion that they are sharing the second shift equally. However, it is clear that the private sphere still belongs for the most part to women no matter how much of the public sphere they have been able to enter.

While men escape a lot of the actual work of raising children and cooking and house work, they are also deprived of the other side of the coin, because those very activities provide feelings of being needed, connection with children, pride in arrangement of their living space, knowledge about the price and quality of food and the outlets for creativity and giving that preparing food can provide. Because these activities are devalued as "women's work," for both the men and women who do them, they are often considered to be mere drudgery.

Whatever tasks have been assigned to women tend to be lower status jobs. We need to look at these tasks again with different eyes to judge their value. I think men miss out on a lot in not sharing these responsibilities. I enjoy creative cooking and the chance to pick out and even grow healthy food. These tasks like gardening, cooking and composting are what keeps humans grounded on the earth and reminded of their places in the habitat.

Men's bodies suffer perhaps even more than women's bodies in certain respects because men define themselves through Mind. Often men do not pay any attention to their bodies at all and someone else, usually a woman, takes care of their bodies. Too busy to eat? To busy to take a moment to go to the bathroom? Override, override. Mind over matter. By ignoring the body, by feeding it fast food and doughnuts, coffee, alcohol and cigarette smoke, they show that they are not interested in the body's alterity. The body is supposed to follow the instructions of the mind. Men treat bodies as objects to be controlled, manipulated—and even more damaging—ignored. We could say that many men treat their bodies like they treat women: no respect for their own value and knowledge, as if they owned them, demanding that they look good, and as if the body were under their control. Athletes in particular learn the ways of transcending pain, going the extra yard at the behest of their mind and their coach, and sometimes with the help of synthetic hormones. These ways of viewing the body are an essential part of keeping the mind/body split intact.

Separation from body puts men in a state that leaves them susceptible to circumstances that could harm their bodies. In her book *Femininity and Domination* (1990) Sandra Lee Bartky asserts that, "In a striking critique of modern society, Michel Foucault has argued that the rise of parliamentary institutions and of new conceptions of political liberty was accompanied by a darker counter-movement, by the emergence of a new and unprecedented discipline directed against the body.... The disciplinary practices Foucault describes are tied to peculiarly modern forms of the army, the school, the hospital, the prison, and the manufactory; the aim of these disciplines is to increase the utility of the body, to augment its forces" (63). In all of these areas discipline has become key to making sure that the body does as the mind tells it. Here I will speak primarily about what happens to bodies in the military where men's bodies are particularly susceptible to that discipline to the point of risking death.

Certain minds, ideologies and power, decide that a war must be waged and send soldiers out to the battlefield to kill and be killed. Again the hierarchy of men comes into play—the low men on the totem pole such as men of color and poor men are seduced into the military by economics, promises of training or by the possibility of becoming a hero. Once in, they are trained to be all discipline.

Philosopher Michel Foucault stated, "A 'political anatomy,' which was also a 'mechanics of power,' was being born; it defined how one may have a hold over others' bodies, not only so that they may do what one wishes, but so that they may operate as one wishes, with the techniques, the speed and the efficiency that one determines. Thus, discipline produces subjected and practiced bodies, 'docile' bodies" (*Discipline and Punish* 138). The military relies both on the power-over hierarchy of rank and also on the mind/body split and the power-over body. In men who are well-trained, the body is not only an object but is an object following orders of rank and trained to behave in certain automatic ways.

War is the ultimate separation of mind from body and of men from mothers, women and children; this feature makes it a magnet for many men who are counting on that separation to establish their identities. It is the manifestation of all they have learned as boys. Their minds (actually the minds of their superiors) tell their own bodies what to do, overriding emotions and legitimate body knowledge, and that discipline is considered the height of achievement.

Those who have enlisted because they are poor and disadvantaged risk their bodies for their country to learn a skill, to move up the hierarchy. It is a gamble with death for the possible gain of power-over. To require men to serve in the military, as in times of the draft, or to be pushed into it by economics or machismo is a tragic side effect of the dichotomization of men and women.

Military leaders, as the mind of the operation, want their men to have strong, well-trained, obedient bodies. They force their underlings to the lowest part of the male hierarchy so that to survive they will exert the only power they have, power-over the enemy, the Other; and power-over their own bodies. The importance of drawing a thick line between men and women and outlawing "feminine" qualities is magnified. The military seals off masculinity from any leakage of power-over or infiltration of immanent power from the outside. They harken back to a time when men were warriors and kings, indisputably in power.

The most crucial aspects of the military are threefold. First, the men must not allow even a hint of femininity inside their borders. Secondly, their minds must exercise complete control over their bodies so that even when their bodies are tortured, their minds remain impenetrable. And third, they must not allow the we/they line to soften in any way; the enemy—whether they be men, women and children—are all bad, all different, all less worthy than We.

The presence of openly gay men in the military threatens the military's barrier against femininity. The model of sex that is unquestioned in our society and in the military, is that of the domination mode of sex: one party is subject and the other object, one party dominates the other. Any thoughts of sex must be power-over sex, domination, and objectification of the sexual partner. Thus, if two men are having sex, one of them must then be put in the object category, the "feminine" category. Sex between men puts the military code at risk by blurring the boundary and allowing the "feminine" to creep in; it is seen as undermining discipline, authority, and the strict hierarchy of power-over.

I deliberately have not talked about women in the military because that phenomenon is similar to women in business or sports or the other traditionally male preserves. Women try to make inroads by being allowed into otherwise male territory. The presence of women in the military does create a strain on the paradigm of "no feminine" and for the most part has survived because the women themselves do not parade their femininity but rather emphasize their ability to act masculine. Women showing their masculinity is not as threatening to the establishment as is men exhibiting their femininity. Additionally, just as in civilian life, most women hold inferior positions in the military and often appear in "support" roles. I would contend that there is still an overriding disdain for women in the military and that any excuse, such as lesbianism, is enough to get a woman expelled; but it is not the focus of the gays in the military debate.

Incidents like those at the Tailhook Convention in 1991 show us the reality that exists in the military—the hatred of women and things "feminine." The tradition of setting aside a time when women are shown their "real" place in the military, like at the Tailhook convention, has been celebrated for years. It was not until some women complained about being treated as objects and demeaned that anything was done about it. For women to break rank and call attention to what was going on at the convention was courageous because it meant alerting everyone to their difference and to their different treatment. Meanwhile, the majority of the military remains male and the brunt of casualties, at least on the side of the U.S., are young men of color.[17]

Even in the military, when the training and emphasis is on power-over and the men are coerced in one way or another to serve, the officials cannot stop the emergence of non-sexual egalitarian relations among men. When men of the same rank spend lots of time together and get to know each other's stories and histories, there enters the possibility of close relationships emerging. In fact, those relationships are sometimes encouraged by the higher ups; men can then work more as a team and not as individuals out for themselves, a factor which would weaken the forces. Cooperative camaraderies are formed among the men such that they consider the whole team instead of just their own individual situation. In extreme situations, a soldier cannot help but be reminded of his connections to and reliance on the others in his unit.

Kent, a man I know who fought in the Vietnam war, looks back with great nostalgia at the relationships he formed with his fellow soldiers. In extreme circumstances, exerting power-over the enemy is not enough to keep a person going. There is the chance in the down time to hear the stories of other men and to share emotions and fears. With the specter of death so close, what is important in life, what is valued over all else is shared; bonds are formed; immanent power is tapped into. Kent looked back at those days in Vietnam as some of us look back at the relationship with our mothers. Both were times when relationship, connections, the sharing of ourselves happened without recrimination. So while Kent was appalled by the overall mission and the horrors that happened while there, he still looks back with longing at those times and those relationships. I find it tragic that there are not more positive ways for men to be allowed and encouraged to form meaningful bonds. It often takes a war for men to find a way to love each other.

In sports, which are often modeled on the military, there is a parallel but less exaggerated example of camaraderie among men. Similar conditions are at work. The men on one team are pitted against those on the other team and are encouraged to see themselves as better than and different from the other team. The ideal of teamwork is applauded but the appearance of anything else that might hint at "femininity" is off limits.

In many of the professional sports teams, however, the presence of power-over in the form of different salaries and benefits for different team members, undermines the possibilities of forming trusting relationships. While coaches work for team spirit and cooperation among the players, power-over differences work to keep the players distrustful of each other.

In the rest of the civilian world men are not encouraged to form bonds with other men. They are mostly encouraged to remain separate, look out for themselves, be autonomous, self-contained, and need no one. Most men have not developed their skills at venturing out of the power-over position with women. With power-over as the ingrained and automatic power of choice, a consciousness raising that few men are willing to undergo is required. A precursor to such a move is for men to recognize the alterity of women, body and everything else on the planet and to interact with it without using power-over. Giving up power-over is seen as a loss of power and, in a way, it is. However, to give up power-over and gain immanent power is not a minor exchange at all, and one surely comes out ahead in quality of life.

In the area of sexuality men are trained to see women a certain way and their bodies have been trained to respond with pleasure to power over women. With pornography[18] men are expected to rise to the occasion, to train their body-minds to get off sexually on the abuse of women. Pornography puts men in the position once again of having to fit into the mold of domination and power-over, thus lessening their ability and chance of reaching their own immanent power. We have thrown up another smoke screen to hide and further confuse ourselves. We simply rise to (or sink to) another level of dichotomous thinking. We continue to split the world and live on the power that comes from splitting instead of searching for immanent power that acknowledges both our alterity and our connections.

6
Shamed if She Does;
Shamed if She Doesn't

We have looked now at how the mind/body, male/female splits affect mind, body and men. In this chapter I will explore how being placed on the down side of the dichotomy along with body and objects has affected both how women see and treat themselves and how others see and treat women.

How Women See Themselves

Here I will look at the development of women's identities, that is, how they see themselves. Self-perception, an internalized aspect of oppression, is not always accessible to analysis. As we saw in the first two chapters of this book, in the stories we repeat from generation to generation, men are the heroes and women are the objects or prizes.

Children are influenced not only by adults' conscious statements to them but also by the stories they see, hear and sense around them. Small children trying to figure out who they are and their place in the world are like sponges absorbing the slightest clues. During their process of gender identification, children look to the stories that surround them to formulate their own narratives.

Carol Tavris, in her book *The Mismeasure of Woman* (1992), tells us that the communications researcher George Gerbner once stated that the human being is "the only species that tells stories—and lives by the stories we tell" (301). Think of your own life stories and where they came from and how you know where to go next—what is part of such a story line and what is not? Tavris states, "They are narratives that provide a unifying theme to organize the events of our lives.... It is here, in the stories that men and women tell about their lives, that we find the greatest divergence between them" (301-302).

The classical men's story is about a hero who goes out in the world to conquer some mean obstacles and returns victorious to win the hand of a sweet young maiden. Tavris puts it this way: "The classic women's story, whether in ancient fairy tales like 'Cinderella' and 'Sleeping Beauty' or their modern equivalents in romance novels and films like *Pretty Woman*, is a narrative of passivity, chance, and fate. Horrible things, all of them beyond her control, happen to the beautiful heroine who awaits rescue by her Prince. Until he saves her, she is doomed to a life of sweeping, cleaning, struggling, prostitution, or corporate executivehood. If she isn't beautiful, pliant and willing to give it all up for love, she doesn't get rescued" (302).

Of course, the latter story has been primarily a white European narrative. There are additional myths that women of color are associated with; for instance, for African American women, the myth is that they are strong and independent, able to handle both the family and the work world. But because this myth directly contradicts that of the passive white woman, black women are often accused of emasculating men, of taking on male characteristics that do not "rightly" belong to them. These two female myths point up the deep-seated contradiction inherent in all women's identity struggles.

What effect does the repetition of these myths have on women's perception of themselves? And how does the subject/object dichotomy and its genderization worm its way into the narratives of boys and girls? These are the questions I would like to deal with here.

Even though we *know* that language has an enormous impact on children's conception of the world and their place in it, the use of the "universal man" is still prevalent in children's books and even in our own speech. Recent studies in linguistics (1992)[19] have shown that a large percentage of boys and girls reading the pronoun "he" still do not envision girls as possible actors. And, in fact, at a very early age both girls and boys are uncomfortable when the protagonist in a particularly action-packed story is described as a girl rather than as a boy. These studies show that, particularly as small children, girls are learning that they are not subjects in their own right.

For her Ph.D. dissertation in 1973, Alleen Pace Nilsen at the University of Iowa conducted studies on this subject. "Using a picture-selection technique with 100 children ranging in grade level from nursery school through the seventh grade, Nilsen found that *man* in the sentences 'Man must work in order to eat' and 'Around the world man is happy' was interpreted by a majority of children of both sexes to mean male people and not to mean female people" (Miller and Swift 27). Nilsen then looked in beginning textbooks of prehistoric people and found that the illustrations of male figures outnumbered those of females eight to one. As these examples show, such biases are still very much embedded in our culture and language.

When we hear phrases like "every man and his brother" or "to each his own," "all men are created equal," and the thousands more like them, neither girls nor boys automatically extend this to include girls; females are left in a never-never land of the outsider. In Simone de Beauvoir's terms (1974), women are the "Second Sex"—the Other.

Erik Erikson, one of the foremost theorists in the area of psychosocial behavior (of boys, though he did not make that distinction) postulated a theory of eight stages of development.[20] What interests me is Erikson's second stage of development, which he called "autonomy versus shame, guilt." This stage is the one in which a very young child supposedly acquires a sense of separateness and an accompanying sense of self-will. But as we have seen, girls are taught that their identities consist of being an object/body that, of course, has no autonomy or self will. This is a classic double bind: as a girl it is wrong to be autonomous; and as a human being it is wrong *not* to be autonomous.

The fault here lies in the linkage of the two dichotomies (male/female and subject/object) such that "subject" is always in the top of the dichotomy along with "male"; therefore, girls experience exclusion. In the words of Luce Irigaray in *The Speculum of the Other Woman* (1985), "We can assume that any theory of the subject has always been appropriated by the 'masculine'" (133). The very concepts of "womanhood" and "subjectivity" are in conflict. Because there seems to be no way to be both simultaneously, women must constantly juggle two extremes, being a woman or being human. Elizabeth Debold, Marie Wilson and Idelisse Malave, authors of *Mother Daughter Revolution: From Betrayal to Power* (1993) state it this way: "As girls approach adolescence, they encounter the two well-trodden paths that women take into patriarchy: conventional femininity and 'girls will be boys,' the culturally approved adoption by women of male models for how to be and act in the world" (57).

She is shamed if she does and shamed if she doesn't. If she chooses the identity of a woman, she may feel shame both because of her inability to be fully human, to be autonomous and also because she is not a "good enough" object—that is, her body is not thin enough, white enough, pretty enough, or sexy enough. For a black woman there may be the additional shame of having abdicated an ancestral myth of being a powerful force in her own right for the Western myth of the ideal woman.

On the other hand, if a woman leans toward autonomy, she may feel shame both over her failures as a feminine object and over her unworthiness as a human. She may feel like a fraud assuming characteristics that have been specifically assigned to the "masculine." Then if she succeeds, she feels she has cheated, expropriated what was not legitimately hers. Sandra Lee Bartky states, "Many oppressed persons come to regard themselves as uniquely unable to satisfy normal criteria of psychological health or moral adequacy" (30). There is shame associated with stepping outside her prescribed narrative and shame in staying within it.

Bartky expresses the double bind this way: "to be psychologically oppressed is to be caught in the double bind of a society which both affirms my human status and at the same time bars me from the exercise of many of those typically human functions that bestow this status. To be denied an autonomous choice of self, forbidden cultural expression, and condemned to the immanence of mere bodily being is to be cut off from the sorts of activities that define what it is to be human" (31).

But no matter what balance women strike, the pressure to be a desirable object must be dealt with in order for them to feel adequate. Girls grow up surrounded by the most powerful socializing tool of all, advertising: glamorized women on TV, in billboards, mandating that women look, smell and feel like beautiful objects. This, they learn, is where female power is located, in a woman's ability to attract a man, to manipulate a man, to compete and win out over other women for a man's attention. Women as bodies, either as sexual objects for the pleasure of men or as mothers at the service of all, are the role models we present for girls. The power-over culture brings us our staples of women's work and men's work and continues to trivialize "women's" work. The occasional pictures we see of women in places of power all come connected to behavior that either mimics the man or is designed to attract him.

Let us look more closely at some of the ramifications of women identifying themselves as objects and as body. When I talk of subject, I am referring to the thinker, the doer of action, the self or the ego. Subject is conscious or consciousness; and when it is in a dichotomous relation with the object, the object is what the consciousness observes or acts upon. Subject is the doer; object is the done to. When we use the grammatical construction, "the dog chases the ball," "dog" is the subject of the sentence and "ball" is the object. Our grammar is quite clear about which is the subject and which is the object and demands that these two remain distinct. The subject acts; the object cannot initiate action but merely responds to the subject's actions or words. There is a distance created between the subject and the object. Perhaps something about what is in the object or what the object has, inspires the subject to act. In this case the ball is moving and the movement is attractive to the dog. The subject does the thinking, assesses the situation, and decides what to do while the object just is and remains at the mercy of what the subject decides to do to it; and, in the case of a conscious object, the object is not necessarily aware that it is an object at all.

Not all languages are set up in this way. Natalie Goldberg in *Writing Down the Bones* (1986) explains; "Our language is usually locked into a sentence syntax of subject/verb/direct object. There is a subject acting on an object. 'I see the dog'—with this sentence structure, 'I' is the center of the universe. We forget in our language structure that while 'I' looks at 'the dog,' 'the dog' is simultaneously looking at us. It is interesting to note that in the Japanese language the sentence would say, 'I dog seeing.' There is an exchange or interaction rather than a subject acting on an object" (62).

Let us look at how these distinctions between subject and object, male and female are reproduced in every generation. We know that children are affected greatly by the adults around them, not just what they say but what they do and how they feel about it.

Take the example of a boy and a girl growing up in a house with two heterosexual parents who both work. Think about how the children are getting their messages.

Imagine that the mother is the one who takes responsibility for the household work and the primary responsibility for the raising of two children. The mother tries to accommodate everyone, keeps peace, does the emotional work of the family. Though she goes out to work, her job is not supposed to be her primary concern. Rather, the relationships in the family are the most important. She attempts to be selfless, to think of everyone else first. However, these attempts create an undercurrent of anger, depression, guilt, and listlessness that manifest themselves in this mother in many ways. The children pick up on mother's unhappiness and powerlessness—even if the mother has not articulated them to herself and feels she is doing everything "right."

When the children are at day care, women serve them and take care of their needs. The majority of parents who come to pick up their children at day care are women just as the majority of adults who supervise them when they go to play at a friend's are also women.

When the children see their father or men in general, not involved in the same way in their children's lives, they assume that men are separate and special. The men appear to be served by the others in the family and the society. In some mysterious way that is not spoken about, all of this is for him. He seems to be the final authority, the power in the family and in the world.

Both boys and girls may find themselves identifying with their father rather than with the unattractive, overworked role of the mother. Even where they appreciate and need her nurturance and love, they would not want to exchange places with her. For the boy that is socially acceptable behavior; but for the girl, it is a different story. She is supposed to want to be like her mother. At some point in her narrative, she realizes that it does not matter what she wants, her story must be about what other people want her to do.

Of course, each family is different and there are some in which the father is the nurturing one or the one to take responsibility for the children. Sometimes mothers or fathers try deliberately to change age-old patterns. But even in such cases the words that are said about the choices that are available to children of both genders do not seem to counteract the primary clues from which children learn. Rather, children pick up on the undercurrents, the power struggles between members of their families. Additionally, the images reflected in the media are powerful even when they contradict the actions and feelings of their role models in the home. The power of these undercurrents and images cannot be underestimated.

When children compare notes at school and try to fit into the power-over culture, they are encouraged to follow the dominant pattern even when it may conflict with what they see in their particular home. Children are hungry to align themselves as a girl or a boy. They seek out information that will help them in this endeavor.

In general, girls are groomed to be the objects to boys' subjects. Girls learn that their identities are wrapped up in becoming like their mothers. And mothers in this society on many levels are treated as objects existing for others and not for themselves. I will look at this issue in detail in Chapter 10, "Contemplating Our Navels: The Dilemma of Motherhood." Mother is food and nurturance for the infant; she gives up any identity she had as a woman or as a person and takes on object status. Girls who are inclined instead to see themselves as subjects run into a major conflict with their explicit training to be like mom. The authors of *Mother Daughter Revolution* state, "Mothers repeat the lessons they learned as girls to their daughters. They teach girls to be women like them, to survive in a world of male privilege and power by pleasing men" (Debold et al 55). There are many ways to shame girls into conforming, even without ever saying, "Shame on you." The more girls resist the feminine role, the more pressure can be brought to bear on them.

Subtle and not so subtle socialization techniques reinforce early dichotomization. Studies have shown that even as very young babies, girls and boys are held differently and the attitude toward them is different. Girl babies are treated more delicately and handled like glass vases whereas boys are roughed up to get them prepared for a rough and tumble world of activity.

Time after time we see sex role stereotypes reinforced. Recently a well-known children's science museum was publicly criticized for its characterization of children scientists in some of its literature. Those pictured were boys except in two cases: one where the experiment was being done in the kitchen and the other where the girl was watching the boys doing the experiments. Eternal vigilance is required to fight these kinds of messages because the fallback, unconscious position continues to be boys as subjects; girls as objects.

Formulating an identity is a traumatic process for those children who clearly do not fit the standard ideas of what boys or girls should be or do. Because dichotomies are not reflections of reality but an imposition onto it, of course boys come into the world with traits that we label feminine and girls come in with "masculine" traits. It is then up to the society: language, schools and parents to teach—often more akin to "force"—a child to take its place in the world.

Recently, I took a friend's four year old daughter into a drug store and she insisted on buying a toy of some sort before we exited. We went down the toy aisle and she had a hard time deciding what she wanted. I made a few suggestions like racing cars or snakes or balls. She became disgusted with me and told me in no uncertain terms that she would not buy "scary" stuff and also that she had to buy something with a picture of a girl on it. That limited us to play lipstick, dolls and doll clothes, mirrors, and in general things having to do with how she looks or how to play at being a mother. This is what I mean by the subject/object dichotomy as it relates to males and females. The female is taught to think of herself as an object; the goal is to make that object as pretty as can be. This child was afraid to identify with the action toys even though she is a physically strong, daring little girl.

This is the same girl who a year earlier insisted on wearing her mother's high heels to the playground where she would climb the monkey bars making sure she kept the oversized shoes on her feet (no easy task). Perhaps she was trying to keep her female identity intact while she did "male" things or maybe just the things she really wanted to do. At four, her bottom line was finding and playing with "girl" things. She tried to manage her shame, do a little of both, juggle her identity. But each year she is at risk of giving up a little more of herself and letting the pictures, the narratives "out there" determine what she will be like.

The images that are displayed for girls and women to emulate are impossible for 99% of women to attain. That means women carry around the shame of not attaining that place of perfection. No matter what else we say to girls, they can't help but notice the energy, the time, the endless conversations their mothers, sisters, aunts, women on television and in the movies have about beauty and weight loss. They feel the desperate, almost frenetic need of so many women to be "attractive" at all costs. They see women spend billions of dollars per year on cosmetics, plastic surgery, diets and fashion, cosmetic hormone replacement therapy, and gyms. And that's just money. Consider the colossal waste of time and energy in pursuit of this chimeric goal.

Girls are drawn away from recognition and acknowledgment of their own desires by the push to become desirable objects. Here is a place they feel they can have some control; unfortunately it is not control over the expression of their authenticity, the alterity of their body-minds but rather, their body image, split from their minds. If we think that this obsession with the perfection of women's bodies does not enter into the development of the identities of both boys and girls, we have our heads in the sand and our bodies sticking out all over.

A nationwide survey done by the American Association of University Women in 1990 contained questions about what boys and girls think about themselves and their potentials. In reporting on the results of that survey, authors of *Mother Daughter Revolution*, stated, "Sixty percent of elementary school-aged girls and 67 percent of boys felt happy with themselves. In high school, only 29 percent of the girls still felt that way, while nearly half of the boys held themselves in high esteem.... The most precipitous drop in girls' feelings about themselves occurs between grade school and junior high" (Debold et al 9). At that age girls begin to exhibit low self-esteem. They begin to think that they are not as capable as boys and they become fixated on their looks. This age is a particularly dangerous time for girls when some begin a journey into anorexia that could destroy their lives. Girls seem to be looking for something, anything, that they can control.

For many women, somewhere in their childhood there occurred a severing of desire either because they were continuously frustrated or they were severely punished by adults for behaving in ways "inappropriate" for girls. Girls' own desires conflict with becoming desirous objects. It's that double bind again with the human part dying for expression and recognition and the feminine part having to be attended to at all costs.

Some women play the role of desirable object better than others. It seems, however, that the closer one is to being successful as a beautiful, desirable object, the more danger there is that her time, energy, and money will be spent on perfecting her body (object) and the less she will be available to seek out her own desires.

There are many components to being beautiful and they are context dependent but at this time in history, an image of Beauty is taking over the whole world. Wendy Chapkis, author of *Beauty Secrets* (1986) says, "The fantasy of the Good Life populated by Beautiful People wearing The Look has seized the imagination of much of the world. This Western model of beauty represents a mandate for a way of life for women throughout the world regardless of how unrelated to each of our ethnic or economic possibilities it is" (37). That image is that one should have a pretty, preferably white face; a tall, thin, firm, perfectly able body with large breasts; unwrinkled, flawless, hairless skin; "good" hair (on the head that is); and be wearing expensive perfume and clothes including high heels. Many of these things a person is born with or is not and nothing can be done about it (though the feeling is that if she can do something, she should). Women are expected to want to change the way they are to approximate Beauty more closely. There is an underlying assumption that one of women's primary goals (along with having children) should be to look as attractive as possible.

This Beauty component is a crucial part of women's identities. As Chapkis explains, "The relationship between Beauty and body is thus extremely problematic, all the more so for women for whom both qualities are central to identity. Approximating beauty can be essential to a woman's chances for power, respect, and attention" (14). Without understanding why she is obsessed with appearance, hers and other women's, she feels shamed or on the other hand enticed into trying to fit the standard. In order to survive, women look for at least some form of power even if it is power-over and not immanent power. One way to get it is through being a great-looking object. There is obviously a reward there if one is successful but it is not the ability to express oneself or to be an autonomous body-mind.

For most women there is something about their bodies that they wish to hide, are ashamed of—whether that be heritage, disability, age, class, weight, a first language other than English, religion, sexual preference, etc. I would add to that list that here is where we carry our wholeness as body-minds, our alterity as women and humans that cannot fit into the standard and that we have had to put in a closet somewhere.

In my own case, I put my disability in the closet. I was always trying to pass, to distract people from noticing I was different. I made sure it stayed a secret—no picnics where softball was mentioned, never went barefoot, ambled leisurely across the street when the light changed— too cool to run, too scared to be seen.

Body image matters to women so much because of what I call the theory of original shame. Embodiment itself carries shame: the shame of nakedness, of aging and of mortality. Because men can and do project a lot of their shame and blame onto women, body shame is not as salient an issue for men. A version of this projection is the Adam and Eve story; we saw another version acted out by the emperor in our fairy tale. The emperor was able to continue his quest for mind-only "truths" by demanding that women assume all of the duties related to the body.

As long as the mind/body split is intact, women have the illusion that dumping their shame onto their bodies will somehow alleviate it. So women treat their bodies just like men treat women—recognizing no alterity, exerting superiority and power-over. In other words, tyrannize it. Make it behave. Refuse it its appetites and desires. Starve it. Carve it. Stuff it. Exercise it to death. Slice it up. Pump it up. Shut it up. Punish it. Sell it.

Being labeled "fat" is a threat held over the heads of women. If we are fat, it is our fault and we should feel repulsed, society tells us. But because fat is a quality that is hard to hide and because it is perceived as voluntary, it is a cutting edge issue in the arena of identity development. Fat women who refuse further dieting or never go on diets to begin with are heroines because, through the worst of peer, societal and institutional pressure, they are saying, "this is how I am and I refuse to hide to protect you from your own body shame." There is currently a magazine called *Fat!So?*—the title expresses this idea nicely.

The power women exert over their bodies is substantial. They try to make them skinny and firm, and some body types are more able than others to achieve the ideal; they exercise extreme control over their desires for food; they paint their faces and have surgery to look better. They elect to have high-risk surgery such as breast implants to force their bodies to be more attractive. Some power may come from these efforts, some power-over men and some over other women. But often the body resists this kind of pressure. The body or the little girl body-mind may refuse to go along with that program.

Let me give an example of what some women do to accommodate their little girl who never got recognition and acceptance for who she was. A friend of mine, whom I will call Marina, remembers that at age eight a huge shift occurred in her self-image. This woman felt strange and wonderful sexual desires when she was a child and was told that these desires were wrong and should be resisted, never acted upon and never allowed to surface. To remain true to her desires she would have had to go against everyone—parents, teachers, friends. How many small girls have that kind of strength or understanding? So outwardly she buckled under the strength of outside forces. Yet within her all these years has remained this stunted eight year old girl who requires—no, *demands*—expression but for whom she feels fear and ambivalence.

Marina fears this little girl and believes that if she ever got loose she would be so angry she would tear up the world, refuse to take baths, lash out at those around her, say what she thought no matter what the circumstance. So to appease her, to keep her alive and yet unsurfaced, Marina feeds her food. She binges for her. She gives her the only socially acceptable outlet for her desires in the form of food and still she is shamed by it. The whole process depresses her but she is unable to stop doing it. She is unable to let that girl go and also unable to allow her to grow up. The girl is blackmailing her and causing her pain and depression.

But an object should not have desires nor speak them. It confounds all of those around her; her desires must remain unspoken, not because they cannot be articulated (though that may be part of it and we will discuss language later in the book) but also because objects by definition do not have desires nor can they speak. If women's desire is to become desirable objects, they become confused because they do not experience themselves as objects only. They have within them, buried however deeply, the capacity to desire that manifests itself in many ways.

And some women crave food. This craving may be an attempt by women's body-minds to thwart the efforts of the mind to make the body conform to object status, or it could simply be the result of prolonged periods of restraint and starvation diets. In a way, weight gain is not self-destructive but quite the opposite; it can be a sign that desire is alive and well but has no outlet. The power-over won by being skinny is not enough.

Hilde Bruch, professor of psychiatry and author of the classic work *Eating Disorders* (1973) stated, "It is impossible to assess the cost in serenity, relaxation, and efficiency of this abnormal, overslim, fashionable appearance. It produces serious psychological tensions to feel compelled to be thinner than one's natural make-up and style of living demand. There is a great deal of talk about the weakness and self-indulgence of overweight people who eat 'too much.' Very little is said about the selfishness and self-indulgence involved in a life which makes one's appearance the center of all values, and subordinates all other considerations to it" (198).

Feminism in general has not yet come to terms with fat-phobia, another code name for women-phobia. Where many other instances of women-phobia have gone underground, this particular issue provides us with a litmus test to judge where we are on the scale of accepting the dichotomous viewpoint. How much do those of us who claim to be feminists continue to find scapegoats for our own body and women phobias?

We must begin to see these stigmatized qualities as inalienable parts of us worthy of acceptance. We cannot be whole powerful beings if we keep parts of ourselves locked away.

In describing the price we pay in political terms by keeping parts of ourselves locked away in shame, Wendy Chapkis states, "But while individual acts of defiance may not be equal to the task of defeating the structural inequalities of racism or sexism, they are in no way unimportant. Fighting the pressure to conform, attempting to hold one's own against the commercial and cultural images of the acceptable is a crucial first act of resistance. The attempt to pass and blend in actually hides us from those we most resemble. We end up robbing each other of authentic reflections of ourselves. Instead, imperfectly invisible behind a fashion of conformity, we fear to meet each other's eyes...'what are you looking at anyway?'" (175).

This issue of shame and hiding in various closets gets in the way of women working together effectively. Shame, especially when it is unacknowledged, makes women act in strange ways toward one another while they work out a relationship with it. "Shame is profoundly disempowering.

The need for secrecy and concealment that figures so largely in the shame experience is disempowering as well, for it isolates the oppressed from one another and in this way works against the emergence of a sense of solidarity" (Bartky 97).

We need to work on both the individual and institutional level at the same time. In speaking about the importance of appearance to the down-under status of women, Chapkis states, "This can only change when beauty loses its distorted power in the evaluation of a 'woman's worth'; that is, when the dependent relationship between women and men has been dismantled. Thus are the politics of appearance inextricably bound up with the structures of social, political and economic inequality" (174-175).

How Women Are Seen By Others

The second area I want to address in this chapter is how women are seen and treated by others, both other people and institutions. We are not simply dealing with a psychological problem that women can overturn by refusing to be ashamed. Change also requires social upheaval.

I think we would all agree that women in the Western world (and, of course, in most other places as well) have historically been in power-under positions. There are some who would argue that women have by the 1990's achieved equity with men and have nothing further to struggle for. Some see feminism as redundant, as having outlived its usefulness. My view is that while women have made some inroads and some progress, for the most part the bulk of their institutional oppression is still very much in place.

I define women's oppression as stemming from the dichotomized world view which splits men from women, institutionalizes the domination mode of power, and puts men in the position of power-over making them the standard to which women are compared. Political philosopher Moira Gatens stated, "From ancient Greece to our own time women have been defined not so much in terms of any positive qualities that they possess but rather in terms of the male qualities that they lack. For the Greeks it was lesser reason; for others it was lesser strength; for Freud women lack (or have an atrophied) penis. The important feature to note is that there is a history of women being defined only in terms relative to men, who are taken as the norm, the standard or primary term" (*Feminism and Philosophy* 94).

Essentially, then, no matter how many women get into positions of power, if the assumption remains that men are the opposite of women and that women must be defined through men, as what men are not, it follows that women cannot escape the power-under position and will be, in my definition, oppressed.

Dichotomous thinking affects women's status in many ways. Let us look at just a few of the major ones. The linkage of the dichotomy of reason/emotion with man/woman has made it impossible for women to share power equally in political systems. As stated earlier, the public sphere (where the political decisions are made) is defined against emotion, particularity and women. In the reason/emotion dichotomy, emotion is on the devalued side and is associated with women, body and habitat. We define "reason" as the transcendence of habitat, body, emotion and females. Because reason has traditionally been something which humans are considered capable of but which animals are not, our very humanness depends on it. We can then see the trap that is set; women, who are placed on the same side of the dichotomy as nature and opposite from reason, are not quite human. Only men have the pure power of reason and can transcend their particular bodies to reach some higher plane of "Justice" or "Truth." Though we may see evidence of an apparent breakdown of these dichotomies in our everyday lives as more women appear in the public world and enter fields such as law, mathematics, science, politics and medicine, the dichotomies are still fundamental in our language, thinking and behavior.

And we continue to link women to the private sphere, throwing further doubt on the question of whether women can be fully vested participants in the public sphere. Can the "he" simply be changed to he/she to include women as citizens and workers? We must also ask, "who does the work of the private sphere—the cooking, shopping, cleaning, child raising, emotional support—if women are incorporated into the public sphere?" It is scarcely as if men are clamoring to be included in the private sphere to take up the slack there.

Will women's inclusion in the public sphere change it? One possibility is that if enough women get into places of power in the public sphere, the dichotomy will teeter and fall; equality will reign. But a closer look will disabuse us of that notion. Why? Because there are two preconditions for women's entry into the public sphere: 1) that women "do" public as men have always done it—that is they leave their alterity at home and 2) that women keep up their end of the dichotomy, the private sphere. That way, neither men nor the public sphere has to change.

The public sphere does not have to be made "impure" by women's bodies or emotions. Women must leave these things at home in the private sphere as men have always been required to do. And men do not have to behave differently at home because the house and family are still firmly in the hands of women. It has actually worked out rather well for men to have women in the public sphere under these conditions—women can do the work that men shunned anyway, the lower status work, and the power structure has not changed. For example men are the CEO's, women are their secretaries and office managers; men are the pilots, women are the flight attendants and so on. No matter how many gains are made by women in the public sphere, while the linked dichotomies are enforced, they will still have to bear the ultimate responsibility in the private sphere in addition to any gains in the public one.

But there is a price to be paid by women forced to fit into dichotomous systems. Either they must accept their place on the devalued side of the dichotomy or they give up their alterity and take on more "male" (as defined by society) identities and go into the public sphere while still holding up the private sphere of the teeter totter. Thus, though "success" for many women appears to have been achieved, the costs to women have not been adequately assessed.

Some women, who are currently struggling in both spheres, doing so much more than their share of the work, may see feminism's "gains" as a farce. When a woman is expected to do all of the private work and work full time in the public sphere, she may find herself blaming lots of sources for her perfectly valid anger. Columnist Ellen Goodman delivered a speech at a conference on women in politics at Laney College in Oakland, California in 1994. She proposed that we look at women's situation using the following analogy: she said that women have kicked the door down to the public sphere with one foot but the other foot is still being dragged along and they are limping at the moment and will be until they can get their whole selves into the door. In other words, women are in the middle, not at the end of the struggle.

When women do enter the public sphere, they are required to try to take on a "universal" subjectivity, which we have already seen is not universal at all. As long as our workplaces are set up on an unacknowledged white-male model and not a universal one, there will be no clear way to raise an issue that arises from the side-effects of having a particular body which is not white and/or male and/or able-bodied and/or heterosexual. Because we cling to the notion of universality, we cannot expose that "ideal" for what it is and we feel compelled to push for more universality, more "equal" treatment in our workplaces.

It is *difference* that is not acceptable in the public sphere—the drawing of attention to *body*. So long as we are the same in body (and as long as it is white, male, heterosexual and able, it can take many different shapes and still be acceptable), we can claim that bodies are unimportant, that they are not a crucial factor in job promotion, career development, competency, etc.

White men's bodies do not have to be entirely abstracted from the workplace because they fit the norm for bodies. If one has a different body, it calls attention to itself. A different body may even arouse the standard body, making a man aware of his bodily desires and thus corrupting his attempt at universality and spirituality and sinking him into particularity, emotions and individual needs (which, of course, were always there but were unacknowledged).

A female body provides ammunition for a woman's exclusion from power. The jokes, the nude pin-up pictures of women, the pats on the bottom are all ways of making sure women know their place is in the body—that they have not and will not achieve the status of bodiless equality.

If, in the real world, we could show up for work as the universal mind, equal to each and every other mind, such things as sexual harassment, of course, would not be a problem. Minds have no genders, right? But pretending that we are all identical as we show up makes the very real issue of sexual harassment a phantom. When coming to the public sphere, workers are supposed to leave their bodies at home, preferably in the care of a good wife. Then how can women be harassed when the deal was that they leave their bodies at home? Admitting to having been harassed implicates them in reneging on the deal made upon entered the public sphere—to leave the bodies at home.

The Clarence Thomas hearings regarding his alleged sexual harassment of Anita Hill are a good illustration of these points. Here was a woman admitting to her difference and denouncing the ill treatment she received because of it. She embodied the contradictions that for the most part go unreported by women. She as much as admitted that she was black and a woman! Of course, that exposure of herself also uncovered the body of Clarence Thomas, something he had successfully been hiding for so long. The rule Anita Hill broke was to question the acceptance of his long-assumed white male role. Hill was doing to him publicly what he had done to her privately—showing her her place by pointing out the body. Now he could retaliate by saying that such exposure was racist and instigated by white feminists. He could feel wronged when it was about race but he could not or would not make the link with gender.

Those of us who are not of the standard body are terribly threatened by exposure of body, because it proves we have not held up our end of the public sphere contract. Many women and men in the African American community rallied around Clarence Thomas because his exposure threatened to expose them as well. In a divide and conquer strategy, those in power say, "Let all of those with different bodies go around exposing each other and we have them where we want them—*they* are body and *we* are mind."

But let's face it—most of us in different bodies, at least in regard to gender, race and (dis)ability are already exposed—we have nothing real to lose. Those who have something to lose are those who are pretending to be Universal. Our energy, then, should be focused on exposing the white male body rather than trying to be included in it. The point here is that *we are all living in bodies* and we are *all* bringing them to work with us.

The contract women made with "the system" was forged under false premises. They agreed to do something that no one can do: leave their particularity at home. It is and always has been an invalid contract because it is impossible to fulfill.

Here is where the shame from the last section comes in again. Since Anita Hill testified and became a role model, monitoring agencies report a large jump in the number of sexual harassment complaints lodged all across the country. As long as women are ashamed of having bodies and our shame is private, they will continue to be harassed, denied promotions, and treated superficially in the workplace. When they go public, they finally stop "passing" for men; they call attention to all bodies at work that are dying for that recognition anyway. We should stop putting our energy into defending the universal-all-are-equal-under-the-skin model of justice and start exposing and deposing the white male standard from its throne.

So what is done with women in the public sphere remains to be seen. Women's entry into the public sphere may be seen as a first step toward upheaval of the dichotomy if it is done with a consciousness of what is necessary to move beyond it. Having women in places of power when women get organized enough to stop "passing" for men would indeed be sweet.

Only by acknowledging the sex and race of the "universal" body, the body in power, will the ill treatment of those people who do not fit the standard be raised legitimately. Without that acknowledgment, all women and men of color are kept in their place: they are constantly reminded through sexual and racial harassment that their bodies are different and are going to keep them from being taken seriously as one of the standardized group.

I realize that the topic of how women are affected by the mind/body split is a huge subject on which many books could be written. Here I am merely trying give the reader a taste of the tenacity of the idea that men are mind/subject and women are body/object; this view essentially has not changed even with all of the efforts made by women to achieve equality. This view has robbed women of their subjectivity and alterity and required them to contort themselves to fit a beautiful object standard or take on a male subjectivity. Attempts to alleviate these problems by further denying women's bodies and therefore keeping the mind/body split intact are ineffective.

Since women are not able to live authentically as subjects in this culture, their choices are impossible. If a woman chooses the body (object) route, she ends up either in the role of wife and mother, self-sacrificing for the children and husband or in the role of whore, both of which rely on power through the promotion and support of others' subjectivity and power. She makes others value her and perhaps even find her indispensable so they will keep her around. Or she can choose (or be forced) to work in the world where only men are really acceptable and deny where possible her gender even when no one else denies it (they pay her less and do not promote her as they would a man). Or she can combine these things and be superwoman, wife, mother and worker and leave herself no time to wonder if she has other desires that are not being fulfilled.

Our efforts to influence our children to see themselves differently are often in vain because we do not adequately deal with the pervasiveness of the power-over splits throughout everyday life. So whatever our talk is, it is just talk; until our attitudes, language, institutions, and behavior change, children will continue to be dichotomized and girls will continue to work toward becoming better objects while boys reap the benefits due subjects.

II.

THE JUICY WHOLE:
A MODEL FOR CHANGE

So far we have been dealing with the critique of dichotomies and power-over. We have defined dichotomies and power-over and given illustrations of how they work. We have shown how insidious and prevalent the splits are in the fields of philosophy, religion, science and medicine, economics and politics. We have looked specifically at the effects which dichotomization has had on all four parts of the mind/body, male/female split.

The world cries out for a new model, one that will move us from the dichotomy model of reality to a more humane view of our relationships to each other and to our habitat. In the next chapter I will propose such a working model. Following the introduction to the model, I will apply it and discuss avenues for getting from where we are now to where we need to be—how do we create a context for ethics such that the prerequisite to resolving ethical dilemmas is not to dichotomize ourselves but, rather, to insist on the involvement of all of our connections?

7

The Between Model

"Between nature and culture, between night and day, between sun and stars, between vegetable and mineral, amongst men, amongst women, amongst gods, she seeks her humanity and her transcendency." (Luce Irigaray, *Elemental Passions* 4)

I invite you to move from reliance on a linear, dichotomized model into the Between zone—between the old and the new, the past and the future. Begin this chapter by letting go of the need to dichotomize: let go of absolutes and mutual exclusivity. Go to your fortress, your edge, your boundary and begin to stretch to the open space of possibility beyond.

I am going to describe the Between as best I can though you will certainly have more to add from your own experience. Please remember that even as I describe this "thing" called the Between, that there is no such thing as "the Between." Naming freezes, solidifies, kills the spirit of movement and constant change. What I shall describe is between names. It is the empty space, the room to move, to grow, to stir, to mingle.

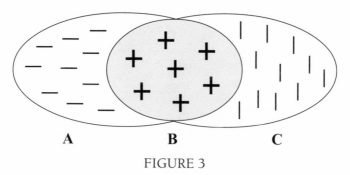

FIGURE 3

The model drawn above is a representation of what I mean by the Between model. There are two circles, Parts A and C, which are linked together by their shared area, Part B: "the Between." Parts A and C represent two alterities brought into relationship.

For example, if we are talking about the Between of you and me, Part A is what I bring, my body-mind, my life experiences and wisdom, my biology, my shape. And you bring Part C, your authenticity as an individual, your particularity.

Our current worldview, which I critiqued in the first part of this book, cavalierly divides us into opposites and discards the space between. The worldview I advocate as represented by the above model is closer to how I believe reality actually exists. It follows that the part we currently excise when we dichotomize is the most interesting and dynamic part of us all.

Imagine any of the dichotomies: me/you, mind/body, humans/habitat, future/past, male/female, reason/emotion, day/night and begin to visualize them in a different relationship, as two circles interlinked, like the arms of two close friends. If we, in all of our encounters with others and with the habitat, were in this form—if this were a reflection of reality—we would understand that we can never be separated from each other without losing large parts of ourselves. We are individuals, yes, but we are also constantly in relationship.

Think of the place between you and me—it is not a constant. You change, I change and our interactions consist of change. Even if we thought of ourselves as solids made up of our own life stories, when we come together and mingle in the Between, there is no way to control what happens. Feedback loops are created that feed us and loop back again, so that even small changes create large effects. The Between is where we overflow the boundaries of either/or. It is all that has fallen into the chasm created by splitting the whole. It is vital and alive with creativity and possibility.

We yearn to predict and control so that we can witness our individual power-over. But this place of Between requires that we let go of that fear of powerlessness. Here there is a power much greater than individual power-over—here is immanent power—yours and mine—the power of wholeness, connection and expression, what I believe gives meaning to our world.

This model requires balance. It requires my alterity and yours equally. You must bring your whole self without fear and shame and I must do the same. We will not be invisible here; we can bring all we have, all we have learned, all of our wisdom and ignorance, and put them together.

But we do not merge. Our alterities are intact and we can always retreat to our home base though we are never isolated and autonomous but rather remain in relationship. I am not you, nor you me—sameness and uniformity have no place here. We can share similar experiences, certainly, and we may feel safer if we do, but we are always more than simply that identity which we have in common.

Pieces of this vision are familiar to you—you have heard similar concepts from sources such as Eastern religion, Riane Eisler's partnership scheme (1987), feminist philosophy, goddess tradition, etc. I have synthesized some elements from those traditions into this model; but this model is also somewhat different from all of those other models. For instance, I am not saying that I am you and you are I and that all is one in the universe. In this model there is wholeness but not oneness. 1+1+1...but never just one. Just "one" leaves no room for alterity and difference but assumes one universal to which all must conform.

Additionally, in this model there is no bridge between you and me. A bridge can only be built between two who are already separated; I contend that we have never been separated in reality, even though we have conceived of ourselves in that way. This model provides a way to envision what, in our linear mindset, we might call paradox. We are together and separate at the same time.

The Between is operating on many levels at once. My alterity comes from the Between of my body and mind; and when I interact with another person or with my habitat in an immanently powerful way (as opposed to one of power-over), I am relating from that center place, from that place of integration of body and mind. In many religious models—both Eastern and Western, there is a push to transcend the body, to use it as a tool or subjugate it. In the Between model an individual's body-mind is the core of the alterity of the individual. We do not attempt to transcend our core to reach universal Truth. Rather, we strive for acceptance of our alterity as body-minds which we can then share in relationship with other individuals, in our social structure and with the habitat. In this way we begin to understand the meaning of universal truth, a collection of all of us living in relationship. The universal is not singular but amalgamated.

Each time you find yourself using a dichotomy in your thinking, I suggest taking that dichotomy and putting it into the Between model, *bewholing* it. "Bewholing" is a word I have coined to indicate taking two things that are presently in a dichotomous relationship and putting them into the Between model, acknowledging their connections and their alterities. We can, for instance, still use the words "mind" and "body"; but the image we conjure will be like the one in Figure 3. If you think you have a mind and a body that are separable and disconnected, as Descartes thought, try imagining instead that your body and your mind are connected like the two circles. You will never hold one or the other still long enough to separate the two spheres. Each entity traditionally thought of as oppositional, with one term fixed as standard and more valuable than the other, now has its own alterity, and its dynamic connection to the other must be acknowledged.

Difference is crucial to the Between. Fertility and creativity rely on difference. Becoming identical to a standard, forcing ourselves to fit, as we are encouraged to do in the dichotomy model, is counterproductive in the Between model.

In the sweep of dichotomization, half of the world has been put in the power-under position as an object. Where are the voices of the silenced ones? We must hear from sexual difference and from all other kinds of difference. Referring once again to the dichotomy figure in Chapter 1, we cannot even begin to detect the alterity that lies in that washed out, pale reflection-of-the-standard, part of our world.

Traits such as receptivity, intuition, cooperation, and empathy that work well in the Between are labeled as weaknesses in our society. Thus, we repress those innate abilities to respect alterity, to cooperate rather than dominate, to nurture rather than destroy, to linger in the Between rather than run from it.

When we dichotomize ourselves, the Between is destroyed, leaving us with an emptiness that cannot be filled independently. We are constantly searching for ways to fill it and our culture tells us, "What you need is a good man/woman, some kids and a load of money and material possessions." We spend our lives on that search. All we manage to do is damage our ability to relate to each other and to experience immanent power. We do not necessarily have to *do* anything. It is the moment we live in; we are in the past and the future in the moment of the Between.

Think of the superstition/science dichotomy. These are the two paradigms we have relied upon historically to help us understand our lives. I am defining superstition as the inclination to call into being gods and entities with supernatural powers as the primary means of interpreting our experience.

But when we move from superstition to the scientific paradigm to give us answers, we put our faith in different gods, the gods of prediction and control. We believe that if we are disciplined enough and study hard and long, we will be able to understand and manipulate the world around us. Both the superstition and the scientific modes contain some truth and some delusion.

I am not suggesting that we retreat nostalgically back to the Middle Ages, get rid of technology, and go back to living in fear of the gods. However, just as dangerous is allowing the traditional scientific paradigm to serve as a model for all of our interactions.

If we think of mind and body, humans and our habitat, as located in a system like the Between model, we must shift our perceptions accordingly. Both the ancient notion that nature was unpredictable and wrathful, and the more contemporary notion that our habitat and body are simply machines to be predicted and controlled by mind and man, are inadequate models with which to describe reality. Instead, while there is a somewhat predictable aspect of both body and habitat, there is also a constantly changing, dynamic, non-linear element which must be acknowledged and appreciated as central to our lives.

We as a society have tended to be reactionary in our development. We react against what we see as superstition and become rationalists, believing only that which can be scientifically proven to exist. Anything outside that model is labeled "superstitious." Or we believe in a god or some form of spirituality and are no longer purely scientists. A way to have both at once was developed around Descartes' time and included at core a complete separation of the two spheres; he separated the scientific from the religious through the creation of the mind/body split.

The Between model gives us a way to have a combination of the two paradigms without splitting them and losing important parts of ourselves and the world. Our bodies and our habitats are neither systems of inert particles, nor are they totally unpredictable organisms. Rather, they have alterity, they are inextricably linked with mind and humans and they have, operating within them, the Between, the ever-changing connected part that is complex, non-linear and full of feedback loops refusing predictability.

If the Between model can shed some light on these controversies, all the better. In my view the sacred is wholeness, which includes both our connections (Part B) and the alterity of each entity (Parts A and C). When we forget our connections or the alterity of others in the habitat, we lose spirituality and the sacred. Spirituality is not something outside ourselves; it is in our connections. It is not hierarchical with a god at the top, men next, then women, then animals, and with body somewhere underneath it all. Rather, it is horizontal and relational—part of the many not dictated to by the one.

Immanent power lies in the Between—not power-over but the power of connection. We can tap into it by respecting the alterity of each entity and allowing ourselves to enter into the Between.

But, immanent power is dependent on the strength of the alterities of each side of the model; the power source is split when we dichotomize our wholeness, eliminating the possibility of a strong Between. Reaching our immanent power means that not only must my alterity be strong but so must the alterity of any entity with whom I am in relation.

It follows, then, that my best interest is to look out for your best interest. These two interests are not mutually exclusive; rather, they are mutually dependent and inclusive. Each individual is a part of the next; when an individual takes care of herself, the whole group benefits. When I take care of you, I benefit as well. We each must take responsibility for the health of our own body-minds as well as encouragement of alterity in other body-minds since both alterities are crucial to the well-being of the whole. Benefited individuals are then able to contribute in stronger, more powerful ways to the community. If, in order to reach one's own immanent power, one relies on others' reaching their immanent power, then one's own success is bound up with the success of the other. I cannot be free until everyone else is free. Immanent power requires a complete redefinition of success, of power, of identity, and of the effects of selfishness and self-indulgence. I cannot be powerful at your expense; I am depending on your strength and cooperation.

As a concrete illustration of the way the Between works and how it contrasts with the dichotomy model, I will talk about the subject of conflict resolution. Think of the ways our society addresses conflict—confrontation and violence using power-over are certainly the most common forms. Child and spouse abuse are on the rise in this country and are only slowly becoming frowned upon as methods of handling domestic conflict. In the public sphere, corporation and government abuse is apparently becoming more acceptable.

The primary sanctioned model for resolving more public conflicts is the legal model, in which the parties are very much separated and adversarial; one wins and one loses. It is not crucial that each side be heard; in fact sometimes the only people we hear from are attorneys. Ideally, the conflict is resolved by determining who under the law was in the right and who in the wrong; who is innocent and who is guilty. That system is based on a power-over model and is designed to discover only one version of the truth. (I won't even get into the inequities here caused by using the "universal" model—see Chapter 2.) The parties are dichotomized and oppositional, usually with the party with more status and power on the top. The parties are enjoined from talking with one another and instead communicate across the divide through attorneys. One is declared a winner and the other pays.

Suppose that, instead of a winner and a loser or a determination of guilt or innocence, what you wanted was a way to work and live together that resolved conflict and reduced animosity? Suppose you wanted peaceful co-existence and not blame?

An alternative to this court process is community mediation. A mediation takes place in a neutral setting and is facilitated by one or more disinterested persons who are the mediators. The rules are simple: each party gets a chance to talk without interruption and must show respect to the other party. The mediators may ask clarifying questions so that the issues presented are clear. The parties talk first to the mediators to make sure their whole story is clear. Then the parties speak together until they have reached a mutually agreeable solution.

Picture this in the horizontal Between model. Let's use an example of a noise dispute between neighbors. In this fictional dispute one of the parties is a graduate student and her neighbor is a 60-year-old man. The man is complaining that the student comes home late at night, often after having had too much to drink and brings home friends with whom she carries on long and raucous philosophical discussions. In addition, the woman has loud parties that go on and on into the wee hours of the morning. Each is given a chance to speak authentically about what they see as the problem. During their opening statements, the man expresses his dismay at the inconsideration shown by the woman and believes that as a homeowner and taxpayer he has paid for peace and quiet. The woman believes that he is oversensitive and has nothing better to do than pick a fight.

Often it is in the mediation that the parties hear each other for the first time without all the shouting and calling the police that may have gone on before. The mediators must be conscious of power balance and keep power-over from being used in the hearing. For instance, in our example there may be a power imbalance created by class and gender in favor of the property-owning man.

The goal in a mediation is to encourage the parties to see their connections and their mutual impetus for resolving the dispute. Neighbors, for instance, are connected simply by the places in which they live and generally want them to be peaceful and anxiety-free.

Good mediators are those who can encourage people to move away from wanting to "win," from a place of rigidly drawn boundaries and great animosity, to one more suitable for resolution. The sides are not drawn as clearly as in a more legalistic setting and it is possible for all to "win"—no guilt or innocence is assigned. They do not have to agree, but each must understand the other's perspective. This part of the process I would call "Hearing and Respecting the Alterity of the 'Other.'" This stage is a prerequisite to a workable agreement.

Thich Nhat Hanh calls this place of comprehension and understanding "non-duality," not-two (*Peace is Every Step* 100). The word "comprehend" comes from "*cum*" which means "with" and "*prehendere*" which means "to grasp" or "to pick it up." It means to pick up something and be one with it. The goal of a mediation is to hold the container for the participants to talk with and comprehend one another and to see their mutual connections. Once the alterity of each party has been acknowledged and the connection pointed out, all kinds of possibilities for solution emerge.

Once the participants have been allowed to fully express their alterity and to be heard, and they have listened to the other party, they can then move from the stances they had upon entering the mediation. From the strength and trust developed in that stage, the parties can feel safe enough and respected enough to move into the Between. Once they understand one another, they can hopefully see their connections as well as their disagreement. They may find they have at least some similar goals such as a safe, pleasant neighborhood.

Once they enter the Between, they are in an arena rich with possibilities for working out solutions. Here lie the most creative solutions; the ideas generated rely on both parties. The parties sitting alone in their homes may not have been able to come up with a single possible solution and may have come to the mediation table with severe doubts about the possibilities for resolution. But together the possibilities come forth. Who actually articulated an idea used in solving the dispute is not important. There is no way to own anything in the Between.

Have you ever felt when in dialogue with others that ideas were coming from a place beyond the limitations of any one individual? Some of my most rewarding and satisfying conversations have been like that.

When the conversation is over, it is impossible to give credit to any one person alone for the ideas that emerged. In the Between, ego takes a back seat to the larger goal of working out the conflict. One idea generates another like a feedback loop in chaos theory.

Now contrast that with a discussion in which people enter in knowing they are right and speak only to convince others of their point of view. They are in it to "win" and they use the power-over model to claim the spoils of their victory. There is no real exchange and mingling of ideas, but rather just a "preaching at."

The ultimate goal in the mediation process is for the parties to actually hear and understand one another. Mediation using the Between model insists on strong alterity for everyone, the willingness to listen to difference and to understand it, an ability to let go of ego in the moment of the Between, and a desire to solve conflict rather than to "win." It is important that the participants are able to see not only their differences but their similarities as well. We would do well to use this model in all of our interactions with others.

Now that we have talked generally about the Between model and seen it at work in conflict resolution, I want to speak specifically about how this model can change the way we conceptualize mind and body and male and female. First I will look at mind and body. Two major changes that we can expect if we bewhole the dichotomies of mind and body are embodiment of the universal and the objective and access to our immanent power.

8

Between Body and Mind,
Woman and Man

Healing the Mind/Body Split

One suggestion for dealing with the complex problems of the mind/body split is offered to us by the French philosopher, linguist and psychoanalyst Luce Irigaray. She gives us detailed analyses of the ways in which the body has been repressed by the mind. What I have more simplistically called "mind" and "body," Irigaray calls the "symbolic" and the "imaginary."

The symbolic (mind) for Irigaray has two major meanings. As Margaret Whitford, philosopher and expert on Irigaray's work, explains it, one is "order of discourse and meaning, the order into which all human beings have to insert themselves and which therefore precedes and exceeds individual subjectivity" (Whitford 90). Language is a major component of the symbolic but it also includes all of the various structures that we as humans have to fit our experience into as we are socialized. Another meaning of the word, however, is that which enables humans to break from the imaginary (body).

The imaginary represents several things for Irigaray: on the one hand, it is what Whitford calls "the unconscious of Western thought—the unsymbolized, repressed underside of Western philosophy" (89). If that is too abstract, think of it as the bottom half of the dichotomy where women, objects and bodies have been placed in Western society. It is the raw material that cannot be transcended or absolutely identified.

But the imaginary is also in some sense something that is yet to be formed by a revolutionized symbolic, something that would change the plight of women and men, mind and body in our society. What is yet to be acknowledged is the alterity of body so that it overlaps horizontally with minds. This lack of alterity is represented in the dichotomy drawing, by the shaded, cut-off lower part. When we use the Between model, this part actually takes on shapes all its own that are, from our perspective in the dichotomous worldview, as yet unknown and certainly unpredicted.

The imaginary and the symbolic are very much intertwined. Whitford states, "the symbolic is structure (form) which is given content by the imaginary, and the imaginary pours itself into the available structures to form representations" (91). The underlying imaginary out of which the symbolic arises is simply the "primitive material of existence: life and death, kin relationship, and the body (either the body surface or speculations about what might be inside)" (60).

In Western thought, the ideas of the symbolic and the imaginary are in a dichotomous relationship, with the symbolic on top. Language, structure, and forms (mind)—the symbolic—are valorized. If something cannot be articulated in a linear, "rational" way, it is not of value. We can see this in the separation of science and art with art denigrated, repressed and devalued and science put on a pedestal as knowledge. The imaginary has been ridiculed, thought childish, seen as in need of transcendence. Irigaray advocates seeing the two as interconnected. Translated into Between model language, making them interconnected would be to ensure that their relationship was horizontal and each of them had alterity—it would mean bewholing them. The body and biology supply the primordial material and the mind and culture impose structure; however, the two do not exist dichotomously but rather in relationship with one another.

How do we get at the body (imaginary) now that we are so deeply in a conspiracy with the mind (symbolic)? The imaginary has been forced deep into the unconscious and it is there that we must search for it. One way to do that would be to minimize our use of linear language; to find other ways to express ourselves like painting, dance, poetry, music, sculpture, play, and dreams. In later chapters we will explore in more detail suggestions on how to get there from here.

This section discusses how to bewhole our knowledge and ethics and how to use the immanent power created by such bewholing to heal ourselves. On the level of knowledge, by re-introducing body into abstract notions of universality and objectivity, we enable ourselves to understand a bewholed world instead of a dichotomized one. On the personal level, bewholing ourselves gives us access to the Between, a place of healing and power which does not require the domination of one part of ourselves over the other.

Embodying the Universal and the Objective

We spoke earlier in this book about the search in many academic fields for objectivity and "Truth." When we examine these ideals in light of the Between model, their ultimate importance fades. To grasp a reality that presents itself in the form of the Between model, new methods of inquiry must be developed. If the "body" can never fully be extracted from an experiment or a philosophy, then that situation must be acknowledged from the start—no more ought we to pretend that we have no body and can be objective or universal in our perspectives.

Embodiment in every field means that scientists or writers must accurately define who or what is the object of their study. For instance, a Lawrence Kohlberg in psychology would not be able to study a small group of able-bodied, upper class white boys from New England and then extrapolate his results to cover the whole universe of moral development. He would be free to study such a group but he would have to limit his conclusions accordingly.

Why should any field of study be exempt from an inclusion of body? Inclusion of body—all types of bodies—in all fields is essential not only to altruistically accommodate people who are not white and middle class, but perhaps more importantly because, as we have seen, a radical change is necessary, and the standard model alone is simply not strong enough or versatile enough to provide the answers. The point is not to eliminate the white middle class, but to embody it and take away its automatic assumption of universality, making it simply one viewpoint among many.

Let's look for a moment at the study of science. An embodied approach to science would include the acknowledgment that what we study has alterity and that we are connected to our objects of study. We talked earlier about Russell's paradox of the set of all sets. We cannot stand apart from our habitat; we cannot see it if we are not in it. Refer once again to the Between diagram on page 127. Since it is impossible to extricate one circle from the other, traditional scientists minimize the dilemma by steering clear of the Between, drawing their boundary just before the Between and conceptualizing that the Other (the object of the experiment) begins at the point beyond the Between, part C. As you can see from the diagram, the method of excluding the Between will not produce understanding of two whole circles interconnected, but rather fragments of two circles with their connection gone.

Scientists must also recognize their own roles in the experiment. The emphasis then is on an exchange of knowledge rather than an imposition of control. It should be possible for scientists to have dialogues with the "objects" of their research, acknowledging their own alterity and allowing for both the alterity of the other as well as the Between where they are inextricably connected.

Scientists like Barbara McClintock take an approach to science that is compatible with the Between model. McClintock was a geneticist who began her work in the 1920's.[21] Her methods for doing science were based on a radically different perception of reality than that of most of her colleagues. Her goal was not predictability, which would demand "purity" and dichotomization of subject and object; for her the goal was the process of discovering a more dynamic and constantly changing universe. McClintock did not draw a seemingly impenetrable line between subject and object. To her, science and reality could not be divided in that way. Instead of aiming to predict and control the world, she worked toward understanding and cooperating with it.

She would sit with plants, get to know them, observe them, and let them speak to her; she did this rather than second guess the answer ahead of time and then plan the experiment to prove herself right. Where traditional scientists might simply throw out certain data as aberrant, as a mistake, she tried to stay open to many possibilities and envision a complex world into which the exception could fit. By "listening to the material" McClintock was able to see the larger picture, a picture in which one could make sense of and accept difference.

By "knowing" each of the plants she could better detect any deviations from the expected. She felt that plants, if she listened long enough and attentively enough, would provide the answers. And she was successful in her efforts even while she was often ostracized by some members of the scientific community for her methods.

By limiting scientific inquiry to the linear world of cause and effect, we miss much of what really happens in the world. We try to reduce the world to mathematics. And even in mathematics, the discoveries point away from the possibility of total provability. When we look only for linear cause and effect, we miss the ways in which the rational feeds the irrational and vice versa in the Between. Out of order comes chaos, and out of chaos comes order.

Chaos exists in the Between of body and mind. It is when we allow body into what was previously thought of as mind only, that is, into our fields of study and into science, that we discover an arena where complexity, change, and unpredictability are the norm. There, small changes make huge effects possible through feedback loops and complex connectedness. When we allow for chaos instead of demanding control and predictability, we discover an unlimited world of possibilities, combinations, and resources we had not known before. It is not a world we can ever "Know" in the sense of prediction and control, but it is a world full of wonder in which we continually participate.

Working within chaotic systems is not easy for scientists trained in the traditional scientific method; however, to approximate an understanding of the world, it is necessary for scientists of every branch of science to allow for the possibility if not the probability of chaos in their fields. Chaos is not found just in the field of physics, but in every one of our so-called sciences. If we were willing to admit it, we would realize that no matter what our field of study, non-linearity, chaos, and feedback loops are crucial parts of our experiments, as are our own alterities.

In philosophy as well as in science, we find the same issues surfacing. In ethics we make the attempt to be objective in order to figure out the "right" action. In so doing we attempt to sever ourselves from the situation and from those involved in the ethical dilemma. But in light of the Between model, the act of dichotomizing the world and denying our connections is the most fundamentally unethical act (see Chapter 3). The precondition we have established for doing ethics—that is, objectivity—becomes the obstacle in our path toward ethical behavior. Since we are, in reality, a part of any situation that arises, to expect us to begin ethical deliberations by severing those ties, forces us to act without regard to our connections in an anchorless and irresponsible way. If we want to know how to act in any given situation, we must first acknowledge our connections to the others involved, be they other humans, other animals, or our habitat; then we have the tools to decide how to act justly.

The information needed to make an ethical decision can be found in the Betweens and not in any one individual person. Ethics need not be a list of rules and generalizations, but must be viewed in a case by case context. How do we create a context for ethics such that our Betweens are strong and accessible and are at the core of how we make our decisions?

To begin to answer that question, let us refer to the hypothetical situation involving Heinz described in Chapter 3. As noted in that chapter, Heinz's wife did not even have a name and we knew nothing about her values. It was supposed to be enough for us to go on to get into Heinz's head to find out what values should have a bearing on the decision. We encourage our students of ethics to fragment and "universalize," thus intimately involving them in an unethical act of violence as a prerequisite for calculating the so-called ethically "correct" answer.

According to the Between model, the information that would actually be required in such a case would be what is going on not only in Heinz's head but in his body; and in the body-mind of Ms. Heinz; and also in their connections to the rest of their world. If the Heinzes knew and respected each other's alterity, lived in a community that understood and valued its interconnections, the context for ethics would be intact and the "right" answers would become apparent. By beginning our ethical search with an assumption of the severability of Heinz's mind from his body and Heinz from others, we stack the deck in favor of compounding that initial mistake.

If objectivity should not be the prerequisite to ethics, you might then ask, what is a fundamental requirement? What is essential in finding "right" answers, is working from a bewholed philosophy—that is, one that recognizes the body-minds of individuals and appreciates that they are inextricably linked to a community and to a habitat. The answers to our stickiest ethical problems lie in the Betweens.

The Between of mind and body is where our intuition, gut responses and abilities to empathize are available. But to utilize these skills, we have to allow our bodies to express their alterity. We must then weave into our systems of knowledge the wisdom of a churning stomach, a constricted throat, and a tearing eye, not so that we can rid ourselves of these terrible symptoms, but so that we can experience our way through a dilemma, not just "think" our way through it pretending we have no emotional reaction.

Just as it is not helpful to separate oneself from the other, it is also not helpful to merge with the other to the point of forgetting oneself. Connection and difference both are keys to a strong Between. *The answer is within you and it is also within the other*. The goal then becomes not to control the other or the situation, but simply to understand them.

A bewholed ethics requires fundamental changes in the way we function and the way we see ourselves. Instead of worrying about objectivity and universality, we need to begin creating a context for ethics that at its foundation recognizes and utilizes the alterity of both men and women. This change is not done simply at an individual level; it calls for a transformation of both individual consciousness and societal institutions.

Whitford, in speaking about Irigaray's work states, "The issue of the body and of sexuality is central to ethics, not in the limited sense of a set of taboos and prohibitions, but in the sense that the symbolic division of labor prevents women from becoming-for-themselves" (150). Because a strong Between is crucial to creating an ethical context and because strong alterities are crucial to a strong Between, a prerequisite to making ethical decisions is the recognition of women's alterity, something which has yet to happen, at least in recorded history. There can be no context of ethics if there is no recognition of sexual difference and if there is no avenue for women to become subjects.

Likewise, we cannot create a context for ethics if the alterities of certain groups—for instance people of color, people with disabilities, gay and lesbian people, people of all cultures, not to mention all of the other inhabitants of the planet—are devalued.

I will offer more concrete ideas of how to strengthen the alterity of women in later chapters. For our purposes here, I will cite a personal experience of mine that has a bearing on this discussion. In 1994, I was part of a diverse group of women called Mujeres Unidas that organized a summer camp for women. That camp provided a model of life in a society with a strong Between.

One major difference between this group and other women's camps that I have attended was that it did not start off as a primarily white women's camp and then realize, "Oops, we need more diversity." Instead, this group began with diversity as its major goal and from the beginning required racial parity (at least as many women of color as white women) on any decision-making committees and at camp. The organizers consciously tried to surrender old hierarchical ways of doing things; instead they worked from a place of respect for each other's alterity. We found that together we could accomplish something which seemed super-human but which was really inter-human. In a group as diverse as we were, a lot of discussion and work on conflict was required as all of us brought our distrusts and our fears with us.

The actions of the organizing committee and the camp were revolutionary because they called into question some of the major premises underlying our mono-culture: 1) one group "knows" best and must be the teachers; 2) predominance in numbers of one group over others is not important, it is the intent that counts; 3) interests can be protected even if the people who embody a particular standpoint are not present; and 4) government must be in the hands of a few "experts."

Camp itself was a miracle from beginning to end. Diversity was sought after like water in a drought, and more than racial diversity—all sorts such as (dis)ability, religion, ethnicity, heritage, sexual identity, age, size, physical appearance. Since all of us bring with us old patterns of power-over and fear of power-over, the organizers built in ways to make sure that the alterity of each woman was respected and nourished.

We had small groups (of about 10) called kitchen circle groups that met together many times and created small diverse communities in which we could share our stories. These groups provided a safe but diverse place for the Between to emerge. Additionally, we had a Culture Fest in which over 40 cultures were represented. I wish that everyone might at some time have the opportunity to participate in such an event to learn that there is no "one way" to express what it is that we, as a society made up of many, has to say. There were skits, poems, songs, dances, stories. The performers were not there in a professional capacity to entertain a passive audience; rather, they were there to express themselves in very personal ways and share in the expressions of others. The boundaries between audience and performers continually shifted as the evening went on.

That camp represented an example of a place of embodiment, a place where the universal was in the All and not just the One and where people stood together without artificial barriers constructed to keep them apart. To me it offered a glimpse into a world beyond dichotomies and beyond the idea that there is One way, a universal way.

So much of what we as a society have accomplished by using the white male model (or the white female model) as standard is to negate the existence of everyone else. When we are living in the Between model, the heroes of our television shows (if we have such things), the characters in our novels, the philosophers we read and the poets we study will be embodied individuals with backgrounds and perspectives all their own. None of them as an individual will be seen as cornering the market on truth or knowledge, because we will know that knowledge requires that we deliberately seek out many different points of view. It is not only more interesting and more fun to be enveloped by diversity; it is also more true.

Ability to Use Immanent Power to Heal

Because we do not recognize the body's alterity and respect it as a source of wisdom, but instead objectify it, we are constantly falling ill.

We cannot hear the messages sent to us across that great dichotomized divide. How do we gain access to that which we have repressed for so long?

We must look for ways to bring the repressed part of the dichotomy up to the status of partner with the currently valued part. If, in reality, our minds and our bodies are connected by the Between, communication between them should not be a problem. But we have learned through the many ways outlined earlier in the book, how to shut the door to that communication and to many possibilities for healing ourselves.

Ideally, the way to treat our body-minds would be to tune in daily to the messages our bodies are sending. We would monitor each system to see if something needs balancing or more attention. We would keep track of how diet affects us. Perhaps on a particular morning we may need to sleep a little longer or take a bath and soak for a while or eat a different kind of breakfast. However, checking in and taking the resulting appropriate action does not fit well into a system where we are forced to go to work at the same time each day, or rush around from the moment we arise until we go to bed.

I am reminded of something I heard writer and teacher Deena Metzger say: we must not leap too quickly to find a cure when an understanding of why we have an illness and what it can tell us metaphorically is the message we need to heal ourselves.[22] In the case of my disability, if I had had the operation as the doctors suggested, but then had gone on treating my feet as if they were not attached to my body or my habitat, I would have remained off-balance and unhealed in that relationship no matter what shape my feet took. By continuing to see my feet as other than myself, objects to be manipulated at will—a concept encouraged by Western medicine—I would be unable to heal myself.

A lot of healing can be done without the involvement of health professionals. I have found ways to heal that do not involve cutting muscles and breaking bones, trying to control the look of the foot. Practicing Tai Chi and yoga enables me to feel the energy flowing from the earth through me and back again. Certain other kinds of exercise such as swimming strengthen muscles that are healthy and stretch and relax those that are too tight.

I still live with some pain in my feet, a reminder that I need to continue to pay attention to them and give them care. I have learned on my own how to relieve some of the pain. But I also have some daily practices. My partner massages my feet both morning and night and has been doing so for ten years. We started with my feet and moved up to the ankles, knees and hips, which are also affected when I walk. I have begun to do the work of listening to my body and responding in the best way I can to what I hear. I am always open to learning new ways of walking—not other people's ways but my own unique ways. And I do not try to pretend that I am "normal" and can do everything anyone else can do.

Metzger suggests that we look at our illness as lessons for ourselves as well as for the wider world. I see my disability as a metaphor for our time. My balance problem and lack of feeling in my extremities may parallel similar problems in human's relationship to our habitat and to each other. We as a society are out of balance and we ignore our teetering by escaping once again into mind and away from our bodies, women and the earth body. We cannot hear the signals sent from our bodies that would assist us. And we no longer hear the wisdom of trees, animals and rocks. We have cut our feet off beneath us. Our feelings are anesthetized; we cannot feel the earth, our feet, our emotions or our passions; and we cannot feel each other.

Surgery would seem an appropriate channel for lots of dichotomous thinking—if something gives us trouble, cut it off. We as a society need to think about the equivalents to surgery that we perform everyday while we run from examining our future or the effect our actions have on the whole.

If we focus on the Between of the land and ourselves, we benefit from that creativity and energy. By avoiding further severance of our connections, we have a better chance of healing ourselves. Surgery is not always the "wrong" thing to do; but in leaping to the quickest cure, we may lose the chance to heal.

We have looked at ways the Between model can heal the mind/body split. Now let us move into explanations of how the Between model could change the male/female split.

Healing the Male/Female Split

"Love can be the becoming which appropriates the other for itself by consuming it, introjecting it into itself, to the point where the other disappears. Or love can be the motor of becoming, allowing both the one and the other to grow. For such a love, each must keep their body autonomous. The one should not be the source of the other nor the other of the one. Two lives should embrace and fertilise each other without either being a fixed goal for the other." (Luce Irigaray, *Elemental Passions* 27)

Constructs of "man" and "woman"

Where the dichotomy model separates out traits that are supposedly female and those that are male, the Between model makes no such claims about what might be essentially male or essentially female. Let's consider what the concepts of "men" and "women" would look like if we did not see them as opposites.

Males and females could be considered to be related in a peer way represented by the two interlinked circles. The fact is that there may be traits that are exclusively male or female; but because each of us has aspects of ourselves that lie in the Between, and therefore, are not just female or just male, we may never be able to assess the essence of "male" or "female." One thing we can know is that certain traits have been repressed and devalued and a whole gender, having been arbitrarily assigned those traits, has been oppressed. Being a woman has meant being silent, or forced into roles that either approximated the male standard or "complemented" it. What we have so often mistaken for essential gender difference, are in actuality learned behavioral characteristics that are demanded by the dichotomized society in which we live.

The Between model gives us a way to conceptualize such differences that does not assume that there exist strictly female or male traits or qualities; it also gives us a way to re-evaluate the dichotomies created out of the grouping of certain traits into mutually exclusive categories. For instance, there is no such thing as pure emotion or pure reason. These two qualities exist together and are connected by the Between. An individual may have more of one quality than another but having great skills in the area of reason does not preclude one from having just as great a skill in the area of emotion—people vary widely, not just between genders but also between individuals.

I am reminded of the writings of various philosophers who had convinced themselves that they were operating strictly from the rationality side of the dichotomy. They claimed to worship pure logic, pure mind, pure transcendence. What I noticed was not how logical they were, but rather how fearful of impurity. Unbeknownst to them, their whole "logical" analysis was firmly built on the foundations of one virulent emotion, namely fear.[23] Think of Descartes' fear of not knowing that drove him to doubt everything his senses told him. Or of Plato's fear of not being totally in control of his emotions and bodily appetites and his belief in a world in which everything was solid and unchanging. In Western philosophy one can trace the deep-seated fear of anything that cannot be fully known, a drive for absolutes which would suspiciously rule out anything so ever-changing and unpredictable as a Between.

When men and women were torn asunder, men were banished from the Between, an "impure" place always mixed with women and which can never be completely purged of them. The split excluded men more completely than women from access to the Between. Men are taught that those qualities needed in the Between such as cooperation, sensitivity, receptivity are "unmanly," and as such, men have been kept from developing those innate skills and qualities. Men have had to be not-woman under the threat of losing status within the power hierarchy and many men have not developed the qualities needed to thrive there.

Women, on the other hand, have been able to develop those skills traditionally assigned to women anyway and have been sneaking off into the Between surreptitiously for years—especially with other women who are not playing the power-over game. Additionally, women have been more able to tap into the Between of their body-minds, the place where emotions and logic come together, or intuition and analysis, where men have been trained to develop only one side, the logical, analytical side at the exclusion of the other. Allowed a certain leeway since they were written off as non-competitors, women were allowed to cry, to be affected by their bodies and the moon around menstruation and pregnancy, etc. Women more easily moved into the helping professions and developed women's ways of knowing that relied on more than book learning.

However, one major drawback in the socialization of women is that they are not taught how to be subjects in their own right. In the Between model women can no longer occupy the position of objects for men—that anachronistic idea comes directly out of a dichotomized mindset where subjects could own objects. Since it is dangerously easy for women to slip back into their socialized object status, they must consciously work against that pull and create new forms. Women and men must develop creation skills and learn how to become co-creators.

If women's and men's alterities do not consistently contain certain traits, then what do they contain? What a particular woman's or man's alterity looks like is dependent on a variety of things: biology, life experience, relationships, and skills and talents they may have. Alterity consists of whatever is in the imaginary of an individual. The only way to explore an entity's alterity is to make sure that each individual has a chance to allow their alterity to emerge without being squashed by the symbolic and by power-over. For that to happen, the definition of subjectivity would have to change such that it became inclusive of everyone, and expanded to include both object and subject relations. The "economy of the same" (Irigaray, *This Sex Which is Not One* 74) would be gone. Our current economy, which treats men as subjects relating only to each other in sameness and as subjects in a hierarchy, would be overthrown for one in which connection and difference are the valued elements.

Once we allow room for alterity for both genders and the emperor's tower topples, all other alterities can flourish as well. Once the standard falls, there is room for—no, demand for—alterity of all sorts, that includes all of what a person brings along including race, ethnicity, ability, class, sexual preference, size, age, and so forth.

On a sexual level, for women to have alterity would mean that they would be able to explore what their body-minds find pleasurable and desirable instead of being constantly consumed by male desire. This change in emphasis would greatly alter the way humans relate to one another. Sexuality itself would have to change from a domination/subordination model to one in which neither sex's desire was subordinate to the other. Irigaray states, "Between us, 'hardness' isn't necessary. We know the contours of our bodies well enough to love fluidity" (*This Sex* 215). What women's sexual alterity is, cannot be told without the space, time and encouragement to locate it, as well as a place of safety from power-over.

When Irigaray is questioned about essential male or female traits, the closest she will come to addressing the question is to say that the contrast may be like that of solids to liquids. We currently live in a world built on a male imaginary and preoccupied with solids, predictability, naming and dichotomizing things into hierarchies. Women's imaginaries, Irigaray muses, may be more analogous to liquids, to flows, to non-linearity. However, while speculation about that arena may be fun and interesting, we do not want to get ahead of ourselves and impose unnecessary limits. We'll just have to see...

"Everything is exchanged, yet there are no transactions. Between us, there are no proprietors, no purchasers, no determinable objects, no prices. Our bodies are nourished by our mutual pleasure. Our abundance is inexhaustible: it knows neither want nor plenty" (Irigaray, *This Sex* 213).

A true sexual revolution should allow people to freely express themselves with each other, not according to rigid roles or sexual stereotypes but according to their individual desires instead of assuming, based on gender, the existence of traditionally male or female traits. It should involve recognizing the integration of body and mind and the particularity of each body-mind. In addition, eroticism should be an integral part of everyday life and should not exist in some isolated part of life relegated to the bedroom.

The Between model allows no room for opposites *or* sameness in sexuality. Instead the expression of the alterity of each individual must be respected and encouraged. Simply involving the Between would bring into the realm of sexuality all the values of immanent power and connection and both men's and women's sexuality would function differently.

We so easily confuse power-over and immanent power. Because the power felt through connection is constantly changing and unpredictable and because it relies on trusting other people, its pursuit may cause us to feel out of control and at risk. But we must be willing to take the risk because it is only through taking it that we gain access to our immanent power.

Power that comes from splitting ourselves and allowing one part to dominate is a short-term power only and is in direct conflict with the attainment of immanent power. Each time we indulge in power-over sex or fantasies of power-over sex, we split ourselves further apart and damage our abilities to connect in a meaningful way. Power-over must be constantly pursued and renewed; the more we do it, the more we "gotta have it." It may feel like a quick fix but in reality that kind of sex perpetuates the damage by splitting the immanently powerful whole.

The Between is the truly erotic, where the flowers of feelings and desires—that we cannot even imagine from our perspective in the midst of our power-over high rises—are blooming. "Stretching upward, reaching higher, you pull yourself away from the limitless realm of your body. Don't make yourself erect; you'll leave us. The sky isn't up there: it's between us" (Irigaray, *This Sex* 213). When we talk of wanting sexual freedom, we must look not to how free we are to dominate and be dominated but rather how free we are to reach the fullness of depth of feeling, how free we are to connect. If the sexual revolution ceases at a point where women continue to be exploited, there has not been a revolution at all, just a new twist on the old oppressions.

Where sex has been built on the male model, a model of erections, solids and power-over, I suggest instead a model based on liquids. "Your skin and mine, yes. But mine goes on touching itself indefinitely, from the inside. Secreting a flow which brings the sides together. From which side does that liquid come? One or the other? Both? So which is one and which is other in that production? Neither? Yet it exists. Where does it come from? From both. It flows between. Not held or held back by a source. The source already rises from two caressing" (Irigaray, *Elemental Passions* 15). Males and females co-existing, interacting as peers, tapping into their fertile Between, co-creating, is what the Between model calls for. It calls for seeing ourselves as we are in our bodies, in our dreams, and in our alterity. It calls for difference and connection.

All of this sounds good in an ideal world. But it is difficult to get to these places with someone from a group that has historically oppressed and exerted power-over you. How can we trust that the "other" will not attempt that again?

As I sit here writing the second draft of this book in a cabin in the woods by myself, it strikes me that if I had been sexually abused or raped in my life, I might not be capable of spending this time here with nature. There are no locks on these doors nor shades to pull. Every evening an incredibly isolating darkness inevitably falls. I am not even within shouting distance of help. I am startled by strange noises and my imagination goes wild. But if I had terrible memories of past abuse, I believe, those, too, would come up along with the fear and I doubt I would have the courage to stay there.

In this power-over hungry society, those in the down side of the dichotomy such as men of color and women often find safety hard to come by. I believe people must create that space together, apart from their historical oppressor at first. When alterity has been so put down, so damaged by power-over, it is almost impossible to coax it out if there is the slightest possibility of harm. This, too, is why women of color need places away from both men and white women where they can feel safe enough to foster and nurture their alterity. In later chapters, we will discuss my ideas about uncovering women's alterity and building safety.

One last note on the issue of dichotomies: a reader might ask whether I, too, am using a dichotomy to critique a dichotomy since I am contrasting power-over with immanent power. I seem to draw on two models of power, opposing them and valuing one over the other. However, the problem is more with language than with the model. We have difficulty avoiding dichotomous thought even when critiquing dichotomies. We are confused by using the model to critique the model; we have no meta-term—that is, terms that can get us outside the model to comment on it. However, if we put the two terms, power-over and immanent power, into the Between model, we see that they are not dichotomous but rather each term has alterity and connection to the other term.

If we use the Between model, we can work toward reconciling those seemingly opposing terms. Each time we see or think of something in terms of a dichotomy, we can introduce it into the Between model. The elements involved need not be defined in opposition to each other but can be seen as two necessary components of a whole. Our language requires us to split, but in order to remain whole we must continuously reconnect. This is an ongoing process. We cannot reconnect once and for all but must be forever vigilant.

iii.

Getting From
Cut and Dried
to Juicy Whole

The Between model is not some kind of highfalutin ideal, but, rather, is a working model that can be applied to the world in every way possible. In the next part of the book, I will concentrate on developing applications of the model for evaluation and analysis of social movements and issues and then focus on how to move our institutions and consciousness from dichotomy to Between.

Various people and movements have identified many of the problems outlined so far in this book and they have suggested and tried different approaches to change. However, I want to show how the new model outlined here can provide us with a consistent analysis that can be applied to any social movement. I will look at just two of the current social change movements, the women's and the men's movements, and suggest ways to critique currents within the movements in terms of what will move us toward a whole future.

9
What's Between the Women's And Men's Movements?

The Women's Movements

Many books have been written about women's oppression over the centuries and, relying on the availability of those accounts, I will not take the time to go through that record. Suffice it to say that women in general—though certainly some women more than others—have been an oppressed group since the beginnings of patriarchy. In the West this oppression dates back at least since the emergence of Western philosophy in the period around the time of Plato, Socrates and Aristotle. Women in general were robbed of both their immanent power and often their outlets for power-over: immanent power was all but destroyed by dichotomization, and power-over was made available to women only indirectly, through husbands or fathers, or if they had a certain privilege (particularly if they were white and/or middle or upper class), through asserting superiority over other races and classes. Women have responded in a variety of ways to this deprivation of power, which, though substantial, could never have been total if women were to survive.

In fact, resourcefully, women have gained some power-over in the form of money and political position. Statistically, however, women in the U. S. still make a fraction of what men make on every dollar. And when the number of women senators increased from two to six (out of fifty), women considered themselves lucky. While women have become more visible in formerly male-dominated professions such as medicine and law, these gains are tenuous at best. A while ago I read in the newspaper that the number of women in law firms in San Francisco had actually dropped in 1994 and when one looks at the paltry number of women partners in those firms, one wonders how long it will take to achieve equity this way.

In each period in history, we can see how methods were created to deal with women who got out of line. Prior to the 14th century in the healing arts, we could surmise that some women were tapping into their immanent power by using their body-minds to heal sick people and assist mothers in childbirth. However, as Barbara Ehrenreich and Deirdre English report in their booklet *Witches, Midwives and Nurses: A History of Women Healers* (1973), "In the century that preceded the beginning of the 'witch-craze'—the thirteenth century—European medicine became firmly established as a secular science and a *profession*. The medical profession was actively engaged in the elimination of female healers—their exclusion from the universities, for example—long before the witch-hunts began" (15). The period from the 14th to the 17th century was marked by the deaths of millions of women who dared to venture out of the arena ordained for them, into realms like medicine that had recently been claimed by men. These women represented a real menace to the development of Western medicine and of capitalism, not to a mention a threat to the systematic subjugation of women.

In more recent history, through the struggles of women, most of the U. S. laws that proclaimed women to be the property of men have been repealed. Along with the lessening of these legal, economic and biological pressures, however, has come pressure of a different sort. Naomi Wolf in *The Beauty Myth* (1991) chronicles what she considers to be the most powerful force holding women in their places now, and that is the beauty myth. "The more legal and material hindrances women have broken through, the more strictly and heavily and cruelly images of female beauty have come to weigh on us" (10). These hindrances Wolf refers to highlight the very core of the dichotomy, the subject/object split, which keeps women in powerless positions in one way or another. Gains made in the acquisition of power-over can be taken away by re-asserting the fundamental place of women in the subordinate object category.

As we have already discussed in earlier chapters, dealing with the subject/object split means also dealing with the mind/body split and with the whole system of power-over. The current period in history calls for women, who are situated in the object/body categories, to lead the way to changes in thinking and living in the world. However, with feminism as with any other movement calling for change, we must be cautious not to fall into the same traps that have historically been laid for us. To plan an effective strategy, we need an overview and some perspective on the various pulls within feminism itself.

A tendency in this culture is to simplify various women's movements into one monolith called "feminism." So when newspaper articles appear accusing "feminists" of this or that or stating that "feminists" believe such and such, they should always be viewed with skepticism. There are many feminisms.

Having said that, I note what I see as four major threads within the movements. I describe these threads because an understanding of where we have been and an evaluation of current practices will better enable us to strategize for the future. Because each thread has had and continues to have relevance, I do not intend to devalue any one of them. I will, however, advocate an emphasis on the fourth approach as a way to heal the mind/body, male/female splits.

For the purpose of this discussion I have coined four terms to describe the four branches of feminism I identify and their relation to the mind/body split: 1) "Equality" feminism; 2) "Difference" feminism; 3) "Deconstructionist" feminism; and 4) "Whole" feminism. Keep in mind that each one pulls in its own direction and calls for divergent and sometimes contradictory actions in a given situation. Some movements draw on all four strategies, partly because they may lack an overview of goals and partly because the four are not always clearly distinguishable.

While this section necessarily contains generalizations and overlooks nuances that exist within each point of view, I believe the analysis can be helpful in determining whether a particular strategy is likely to work toward healing the mind/body split.

Equality Feminism

This term describes the branch of feminism which asserts that the primary goal for women is equal rights. Those ascribing to this viewpoint believe that women are equal to men and can and should perform the same jobs at the same pay. Their primary strategy is an emphasis on the similarities between men and women while minimizing difference. They lobby for the inclusion of women into the traditional public world of men.

Simone de Beauvoir was an articulate spokesperson for this branch of feminism. She accurately identified the problem of women's being considered the "Other" to men's subjectivity. And she recognized that women had been lumped into categories such as nature and subordinated to men; she was appalled by what she considered a disregard of women's importance and possibilities. In assessing the problem, though, Beauvoir concluded that it was the links between women and nature, women and body that constituted the essential fallacy and needed to be severed. She believed that to achieve equality women as well as men could transcend their bodies and the earth, the primordial realm, and become emancipated. Beauvoir's envisioned emancipation was one of humans free from their habitat. Thus, she opposed attempts to tie feminism with ecology since that would further entrench women in the mud of their environment.

Looking at this branch of feminism from the point of view of the Between model, we can see that implicit in the arguments is an acceptance of the division of mind from body. The male/female split is recognized as a problem while the mind/body split is not. One of the strategies of this branch of feminism, then, is to agitate to make sure that women are put onto the same side of the mind/body dichotomy as men—that is, on the mind side.

Equality feminists fight for parity for women, for equal rights, for equal pay, for non-discrimination in hiring and promotion. These theorists assert that men and women are equal and, in fact, the same, because both men and women as human beings can transcend body. Based on that premise, women can be just as "rational" as men, though their minds have been unfairly overlooked and denied. That women can be as "rational" as men has certainly been proven time and time again as women move into the public sphere, but the mind/body dichotomy remains.

Included within the ranks of equality feminists are what most people call "liberal feminists" who are calling for inclusion in the already-existing political and economic structure while not necessarily trying to change it. But there are "socialist feminists" who, while wanting to distance themselves from the liberals, also tend to emphasize the sameness of men and women and their distinction from the habitat. In *The Dialectic of Sex* (1971), Shulamith Firestone advocates technological advances that would free women from having to give birth. The key to women's liberation, in her view, is as complete a freedom from body as possible. Both Beauvoir and Firestone "posit the necessity to transcend the female body and its reproductive capacities without questioning the ways in which the significance of the female body is socially constructed and its possibilities socially limited" (Gatens 3). The body takes on a lion's share of the blame for women's troubles. Body is once again the fall guy for humans' inability to transcend their "lowly" existence.

Equality feminism has been extremely valuable to women because of the stark realities of their lives—their lack of access to the legal system, to financial resources, to certain kinds of jobs, to political power—in short, to the sources of power-over. Due to the work of such feminists, we are now able to see beyond the goal of equality to different goals, ones which deal with the fact that the system in which parity is sought is still a patriarchal system. Sonia Johnson states, "Having to keep cleaning up the bloody mess patriarchy makes of our lives further entrenches us..." (*Going Out of Our Minds* 329). She uses the analogy that for centuries women have pounded on the door of patriarchy with a long ramming pole. They gather strength and run for it, bashing it over and over. Meanwhile, the more headway that is made, the more the men inside reinforce the whole structure. She imagines women finally breaking through the door and bursting in only to find that they have not achieved the Promised Land, they have merely landed in the belly of patriarchy.

Women have worked hard to dissociate themselves from their bodies. Of course, as we have discussed earlier, it is not possible to transcend our bodies and reach a universal sexless, genderless kingdom of Oz. In reality, while believing that we can reach Oz, we unwittingly take on the idealized perspective of the standard white male—and we learn well how to keep our mouths shut about the emperor's state of undress. Now that we have more perspective on this issue, we can see that the ultimate step in equality feminism is a complete dismissal of our own unique experience and who we are in our bodies, and may even require a sex and race change. Winning this game, that is, playing the patriarchal games better than men do, may provide us with pride at a job well done, but it is the job itself that must be questioned. If indeed there is a major problem with a society based on the idealized perspective of the white male, then our energy and our desire to "win" is sadly misplaced.

Difference Feminism

This branch of feminism (sometimes called cultural or radical feminism) arises at least partially in reaction to equality feminism. These feminists advocate emphasizing and glorifying the ways in which women and men are different. They cradle the body cast aside by the equality feminists and breathe life back into it. These theorists believe that to leave out body is to leave out women—it is analogous to throwing the baby out with the bath water. They believe the body is good and valuable and desire to be aligned with it. The emphasis is to value what has previously been devalued, the body and women, and find virtues there. Thus, rather than challenge the link between women and body, they advocate flipping the dichotomy over and elevating what has heretofore been maligned.

In other words, difference feminists accept that there is a mind/body, male/female split but assert that society's goal should be to value the body, female side of the dichotomy. From this group comes the idea that ways women have traditionally functioned in the society provide a model for all citizens in a better society. The traits that have traditionally been associated with women, such as nurturing, listening, receptivity, cooperation, peace-lovingness, emotion, self-sacrifice, etc., are the important values for us as a society and should be stressed over the traditionally "male" virtues of independence, autonomy, competitiveness, aggression, and egoism. The dichotomy between men and women, mind and body, is not questioned here, but its arrangement is considered to be faulty: women and body should be on top.

Difference feminists accept the hypothesis that women and our habitat are linked in a positive way. The human/nature dichotomy becomes literally a man/nature-and-women dichotomy and women pride themselves on being more in touch with the animals and with our habitat. Some ecofeminists have fallen into this trap by accepting these divisions and talk about how women have a privileged position with nature by virtue, perhaps, of their ability to menstruate, give birth, and nurse. Some of the very same arguments that philosophers like Descartes or Kant used to exempt women from rationality are used by these feminists to exemplify positive rather than negative traits.

But implicit in this discussion is an assumption that because women do these things or have acquired these skills, they are inherent in women's essential "nature." Many of these values and skills have clearly been socialized into women and do not necessarily emanate from women's bodies or from any kind of "natural" state. Women have been taught to take care of the emotional needs of those around them, just as men could be taught to do. All women do not possess these attributes nor do all men lack them. To say that these values are "women's" values is to accept the dichotomy between male and female and to accept once again very distinct roles for men and women in our society. Difference feminism accepts a deep split between male and female categories based solely on real or imagined biological differences.

An example of a difference feminist is writer and scholar Mary Daly. Although Daly denies that her thinking is dichotomous, she perpetuates the idea that men and women are opposites and essentially different. Daly makes numerous statements such as: "Since female energy is essentially biophilic, the female spirit/body is the primary target in this perpetual war against life. Gyn\Ecology is the reclaiming of life-loving female energy" (*Gyn/Ecology* 355). The claim is that women, due simply to their having been born women, have some essential thing that makes them more ethical, more caring, more intuitive than men.

There have been many attempts to encourage women to tap into that "female power" and to explore its special qualities. I am reminded of another summer camp for women that I attended a few years ago. The goal was to focus on the "Feminine," which was supposed to be something all women had in common, and in so doing we could forget our "petty" differences and act in unity. Race and class were supposed to be subsumed by the category of the Feminine and those who brought them up as core issues were labeled divisive. What became clear to me in examining the work of the camp was that the majority was once again universalizing a particular point of view—that of the standard white female. When problems arose with this framing of the issues, those in power retreated to the safety of what they considered to be an apolitical universal Feminine. Unfortunately the experiences of poor women and women of color did not seem to be congruent with that ideal.

At the camp, the door to the passageway through the mind-only rule was opened long enough to include some women but then was quickly slammed shut again, plunging the focus back to a disassociation from difference and from body. The Female was given the authority to speak but the alterities of individual females were ignored. Subsequent broad universalized claims read just like the institutionalized "white male" proclamations. However, instead of an emperor, there is an empress who allegedly speaks for "all." But the same accusations of racism and exclusivity we leveled at the emperor must also be directed at the empress.

When we imply that there is one thing that is inherent in all women— i.e., that transcends all of our diversities—what emerges is not transcendence at all, but merely the idealized perspective of the standard white woman which defines the "Feminine" and silences those who dare to raise alternative experiences.

Such attempts to reify femininity go from embracing body to attempting to "purify" it and fit it into the old familiar dichotomous mindset. The Feminine is made the opposite of the Masculine. These are abstract concepts which do not correlate with a reality that includes a mix of the many instead of a freezing into One or Other.

With that said about the dangers of difference feminism, it is important to recognize the value of the work women have been doing for centuries. It is true that many of the qualities that have traditionally been
associated with women seem to be exactly what we need in our world
today. In many ways the skills women have learned and the roles they
have assumed can be seen as indispensable to the functioning of human
society. Women's nurturance of relationships has often been the glue
holding our society together. Without it, quality of life would suffer greatly
and we would stand to lose much of the joy of being human. For women
to feel competent and worthwhile by valuing their contribution, whether
it was chosen freely or not, is a significant and healthy development.

Equality feminism and difference feminism are actually merely opposite sides of the same coin: as long as the power-over, mind/body split
worldview is dominant, women are required to give up their alterity.
Whether women try to take on an idealized male identity, ignoring their
differences, or in the alternative, attempt to value that which has been
devalued and elevate the body and women while leaving themselves
open to discrimination, they remain disconnected from themselves. Since
neither strategy deals with the core problem of the mind/body split or
the exclusion of the Between, the solutions will be piecemeal and temporary at best. These "solutions" must fail in the long run. Carol Tavris
(1992) asserts that "Framing the question in terms of polarities, regardless of which pole is the valued one, immediately sets up false choices
for women and men. It continues to divide the world up into *men* and
women as if these categories were unified opposites. It obscures the fact
that the opposing qualities associated with masculinity and femininity
are caricatures to begin with" (60).

With such disparate views labeled "feminism," it is no small wonder
that that conflicts arise. Feminists find themselves in the vicious circle
of identity versus difference and lack clarity about how to escape it.

Deconstructionist Feminism

Deconstructionism is a branch of philosophy which deliberately
breaks down the dichotomous categories of thought that have kept
Westerners imprisoned for so long. When I first began to study the
deconstructionists, I was thrilled by the freedom it offered. Dichotomies
were critiqued and held up as inherently false; and assumptions were
pulled out from under the theories and theorists who had remained in
power for so long. I was excited by Nietzsche's lion who would rip up all

of the previously sacrosanct notions of identity and of thought. No longer would we have to bow down like camels to those theories that had heretofore been claimed as universal.

Deconstructionist thinking has been crucial in freeing feminist theorists within the academy to question "universality," and to emphasize context. A whole generation of feminists has been inspired to work in this arena and to experiment with its possibility. However, to maintain one's credentials in this field, one must ward off any and all accusations of being labeled "essentialist."[24] In order to avoid that label, some deconstructionist feminists have gone so far as to suggest that there is no such thing as a category which can be called "woman" (Kristeva, Butler). These theorists realize that such arguments make political struggles of "women" untenable (if there is no category of women, what, then, is the women's movement and what is feminist theory?) and try to distinguish the use of the category of "woman" as a political tool from the use of it as an ontological category. Judith Butler in her essay "Gender Trouble, Feminist Theory, and Psychoanalytic Discourse" states, "If the inner truth of gender is a fabrication and if a true gender is a fantasy instituted and inscribed on the surface of bodies, then it seems that genders can be neither true nor false but are only produced as the truth effects of a discourse of primary and stable identity" (337).

As much as the deconstructionist point of view appeals to me, I believe that taking deconstructionism to its logical conclusion, we are left with no body, no women and no habitat from which to create alterity. It seems to me preposterous of humans to argue away, for instance, an essence in our habitat—to say that nature is only culture, that there is no earth prior to our thinking it.

Another large problem with deconstructionists is that even while they argue that particularity should be included, they construct their arguments so abstractly that they make sure they are *a priori* devoid of body, an academic requirement. So even when the mind/body dichotomy (and many other dichotomies as well) is critiqued, the very methods used in that kind of theorizing eliminate body. The mind/body split remains untouched as an underlying assumption in the methodology. The audience for deconstructionism consists mostly of other academics; it does not include people who do not have access to or do not wish to participate in the system of "higher" learning. The language used is often exclusive and jargonistic (refer to the Judith Butler quote above). While some of these feminists have successfully challenged the traditional parameters of academic study by including personal experience, emotional content and contextualized study, many become caught up in following the rules of that game in order to be taken seriously by the world of academia, even though the rules are often contradictory to the content of their theories.

Whole Feminism

A fourth branch of feminism is emerging which I will call "whole feminism," that is, the effort to see the whole without dichotomy, to recognize the alterity of men and women but also to recognize the Between, the part that is neither one nor the other. Men and women in this view are not seen as opposite and mutually exclusive entities. What whole feminism emphasizes is that those values and skills mentioned above as those associated with women are simply those that the power-over society discarded when men were dichotomized from women. They are not essentially women's qualities but are quite possibly skills and values that are as much a part of men as of women; men have simply had these qualities "socialized out" of them.

Some ecofeminists join in this project and recognize the dichotomous mindset as a trap. Catherine Roach, in an article called "Loving Your Mother: On the Woman-Nature Relationship" in the Spring 1991 issue of *Hypatia* states, "dualism [culture/nature and human/nonhuman] is unsound because it encourages the belief that 'culture' and humanity are quite apart from 'nature' and that we humans may thus use and abuse the environment at will, without ourselves suffering from the damage we inflict. Any understanding of the world that posits an important or unbridgeable difference between the realm of the human and the nonhuman risks creating a gulf between the two in which the human, because of our inherent chauvinism and anthropocentrism, would inevitably be more highly valued than the nonhuman" (54). The recognition that the dichotomy itself is dangerous helps us to avoid the trap of glorifying one side over the other.

Ecofeminism can be an example of whole feminism when it links the trashing of our habitat with the oppression of women to show how it is dichotomization and power-over which bind women and habitat together in oppression. Women are in a unique position to observe our habitat, not because we are inherently linked but because we have been tied together by patriarchy. Women have the experience of being silenced, of being used as objects, of being denied alterity. What women's alterity encompasses is not clear; it is as yet an unknown terrain, one which cannot be plumbed until women are free and safe to express it. As Irigaray (*This Sex*) believes, it will not be just one thing.

I was at a conference recently with a woman who taught religious studies and the feminist strains in that field. As a dedicated vegetarian, she could not understand how women who were so adamant that they be respected, could continue to oppress the next most powerless "level" in the hierarchy—animals—by eating them and participating in the continuation of domination. Why did they expect such respect for themselves when they continued to deny it to other beings? The linkage between women and animals is easy to extol but hard to accept when it means that we ourselves must change how we interact with others. Both women and men have ways of rationalizing our behavior as we continue to buy into the system of power-over. Whole feminism is an attempt to bring those behaviors into consciousness so that wherever we can, we act out of the connection, not out of the split.

Women are both the same and different from men, and from each other and from other animals; and until that paradox is recognized, confronted and acknowledged, women will find themselves and their identities out of sync with reality. We need an approach that includes both difference and conjunction. We need an approach which questions the mind/body split, recognizes women's alterity and considers the whole.

To bewhole our world means to acknowledge that we are always coming from a particular perspective, living in a particular body. Women may, in fact, share certain things as females, based on differences in body, as may men as males, but these things can never be known because they are always mixed up with our diverse experiences. Embodiment requires openness to both the recognition of difference on account of body and the flexibility not to universalize that difference. It requires accessibility, difference, contextualization, and the perspectives of all of us with no one privileged standpoint.

Comparing the Branches

Let us look at a several examples of how the four branches of feminism might deal with some of the dichotomies (reason/emotion, autonomy/connection and mind/body) that arise within society.

1. *Reason/Emotion*
Consider the relationship of the qualities of reason and emotion. Continuing to see these two qualities as dichotomous, with reason on one side and emotion on the other, equality feminists would argue that

women are as capable of reason as men and would urge women to separate themselves from emotions and emotional arguments and instead develop strong skills of logical analysis. Equality feminists are critical of an appeal to emotion as, for instance, a foundation for a system of ethics and are embarrassed by women who advocate reliance on it. They believe that women have nothing special to offer in the area of ethics and, in fact, women are as capable of arguing abstractly about principles of justice as are men. The further back one can stand, the less invested one is in the situation and the less one's emotions play a role in ethical decision-making, the better.

Difference feminists, on the other hand, will deliberately favor the side of emotion and will use emotion as a valued starting point. They are mortified by the equality feminists' acceptance of the devaluation of women's side of the dichotomy and are insulted by the self-effacing denial of what they see as women's strengths. Difference feminists assume that women are better at the emotional side of things than men are and would claim emotion for the Feminine. Reason can then be identified as a "masculine" quality.

Nel Noddings (1984), a difference feminist, advocates "care ethics" which urges us to assume a receptive stance and pay attention to our bodily responses so that we can understand how to act—something whole feminists might also advocate. Equality and whole feminists, however, might point out that our gut-level, emotional response, trained with bigotry and hatred may not be reliable in many situations. They might suggest that unless these issues are brought to consciousness, emotional responses could be conservative—that is, simply reinforce the status quo. An example of that kind of conservatism is the prevalence of meat-eating in this culture. Training can overcome an initial aversion to meat eating so that without a certain amount of consciousness raising, people either do not experience negative emotions when eating dead animals or they successfully override them.

Whole feminists would claim that such a valuing of emotion as "feminine" further reinforces the divisions in our society and does not allow room for difference from a standard. Whether that standard is feminine or masculine, the problem is having a standard at all to which people are forced to conform. Whole feminists might argue that masculine and feminine traits are not associated with gender but are qualities that each of us has to some extent. Why then do we need the labels of masculine and feminine?

Deconstructionist feminists might say that the dichotomy should not exist and that emotion has a place in knowledge and in study. But in the process of stating this position, the academic feminists will use language that excludes the majority of women in this country and will use the format and framework provided by the university. I have read many a feminist critique which begins with lip service to personal experience, context and perspective but then goes on throughout the text to speak completely abstractly once again, divorced from emotional content and context until the concluding paragraph. It is extremely difficult not to fall into that trap and I have probably done it more than once in this book. We are so used to speaking abstractly and to excluding the body that we often fail to identify it as a problem.

Instead of dichotomizing reason and emotion, whole feminism recognizes that each has alterity and that there is also an overlap, a Between. These two values cannot not be linked with gender making one exclusively a male quality and one exclusively female. Instead these qualities are located on a continuum and shared by all in varying degrees; the goal is to use both at the same time, to operate out of the Between. Whole feminists thus would not accept the analyses of either the equality feminists or the difference feminists. Carol Tavris states, "But if women's daily behavior, like men's, is more influenced by the roles they play, the ideologies they believe in, and the work they do than by anything fundamental to their gender, then we need to transform roles, ideologies, and work so that humane qualities can be encouraged in both sexes" (62).

2. *Autonomy/Connection*

Since these qualities have already been thoroughly dichotomized, it is easy to see them as opposites, as mutually exclusive and mutually exhaustive. Think of our dichotomy diagram again and visualize these values as separated by a gulf. One cannot be autonomous and connected at the same time. And autonomy is the valuable quality, the one we must have to be successful in this society.

When this dichotomy is linked with the male/female dichotomy, men are associated with autonomy and women with connection. Success is linked with the male half, with autonomy. This puts women in a dilemma—if they go after success, it conflicts with a quality crucial to their identities: connection. If they let go of connection, they are ridiculed as masculinized or overly ambitious. As we discussed earlier, women have to walk a fine line to keep their own identity intact while trying to be successful in the world.

I picked this example because in the Between model, connection is a quality valued in the Between and not in the male or the female part *per se*. Connection which is associated with women, could be seen instead as one of the values that has been forcibly cut away from men through the process of dichotomization. It is a value that would be heartily claimed by difference feminists. However, in current conceptualizations, connection is not necessarily a *female* trait but rather, "not-male." Thus, since women are not defined in opposition to connection, this quality seems easier for women to claim.

If we simply flip the dichotomy over, putting women and connection on top, and still define autonomy and men as its opposite, we are stuck with the idea that we are either connected or autonomous. And that men who represent autonomy are the enemy over which women must triumph. What remains is a valorization only of women and their connections to others. The problem with this line of argument is that women become stuck in figuring out how best to serve others often without the acknowledgment that they are autonomous beings with alterity and needs and wants of their own.

Some feminist ethicists belonging to the school of difference feminism have argued that "care" rather than "justice" should be the guiding principle in a system of ethics. Nodding's ethics of care referred to above is an example of this kind of thinking. The connection, the relationship is the most important value, which requires at certain points that one place one's own needs into a secondary position while serving others that one cares about. Sustaining the relationship counts more than the needs of one or the other party in the relationship. Feminist philosopher Claudia Card argued, in an article in *Hypatia* called "Caring and Evil" (1990), that this approach would seem to lead toward encouraging women to stay in abusive and dangerous relationships—rather than breaking off the relationship, one stays to help him/her get better (101-107).

Equality feminists would argue that women can and ought to be as autonomous as men. Achieving autonomy is necessary if one is to succeed in the business world as it currently operates. Proposals such as the Mommy track, which allow women to take time out from career to have children, are seen by equality feminists as a step in the wrong direction because they emphasize women's difference and suggest that women have a need to be more connected to family than men do.

In a whole feminist approach, the quality of connection would exist in the Between, that place where all are connected—the fertile, creative, unpredictable area that we have repressed. We can conceive of ourselves in the Between model as overlapping circles which are both separate and connected. Neither connection without considerations of alterity nor alterity without consideration of connection will be satisfactory. Both are required.

3. *Mind/Body*

Let's briefly compare the branches with regard to the mind/body split itself. The contradiction on this issue between difference and equality feminists is self-evident. On the issue of body, difference feminists might say that women are more influenced by their bodies than men are and that that is positive. However, this kind of body talk blatantly conflicts with the philosophy of the equality feminists who argue that we must deny all difference between men and women for the sake of equality. If we focus on body, we must face the fact that we are different. Difference has certainly been used against women—as fuel for the arguments that women are inferior, weak, non-rational, belonging only in the private sphere, etc. The double bind, of either denying difference and transcending our bodies or identifying with body and risking the loss of rights equal to those of men, remains.

This is the place where some deconstructionist feminist thinking parallels that of equality feminists: both deny the importance of body in constructing an identity. Liberal feminists, for instance, might argue for the idea of essence, but they would say that female and male essences are the same. On the other hand, many deconstructionist thinkers, feminists included, might argue that there is no essence in body and gender and therefore, nothing unique can be claimed for women, people of color, gays and lesbians, etc. and we arrive at a similar endpoint to that of liberal feminists, at a transcendence of body. Descartes thought that we could only know our minds and started his foundations of knowledge there, separating himself from body. Deconstructionists do away with essences altogether so that there is not only no body but also no mind.

I understand the impetus of both equality and deconstructionist viewpoints on this subject—not to give the male-dominated hierarchy one iota of leverage to use for justification of women's oppression based on difference. And as long as we are seeing the world through dichotomized glasses, perhaps women have no other feasible way to protect themselves; but keep in mind that these strategies do not pose a threat to a system of splitting and of power-over. The position of whole feminists is that we must realize that we are all a complex mix of both "culture" and "nature" and that we cannot determine which is which in order to split them apart. Whole feminism would demand that we both acknowledge differences inherent in each individual based on bodily difference, and require a society that does not base its values on a power-over, dichotomous mindset, but rather, insists on alterity for all.

Confusion in the women's movement, then, has been largely due to a reluctance to upset the dichotomizations that run rampant in the Western worldview. We have seen that when women accept that model as a given, they contribute to their own oppression and the oppression of their bodies. At times, working within a dichotomous worldview seems to be the only way to make a real change that benefits women, e.g., working for equal pay for equal work. I would suggest, however, in such a situation, we take care to acknowledge that tactic for what it is. The end should never be only to secure equal pay for equal work; it should be to use the newly won resources to work toward changing the dichotomized worldview itself. In the last chapter of this book, I will talk more about concrete ways to heal the dichotomies.

The Men's Movement

The men's movement has arisen in response to ways in which men are affected by our current thinking about what men are or are not and what they can and cannot do. Like the women's movement, the men's movement is complex and no one ideology or approach is consistently taken. Different people have different priorities they wish to concentrate on. In a collection of essays from the magazine *Wingspan* (1992), editor Christopher Harding identifies four main branches within the men's movement (xiii-xvi):

1. The Mythopoetic Branch is the largest and fastest growing segment. Harding describes it as "a freewheeling exploration of male spirituality and male psychology (especially from a Jungian perspective). It encourages men to delve into their psyches by reintroducing them to literature, mythology and art" (xiii).

2. The Profeminist/Gay Affirmative Branch was started in the seventies and grew up alongside of the women's movement. This branch focuses on correcting societal "isms" such as racism, sexism, classism and heterosexism where they exist in institutions, behavior and thought. Its members actively lobby for women's rights, gay rights and other minority causes.

3. The Men's Rights/Father's Rights Branch is identified by Harding to be "largely focused on changing laws and the public's perception of men.

Father's rights groups lobby for changes regarding child custody, child support awards, rights of unmarried fathers, and abortion issues" (xiv).

4. The Addiction/Recovery Branch grew out of groups such as Alcoholics Anonymous in which men often confront grief over their difficult relationships with their fathers.

I would add one more branch that has emerged more recently which I will call the Redemption Branch.

5. The Redemption Branch includes both the Million Man March (October 1995) and its aftermath and the Promise Keepers movement.[25] Both of these groups emphasize that men have gone down the wrong road and need to redeem themselves by returning to religious models of behavior. Both the Promise Keepers which is predominately white and the Million Man March which was aimed at African American men urge men to ask for redemption for their sins and re-assert their rightful place in the family as head of household.

Comparing the Branches

Each branch of the men's movement has positive features, but there are also features that require re-thinking in light of a Between model of reality. The Between model gives us a way to analyze various parts of the men's movement and identify which actions and philosophies actually threaten the status of the patriarchy (the dichotomous worldview and power-over) in this country and those which seem to reinforce it. I will deal primarily with the mythopoetic, the redemptionist and the profeminist branches here.

Working from the Between model, it appears that the work of the men's movements ought to be at least twofold: 1) working toward building the alterity of men, women, bodies and our habitat; and 2) seeking to move out of power-over positions and experience the pleasure of moving into the Between of men and women, humans and our habitat, mind and body. These goals would destabilize the dichotomy and would move us as a society toward greater immanent power.

Part of the problem I have with aspects of the men's movement, particularly the mythopoetic branch, is that they have not defined masculinity in a precise way. Instead, they seem to rely on what Robert Bly, a leading spokesman for this branch, calls "the deep male" (*Iron John* 6). It is as if this "deep male" is an inborn universal that each and every man must discover and actualize in order to be happy. My concern with that view is that if the concept of masculinity is not debunked of its cultural components, which were formed by a patriarchal society, then it can only reinforce the same old traditional traits of male dominance that led us to our current predicament.

As I stated earlier, men suffer considerably under patriarchy even while they benefit from it, but focusing only on the ill effects of patriarchy on men and trying to fix those does not address the problem of patriarchy and dichotomization at all. The mythopoetic branch never locates the fundamental problem in the construction of men's identities: that is, the assumption of male centrality. Patriarchy is therefore repeatedly reproduced. Robert Bly makes it easier on men to live in the patriarchy, finding ways to minimize damage to their selfhood, but taking the patriarchy as a given.

Bly diagnoses the problem with men in the 1950's as being too afraid to venture out into emotions and feelings arising from the body. Men were stripped of all receptivity and emotional life. Their borders were heavily patrolled. Then women started to make some inroads into the areas that had been defined as exclusively male, such as medicine, law, construction, the art world, etc., and it became less clear what real men were supposed to do and how they were different from women.

The men Bly calls "soft men" are those who, in reaction to that stifled position, started to share power with women by accepting them into the "upper" half of the dichotomy and allowing themselves to dip into the "lower" half; some of those men may even have decided to ditch the patriarchal divisions and relate as peers to women. Bly finds these men to be unhappy. He states, "They're lovely, valuable people—I like them— they're not interested in harming the earth or starting wars. There's a gentle attitude toward life in their whole being and style of living. But many of these men are not happy. You quickly notice the lack of energy in them. They are life-preserving but not exactly life-giving" (2-3).

I agree that these men have a hard time, especially in the face of condemnations like Bly's. It is a challenge to allow oneself to cross boundaries that have previously defined one's identity, particularly if one has no support from one's culture, or even meets with ridicule for those actions. But Bly does not talk about what such men gain if they persevere in this attitude. These men could have a great advantage in engaging with women and other men in peer relationships, building alliances such that they could develop their alterity and tap into the Between. Judging from what a majority of the men in this society are interested in—from football to video games to violent movies, I am thrilled to see so-called soft men who have given up the ideas of war and destruction of the planet.

When I hear of the mythopoetic leaders making a concerted effort to separate themselves from their mothers, and identifying men's major problem as being overly connected to their mothers, I am indeed suspicious. This goal is a retreat from the Between, both the Between of women and men and the Between of mind and body. Reaction against the bonds formed with one's mother seems to be anti-connection and anti-immanent power. After all, what we felt with our mothers when they were pregnant with us was our first experience of the Between. Instead of dissociating from that connection and connections in general, men should be encouraged to seek ways to make comparable connections in other parts of their lives.

Bly may identify some of the problems boys have growing up in the home of a single mother, but his proposed solutions only make matters worse. Bly states, "When women, even women with the best intentions, bring up a boy alone, he may in some way have no male face, or he may have no face at all" (17). The assumption is that he needs a hairy role model like Iron John to grow up to be a manly man. He states further, "A clean break from the mother is crucial, but it's simply not happening" (19). Denial and disconnection from the mother is a sign of fear of the body and fear of women. Charlene Spretnak in an article in the anthology *Women Respond to the Men's Movement* (1992) states, "Many non-patriarchal societies have responded not with fear and resentment but with true respect and awe for nature and the elemental power of the female body" (175). This response to the mother is a possibility far from the mind of Robert Bly.

We in this power-over society already have more than enough separation; further separation moves us toward more mind control of body, more men's control and definition of women. In fact, when a parent hinders the alterity of a child of any gender, there is a problem.

The answer is not what Bly would have us believe, a retreat back into men-only space to retrieve the lost masculine, the undisputed king of the jungle. Rather, the answer is to join together to resist the patriarchy that is making both men's and women's lives miserable—the solution is to eliminate power-over modes, not to further damage our Betweens.

That aspect of the mythopoetic branch which encourages men to feel and to get in touch with their bodies and their habitat can be seen as positive. That effort can help to overthrow the dichotomy between mind and body and humans and animals and puts men in touch with a source of their wisdom. But if the patriarchal source of power as power-over is not identified as the problem, it follows them into the woods and may push them even further into aggressive stances toward women, habitat and body—a kind of hunter mentality.

Also I would encourage the leaders of the men's movement not to try to push men into discovering a lost manhood that is somehow the same for every man (a universal archetype—which, of course, by definition includes power over women). Rather I would hope that they could encourage men to explore their alterity, to see what unique emotions arise, and what stories indeed need to be told to feel strong, but strong not in opposition to women, but as peers with women and each other.

At the heart of the philosophies of the men's movement should be a strong denunciation of violence against women. Discussions of how to eradicate hierarchy and male violence are needed so that women and men do not have to live daily in fear of physical and psychological abuse.

The philosophy of the redemption branch has some parallels to the mythopoetic branch. They seem to agree that men must re-assert themselves as heads of the family—that is, become more iron-like. Minister Louis Farrakhan at the Million Man March criticized men for their lack of respect for and violence toward women. He then said that such disrespect is wrong because "women are the mothers of our children and the producers of our future." He is joined by many in this society who see women as important only in relation to men and "their" children.

This branch, instead of harking back to old "archetypes" of masculinity as do the mythopoetics, idealizes a religious model of maleness. Part of the Promise Keepers' philosophy is that we should return to a model of divine fatherhood and that men should take the spiritual leadership in the home. Both Farrakhan and the Promise Keepers evoke the image of a paternal God figure for men to model themselves after. The question then becomes whether this god-figure ought to be beneficent or rigid. The power-over hierarchy of God···father···mother···child··· animal remains untouched in these philosophies. Rather it refers us back to a time when only men were thought to have souls and women were their helpmeets into heaven.

Men's feelings of alienation are not just personal problems to be resolved by a weekend away from home or by prayer; rather they need to be continually addressed back in the real world and within the real power structures where these men may have some impact. An alternative to the activities of these marches and rallies might be for men to form on-going groups that deal not only with their own emotions but also those of men in general in the society. Bly rightly critiques forced competition among many men, but to adequately address the issue we would need also to have a critique of capitalism and a movement for a different economic system which helps humans work cooperatively, not one that consistently rewards them for a total disregard for others.

The part of the men's movement that does real-world organizing of men against violence against women is the profeminist branch. This branch is very much in keeping with a critique of the dichotomy model. As a representative of this branch, John Stoltenberg constructs a well-thought out critique of "manhood" that does not accept, as Bly does, an instinctual manhood. Stoltenberg states (1990), "Male sexual identity is entirely a political and ethical construction, …and masculinity has personal meaning only because certain acts, choices, and policies create it—with devastating consequences for human society. But precisely *because* that personal and social identity is constructed, we can refuse it, we can act against it—we can change" (*Refusing to be a Man* 4).

He would redefine maleness without its reliance on domination of women and hierarchies among men and would create room for individual difference. Profeminist groups work toward making sure women's alterity is supported by opposing male violence and violent pornography which helps make women safe enough to develop their own alterity. The refusal of men to take the dominant role also frees them up to enter the Between, to allow their emotions to surface and to enter into dialogue around making the planet a livable place for all of its creatures. They can contribute to changing a dichotomized world view into one in which each of our particularities is respected.

Many women scoff at parts of the men's movement because it seems absurd that men need to be more confident of their positions in this world. From women's perspective men have always had definition and power; it is women who have lacked definition and the ability to express their desires. However, men's identities become an issue when men see women intruding into their once-exclusive space. Men are threatened not so much because they do not already have power-over, but rather because they are used to having so much; and it is *all* they have. Threaten their space, their egos and their privilege, and you threaten the mainstay of male identity. Men are virtually excluded from finding identity through connection in the Between; they fear that connection would jeopardize their standing in the world. So they cling to, glorify and seek to ever expand their power-over, not wanting to give any of it up to others.

Though men appear to have all the advantages, it is clear that those advantages greatly diminish if our goal is not power-over but immanent power. More so than women, men have been forced to forfeit their immanent power by being required to stay inside "maleness" and "mind." Men struggle to hold onto their own power-over because it is the only form of power to which they have "legitimate" access. But continuing to wage a war of power-over hurts all of us; even if we win the war we split ourselves apart and in the process sacrifice our wholeness as human beings.

The men's movements would be more effective by focusing on the areas I described earlier—promotion of the alterity of women, men, the body and our habitat and the refusal to use power-over, while at the same time developing skills for entering the Between. I will discuss the specifics about how to proceed in later chapters.

We have now looked at both the women's and the men's movements in light of the Between model to show how to evaluate social movements for their attention to the mind/body dichotomy. Now we will turn to an analysis of a controversial institution, that of motherhood. How can we apply the analyses of the Between model to current social issues?

10
Contemplating Our Navels: The Dilemma of Motherhood

We have seen how pervasive the mind/body split is historically; we have looked at the harm caused to women, body, men and knowledge by enforcing the split; we have proposed a new model and have used it to analyze the women's and men's movements. Now we turn to one of Western culture's most tortured, blamed, puzzling institutions, the institution of motherhood—from the points of view of the dichotomy model and the Between model. This chapter will give the reader practice in examining issues and applying the new model to them.

I devote this chapter to an analysis of motherhood because of its extreme importance in our society and because of its just as extreme perceived failures. It is not my aim to blame mothers or to make further demands on them. My aim, rather, is to expose the impossibility of mothers' situations and to suggest avenues for change. Additionally, since the mind/body split plays an important role in how children are raised and the status of those who raise children, we need to investigate it in some detail.

Remember, I am speaking here as a philosopher, not as a psychologist. What I question are Western conceptualizations of women, mother, and child and the dilemmas these cause; I want to suggest another approach that is consistent with the Between model and that can help us out of the jam. I am looking underneath the studies, underneath the rocks of dichotomous thinking and imagining what lies there. What I urge is a change in consciousness, in how we view the world and certainly in how we view women and mothers.

First consider the mind/body split and the placement of women on the body side of the dichotomy. Nowhere are the problems with this placement clearer than in the characterization of woman as mother/body. The male/female dichotomy already places the female into the lower half of a hierarchical relationship where she becomes a mere reflection of the male. She loses her subjectivity, seeing herself and being seen by others as an object. Then "woman" becomes synonymous with "mother," an entity also lacking alterity but even more completely an object without choices, a body that produces a baby—a baby machine. The male/female dichotomy is collapsed into the subject/object dichotomy.

In the subject/object dichotomy, the idea of ownership plays an important role. An object has no independent standing but functions as property to be disposed of by the owner. The capitalist system is built on the notion of private property and the rights of property owners to dispose of their property as they wish. When certain human beings are forced to follow the same rules as property, we get some strange, often counter-intuitive, results. For instance, in the early days of this country, some human beings were legally owned property to varying degrees; black people were slaves, and wives of white men were, at least from a legal standpoint, their property.

Now we are more sophisticated about who is legally owned—ownership of grownups, at least, is frowned upon. What we have not yet come around to outlawing, however, is either the ownership of others' bodies (or body parts) or the ownership of children. Although there has traditionally been a gut reaction against the buying and selling of babies, it is not out of the realm of possibility because the notion of the ownership of children is still viable. Still ingrained in our thinking is the notion that children are someone's property. How often have we heard men say, "She is having my baby"? From the idea that children are property arises the notion of surrogacy, where a woman carries a fetus she does not "own" and sells it or gives it away after birth. The mother actually carries someone else's baby.

Using an ownership model of motherhood, we can imagine a woman renting out her body for a period of months to produce a baby and we can consider that the product that she has produced will be sold to an interested buyer. Because of the mind/body split, a woman can separate herself enough from her body to sell or rent it and not be thought of as selling her soul; we can live with that. Her body is a machine that will do as she or someone else tells it.

Barbara Katz Rothman, in *Recreating Motherhood* (1990), draws a parallel between production and reproduction under capitalism. Mothers' bodies are the resources from which a product is made. She states, "Under capitalism, workers do not own or control the products of their labor.... What ties together the new technology and the old technology, the legal, the medical, the political, and the psychological re-creation of motherhood... [is the] commodification of children and the proletarianization of motherhood" (65-66). What the discussion becomes, then, under a dichotomous (owner/owned) worldview, is one of laborers and their products, neither of which are self-controlled. Additionally, in extending the analogy of the means of production to women's bodies, the profit motive is primary and it is understood as an acceptable as part of the process. To further extend that same analogy, women's liberation could mean that women should have ownership rights of their bodies and what they produce. Some of women's gains in the area of reproductive rights have taken this exact form.

A push for women's rights to control their own bodies has been a crucial step for women in the legal sense by securing them access to birth control and abortion, a prerequisite for women's alterity. But these gains should not be seen as endpoints. The idea that what mothers are producing is equivalent to widgets that can be bought, sold and owned at all is a problematic one. The discussion needs a new framework, terminology and approach which does not rely on a capitalist model where ownership rights and products are central.

At its core, liberal philosophy's emphasis on rights of ownership separates mind from body and perpetuates women's object status, either as the means of production or as the product. This kind of mind/body split thinking has been a large part of humanity's view of the habitat and body as a resource to be exploited. When women, who are often equated with mothers, are seen as a resource to be exploited, the liberation of women is once again out of reach no matter how liberal the philosophy sounds.

Additionally, every child is related to those of us already here. We cannot separate any child's future from our own. When we base our relationships with children on a property model, only those who have ownership rights ought to be involved—owner and object. It could be that it is this very concept that has fired the debates in Congress about "welfare mothers." Since mothers are themselves objects, if they are not married and do not have a "real" owner for their children, then they either should not have children or society should own them—in orphanages or group homes. However, that conceptualization lets the rest of us who do not "own" children off the hook when it comes to children who already have owners. Instead, it should be the job of the society to make sure that each child's relationships—in whatever form they take—thrive so that the child can contribute its share to common good.

Do we want to think in terms of who owns a child? When we deal in ownership, we are forced into determining the criteria for ownership. Is it determined by who put in the labor? By whose sperm and egg it was made up of? By who paid for it? By who controls it now? I want to suggest that we need a new framework for envisioning the relationships between children and parents. We need a model that does not rely on the power-over, dichotomized view.

Largely driven by the Christian Right, there is currently a heightened interest in motherhood. Our society praises technological changes that make it possible for people who are otherwise unable to procreate, to have children who are "theirs"—that is, genetically related to one or both parents.

Irigaray asks a good question in this regard:

> "Will all this [technology] help us [women] get away from the pressure to have children, our sole sexual 'vocation' according to the patriarchs, so as to get to know ourselves, to love and create ourselves in accordance with our bodily differences?... I think it shows that the goals of our liberation have remained tied to a culture that offers women no subjective opportunities, and that, for want of an identity of their own, many are, in a vague sort of way, trying to find a niche for themselves within a technological era that needs their energy to give itself to the illusion of a future. It is sadly repetitive, wearisome, and rather discouraging, even if on the surface diverting attention in this way suits a good number of people..." (*je, tu, nous* 135-136)

Part of the reason we need to discuss motherhood and the controversial issues surrounding it is so that women are not repeatedly trapped. The trap takes the form of either compulsory motherhood or a generalized reaction against having children. As feminists learned in the seventies,[26] it is not helpful to, with a broad stroke, react against and condemn as retrograde those women who have children. By the same token, however, we must be careful not to glorify motherhood and assume that it is the top priority task of women's lives. How can we move beyond the either/or of having children or not having them such that women have real choices?

Thich Nhat Hanh has a section in his book *Peace is Every Step* (1991) that deals with the connections we as humans have between us. He states that these connections are all "mothers" in a certain sense because they nourish us. His sense of mother includes much more than what our society would technically consider to be "mother" (116-117). Try visualizing Hanh's "mother" as the Between, the connections between us. Certainly in our pregnant mother comes our first experience of the connectedness required to yield new life.

This society's obsession with women's breasts is another manifestation of this longing for something one can never fully recover. Marilyn Yalom in *A History of the Breast* (1997) states, "The more daunting the world becomes with its awesome bureaucracies and endless inventions, the greater the nostalgia for intimacy and basic connections. The breast we knew as infants, or we internalized through the vision of others at the breast, keeps getting further and further away" (277-278).

The original relationship with mother is so ripe with emotion that we often spend our whole lives trying to unravel it. Some of us try to return to that feeling of connection we had when we were still in the womb or were very young infants. Some of us blame our mothers for not giving us enough connection or for cutting us off too soon. This often obsessive focus on mothers is too much strain on that one relationship. If we had a society which valued connection—not just from mother to child but in all kinds of relationships—we could take up the slack for mothers. That singular relationship would not have to carry us throughout our lives with no future relationship ever being enough. But since we do not have such a society, we keep putting that one relationship with our mothers under a microscope, looking for understanding. Since we have systematically destroyed our other "mothers"—our connections with each other and with our habitat—our relationships with our mothers has taken on exaggerated significance.

The optimum pregnancy using the Between model would be one in which the most important thing was relationship. First there is the relationship between the mother and fetus (here and following I use the term fetus to refer to what is technically first an embryo and then a fetus) and then, after the baby is born, between the parents (whoever is there to nurture the baby, e.g., the father, mother, significant other, grandmother, aunt, friends, etc.) and the baby.

The mother and fetus are intricately connected during pregnancy; the mother nurtures a creature that has little alterity at first, so she is doing most of the work. This earliest labor is demanded of the pregnant woman. What can we do to support the Between of mother and fetus? Our best approach to that dyad is to support the woman's alterity as a human being and subject of her own life. If we value Betweens and want to encourage people to have the capacity to move freely into them, we should place a high priority on the nurturing of this first one.

If a woman were not willing to enter into a relationship with this fetus, then we as a society would want to guarantee that she did not have to enter it—which means safe, effective and low cost or, better yet, free birth control and access to abortion. If women and men were more in tune with their body-minds and trained to value them and be receptive to them, more energy would be devoted to discovering and sharing new methods of controlling birth. With a different view of pregnancy would come new approaches to these issues, creative ways to involve the body-minds of women and men in becoming or not becoming pregnant. If researchers themselves involved the Between in their experiments and found ways not to over-power the body but to cooperate with it, we would find more humane methods of birth control for both men and women.

Forcing a woman to have a baby, to enter the Between against her will would simply damage that Between for both her and the baby and thereby harm all of us who are connected to the child or the mother. If the relationship of mother and child is the highest value—and I believe that it is—then of greatest relevancy is the mother's freedom to choose whether or not to enter into the relationship with the fetus.

Another large factor in choice is that a woman must have a real, viable choice not to become a mother, ever. She needs to know that as a subject in her own right, she may choose to do something entirely different with her life that does not include having babies. She should not have to have a baby to express herself, to feel she has contributed, or to feel power. Her alterity cannot rely on whether or not she has a baby.

As a society we should support any expression, artistic or reproductive, that a person wants to devote his or her time to. There are many ways for women to express themselves; unfortunately, so often women have been restricted to having babies and devoting themselves to child raising, as their only viable options. Likewise, men who would choose to be nurturers are eliminated from consideration, simply based on their gender. If a man wants to be the nurturer in the relationship after the baby is born, he, too, should be encouraged to express himself in that way. We need to make use of nurturing skills wherever they appear, since for so long we have done our best to devalue and repress them, especially in men. We do not have to see birthing or nurturing a baby as so different from any other creation so long as we give both men and women that opportunity.

At this moment in history we do not need to require women to have babies rather than do something else. We do not need so many babies in a world whose resources are dwindling because of human over-consumption.[27] And we desperately need women's undivided attention focused on world problems. The world cries out for the very skills that women have developed over the years—skills like cooperation, nurturance, connectedness, emotional maturity, listening, etc. If women are free to open their body-minds to all of the possibilities instead of limiting them to only one, they can use their creative juices to explore better ways of being in the world.

Currently in our language there is a lack of clarity regarding the concept of "pregnancy." There is no way to make a distinction between a pregnant woman who decides not to enter the relationship with the fetus and a woman who decides to carry the fetus to term. This distinction is crucial since it is a necessary though not sufficient consideration in determining whether or not a baby is born. There simply is no possibility of a baby being born if the mother does not enter into relationship with the fetus. The decision to form the relationship must come after the egg has been fertilized and the woman becomes aware of it. It is the next hoop this embryo must jump through, like an entrance requirement, if you will. The first necessary requirement is that the egg be fertilized and the second is that the woman decide to carry the fetus to term. This decision is *not* a passive act that happens to a woman; nor is it something someone other than the woman herself can initiate or force.

To emphasize the paramount importance of that decision to enter into relationship with the fetus, I am going to coin a new term—"fetal adoption"—to represent the action that happens when a woman decides to commit herself to bringing the fetus to term.

The word "adoption" has two meanings that apply here. According to the *Oxford Universal Dictionary*, the word "adopt" means "to take voluntarily into any relationship" and "to take as a matter of choice" (25). Before the baby is born, the only person who can adopt the fetus is the pregnant mother. She must make the decision whether or not to commit to the fetus. Then, after the baby is born, the woman who carried the baby, or others whom she designates can make the commitment to voluntarily take a child into relationship and adopt it.

At first the baby's only possible relationship is with the mother, and if she decides to adopt the fetus, that relationship becomes sacrosanct.

It is not human life in isolation that is sacrosanct, nor is it someone's property; it is the relationship between the mother and adopted fetus which is sacrosanct.

Let us look at some of the issues surrounding motherhood—abortion, fetal adoption, surrogacy, adoption of children, and infancy—to expose the assumptions involved in the way we treat mothers, fetuses, babies and bodies.

Abortion

I alluded earlier to the implications of dichotomous thinking on the debates aroud abortion. Key to these debates on both sides, pro- and anti-choice, are assumptions that the body is separable from the woman and is an object. Pro-choice advocates speak of the woman's body as her property to which she has inalienable rights. The fetus is in her body and she should have the right to do with it what she wants. While this position has helped women obtain the right to abortion, it has not transcended dichotomous thinking. This conceptualization of body as woman's property over which she has certain rights leaves intact the notion of a body and a baby as someone's property. What is up for debate, then, is merely whose property it is: the mother's, the state's, the father's, God's? Objectifying both woman and baby and then debating over which object has more rights is problematic, especially in a society in which women are already stripped of their power and men make the rules. Property rights can be manipulated, bought and sold, taken away, etc. Then even if women get the right to abortion, that right and the funding for it can later be argued away.

Advocates for abortion rights are left arguing that the woman's rights should take priority over the rights of a fetus. Minds argue over how to treat bodies. Remember that women, in general, are equated with body, therefore, it is not just mind arguing over body, but in a very real sense, men arguing over what to do with "their" babies, which happen to be inside women. The subjects determine what happens to their objects, their property. In choosing sides, some men, of course, come out on the side of their property, women; and some come out on the side of their property, babies. And the debate goes on. Pro-choice women end up advocating for their own importance over that of the fetus. Anti-choice advocates argue the importance of the fetus. Which object has more value?

This debate must be reframed; the intervention of the Between model can assist us in that reframing. The decision to abort, in the Between model, need not evoke heavy philosophical debate about whether life begins at conception, at quickening, or at birth. A new life is possible only after the mother decides to adopt the fetus and carry it to term. With a decision not to do so, there is no possibility of a new life. The mother is not an object to be argued over paternalistically; she is a subject in her own right and as such should exercise the immanent power to choose whether or not to enter into relationship with a fetus that has begun to grow in her body. The fetus at this early point has no alterity and cannot be consulted.

The 1987 Washington D.C. case of a pregnant woman who was dying of cancer is a good example of a forced decision. Both she and her husband agreed that she should have a abortion because the pregnancy was too hard on her weakened body; but the hospital authorities forced a judicial determination and the court ordered that the C-section be given, even over the mother's objections. The baby lived only 2 hours, and the mother died two days later. The baby in this case was seen as occupying the top of the dichotomy and as such the mother's and father's feelings and health were overshadowed by the baby. It is practically written into the code of motherhood that the child comes first. If the mother and baby were not dichotomized to begin with, the idea that one could "come first" would be out of the question. The fetus's alterity is completely dependent on the mother. If the mother's alterity were respected and if the baby were seen as part of the mother's body, which relied on her for everything, the outcome would have been different.

It is unthinkable that anyone other than the pregnant woman herself in the fullness of her body-mind could determine that she should start or continue a relationship. How can a politician tell her she must have this relationship? How can a person protesting the sanctity of life tell her she must enter this relationship? These alternatives make no sense when relationship is the critical factor; and if one side is being forced, obviously the Between will be irreparably damaged.

Objects are not in question; property is not in question; rights over property are not in question. What is in question is whether the body-mind of a particular woman wishes to enter into relationship with this fetus at this time. The woman's decision regarding that fetus should be as free and well considered as possible. She should not be subject to peer pressure, pressure from church groups, or pressure from economics. The optimal relationship is one that is freely chosen. Society's task should be to provide that freedom. A woman should not have to give up her alterity to become a mother; in fact, it is then more important than ever to make sure she maintains a strong alterity. If she chooses to adopt the fetus, she should be supported; if she chooses not to, she should be supported.

The decision to adopt a fetus or to have an abortion need not be one of power-over the fetus making it the "Right" of the woman. Rather, the decision should come from a place of immanent power, of connections. This kind of decision making happens intuitively all the time. Sometimes we see a pregnant woman grieving over the loss of a fetus that she has adopted and which was then aborted; another woman who is carrying a fetus of the same age has no feelings whatsoever about the fetus and has an abortion without great sadness or remorse. The big difference lies in how the woman views that fetus and whether or not she, as a body-mind, decided to adopt the fetus. Hopefully, her mind only, cut off from her feelings, would not make the decision; on the other hand, hopefully, she would not make that decision based solely on her feelings without consideration of the quality of life for both herself and the baby.

Fetal Adoption

Now let us talk about the same woman once she has decided to adopt the fetus and remain pregnant. Consider the terminology itself. We once used the phrase, "with child" to describe a pregnant woman. That phrase shows a concern for the woman in relation to the fetus. When we use the term "expecting," the connotation is that nothing much is happening yet; it is all going to take place in the future when the expected baby leaves the mother's womb. Pregnancy is merely a waiting period. From a male point of view, the important events are conception, when father is involved, and birth, when he can see the baby. What is in between is down time. This view would not have originated from the pregnant women themselves.

Barbara Katz Rothman does an excellent job of discussing these issues. She states, "When we think of the newborn as having just gotten here, we ignore where it has come from. But children do not enter the world from outside the world; they do not come from Mars or out of a black box. By the time they are born they have been here, in this world, for nine months: not as children, not as people, but as part of their mothers' bodies. A baby enters the world already in a relationship, a physical, social, and emotional relationship with the woman in whose body it was nurtured" (91). There is evidence that fetuses can hear voices and music while they are still in the womb, that they recognize after they are born.

Conceptualizing pregnancy as a waiting-period leads us to the wrongheaded notion that somehow all that is involved is the mother's body (an already low-rated institution), and the fetus, also just a body until it pops out. We put our emphasis on the physical ingredients that go into the fetus through the mother's system and we often forget entirely about the mother's effort and her need of support and assistance during this time. She starts at this early point to realize that she must be unselfish; she must think only of the fetus; she must give up her desires for the needs of the fetus. A major dichotomy is at work and harm is already being done to the mother, to the fetus and to the relationship.

Rothman talks about how the uterus used to be seen as a safe haven for babies, an impenetrable place of sanctuary. However, as we as a society become more and more medicalized, the woman's body is beginning to be seen as a danger to the baby. It is what the mother takes in that can harm the baby; and the mother is responsible for that. Babies need to be protected from their mothers. I do not mean to say that this scientific information should be discounted; but it needs to be contextualized, tempered by a view of the whole. The context is not just the mother's womb but the whole woman, the fetus and their relationship.

By being obsessive about the unborn fetus, we miss the importance of relationship and the importance of the mother's well being. We see signs in the subway urging pregnant women not to drink or use drugs. We hear talk of imprisoning pregnant women to keep them off drugs until the baby is born, not for the welfare of the woman (who must be punished), but for the alleged welfare of the fetus. We worry about the effects of the drugs on the unborn baby to the exclusion of concern for the mother.

We see the mother at worst as public property; or, not much better, as the keeper of our property. We think we have the right to control her actions under the guise of protecting our property. We might think, for instance, that we should put the mother in jail if she uses drugs or smokes cigarettes, in order to protect our property, the fetus. If we are only thinking of the unborn baby, we may end up imprisoning all pregnant women so we can control completely what they eat and how they live.

A philosophy of the whole would suggest that such attitudes are harmful since they do not enhance (and in fact detract from) a woman's alterity, the primary factor in having a healthy, connected start to life for her child. Our exerting power-over the mother, coercing her into jail or wherever, is counterproductive. Marilyn French in her book *The War Against Women* (1992) states, "It is a major irony that the only developed nation in the world without free medical care, government-funded day care, home health visitors for mothers, or allotments to subsidize childrearing, is jailing *women* for improperly caring for the babies in their wombs" (146). This skewed thinking makes it almost impossible to have a thoughtful, intelligent discussion of strategies for change.

Societal attitudes reflect the posture that women are somehow accountable to all of us for what they do during pregnancy, instead of vice versa. For example, suppose a visibly pregnant woman takes a ride on a crowded bus and is forced to stand up. Having not had a chance to eat lunch at her job, she eats a chocolate bar to give her energy for the ride home. A fellow passenger is quick to inform her of the latest studies about pregnancy and chocolate and urge her not to eat the candy bar. The importance of the woman's own health and well-being as she holds on for dear life when the bus lurches, is not even noticed; it is overshadowed by the notion that the fetus is most important and the fetus is the property of us all. No one bothers to get up and let the woman sit down; no one worries about the hard work she is doing just to make ends meet and the stress she is under at work; no one worries that she does not have dinner waiting for her at home; no one worries that she is undernourished; no one worries if she did not want this child. But they worry about the fetus in isolation, as if such a thing exists. They want to control her as one might set the dials on a microwave to be sure the brownies do not come out runny. The final product viewed in isolation from the mother is what is deemed important and that final product is seen as a product of a body split from the mind of the mother, a mother split from her alterity as a person, as a woman, and as a subject.

Instead of criticizing the way a pregnant woman is living, we would do well to think about all of the things which are affecting both her and the fetus that we may have some control over. For instance, worry about the fumes from the bus, the polluted water she drinks from the city supply, the closeness of her house to electric wiring, the proximity of nuclear test sites or toxic waste dumps, the almost routine emptying of smokestacks and the accidental spills and leaks. Worry about her access to decent health care. These must be areas of concern if we recognize our interdependence with the mother and fetus.

It is in society's best interest to be certain that women are cared for during pregnancy, from economics to good health services. We should see to it that she has enough to eat and that the food she eats is not loaded with pesticides and additives. These are productive and mutually beneficial goals that do not take away a mother's civil liberties but which guard against a sub-standard prenatal habitat.

The primary metaphor of pregnancy in the power-over culture is woman as body, as womb, and fetus as the father's property or prize. The doctor's job, then, is to "deliver" the father's baby from the womb of the mother, to the father. There are a number of problems with this model; I will explore in particular the medical model and its emphasis on the body/object of the woman.

Under the medical model, the emphasis is on making sure the baby is healthy physically, at least according to currently defined standards; the woman's experience of pregnancy and birth is discounted. The woman herself is almost an incidental thing, an incubator, existing for the fetus. Doctors have long fought the practice of natural childbirth because they preferred to have a compliant patient who would simply bring them her womb so that they could successfully remove the baby. If drugging the woman is the easiest way to meet that goal, then they do that. If doing a C-section or episiotomy is the easiest way, then they choose that option. Sometimes doctors give epidurals or induce labor for their own convenience, both of which increase the chances of having to perform a C-section. The woman can come out of the birth experience even more alienated from her body and scared of its workings than before she became pregnant and her recovery time may be greatly increased:

In the traditional medical model, the woman will be told very little about what to expect. She may get an ultrasound and pore over the pictures of her baby. She may or may not be told not to eat certain foods, to avoid alcohol and caffeine, to stay out of hot tubs. But the emphasis will be the telling by the doctor and the requirements of the fetus. Or the doctor may tell her very little and simply attach her to machines and monitor her condition from time to time. If the woman has been raised in the power-over culture, her own knowledge about her body is probably limited and what she does know is considered to be irrelevant. Women's habits in relation to their bodies have developed over a lifetime and do not just start at pregnancy. Pregnancy is, of course, a big change about which an inexperienced woman "knows" nothing and about which the doctor "knows" all.

The woman will be treated as if pregnancy is an illness from which she will recover after the baby is born. It is something to be endured with self-sacrifice and "motherliness." The doctor's job is to separate the baby from the mother by "rescuing" it safely from her body. A hospital birth is the best because it can assure the presence of all the technical tools available. Medicine has the facts about pregnancy and birth and the doctor knows best what this woman should do.

The woman is often not acknowledged for all this "preliminary" work until the "labor" begins and then everyone gathers round hoping for a quick delivery. And there will be a flurry of attention for a little while. A good friend of mine who is a midwife tells a story about a birthing in which she assisted the mother. During the early hours of labor, no one else was around except the midwife. Finally, when birthing was near, the husband and nurses gathered around and screamed for the woman to push. It sounded like a football cheering section. And what the crowd urged was not appropriate for the woman at the time. She could not even hear the midwife telling her to go with what her body told her and push when that felt right and stop when it did not. Once the baby was born, again the room cleared and everyone went over to view the infant and ignored the mother's pain and her accomplishment.

Childbirth in our culture tends to be isolated from the rest of the woman's life. As we saw in previous chapters, the science involved often requires a separation, a controlling of factors in order to be good science; it is the same with "good" medicine. Using the medical model, we remove the pregnant woman from her life and her alterity and concern ourselves with the fetus. The Between is ignored and we proceed as if this description of reality is the "truth."

Midwifery is an approach to pregnancy that has been around for thousands of years. The advance of "Western medicine" caused the decline of midwifery and convinced the society that it is not safe to have a baby outside the hospital and/or with a midwife in attendance. Even through this adversity, midwifery has continued to provide a philosophy in direct contrast to the attitudes and procedures commonly practiced in the medical model. Rothman states, "The very word *midwife* means *"with the woman"* (170). With the woman—that sounds to me like the idea of supporting a woman's alterity. The emphasis is the woman's experience of wholeness, of strength and of wisdom in her body-mind. "Midwifery works with the labor of women to transform, to create, the birth experience to meet the needs of women" (Rothman 170). Midwives reject the mind/body dichotomy and the dichotomy of woman and fetus. They work with wholeness, in context and their methods are individualized to particular women.

The midwife emphasizes the whole experience from conception to motherhood and demystifies the process. She treats women as whole human beings, with desires and connections to others and with experience of their own bodies. Strictly scientific knowledge is tempered by experience, that of the midwife and that of the mother. Experiences are located on a continuum with sexual experience and birth control, birth and parenthood as part of the same process. The midwife works with the pregnant woman long before the birth, helping her to understand the changes going on in her body and listening to what she is experiencing. The midwife gives a pregnant woman support and encouragement to take control in her life. She teaches the woman about her body and what is normal and expects the woman to bring to the midwife's attention anything that is happening that does not feel right. They work together emphasizing that her body has wisdom. The woman needs empowerment all along the way and she needs assistance in her decisions. Teaching and listening are both midwifery skills that cannot be underestimated.

The difference between the midwifery model and the medical model is not just a matter of fine-tuning; it is a difference in goals. The medical model isolates birth from the rest of life and calls it success when the baby's umbilical cord is cut and the baby is breathing. Midwifery's goal is much larger and more inclusive of context. The midwife's goal makes the wishes and hopes of the woman primary and then blends those with knowledge of physiology and science so that complications can be recognized. The midwife supports the woman after she has adopted the fetus and as she gives birth, coaching her and helping her cope. In contrast, often doctors want to be called in at the last minute for the "important event." Midwifery's goal is much less quantifiable and at the same time of utmost importance to the strong, healthy continuation of human life. The mother is not incidental or important only as a vehicle for the delivery of a man's baby; she is central in the renewal of healthy life.

The midwife will ask about the woman's home life, the context she finds herself in. She may ask about the woman's other children and how much help she is receiving from her partner if she has one. She talks with her about the side effects of having adopted a fetus and listens to her concerns. The midwife may speak about ways she could be relieved from some of the stress in her life at least temporarily. The woman is free to ask questions and to receive explanations that she can understand.

If there is a co-parent and other family and support groups involved in the woman's life, the midwife also makes sure that, if the woman wants their involvement, these people are not cut off from the woman during the process. There is the recognition that the woman brings with her into the birthing a context that has affected her and will continue to affect her and the baby. It is imperative that these relevant people are informed of what is going on and involved in assisting the woman.

The midwifery model is compatible with the Between model. We as a society would do well to investigate the methods of midwives and adopt the values they have been putting forward for years in the whole area of pregnancy, pre-natal care and follow-up after birth.

Surrogacy and Adoption

Now let us look at what happens when a mother decides that she wants to give her baby up for adoption. We will look at both the circumstances of surrogacy and of adoption.

In the case of surrogacy, a woman enters into a contract with someone who wants a baby, and she agrees to have one for them. I will not differentiate here between those cases in which the surrogate's egg and the want-to-be father's sperm are used or where the fertilized egg of both of the want-to-be-parents is implanted in the woman. Genes do not endow one with ownership and neither does paying for the child. Those considerations are clearly part of the child-as-property model held in place by dichotomous thinking. What we want to discuss here is how, from a Between model approach, we might view the issue of surrogacy.

The key components of surrogacy for the purposes of our discussion are that the potential mother signs a contract before she gives birth (and generally before she is pregnant); she receives assistance from the expectant adopted parent or parents with medical bills, etc. She may or may not receive payment for her labor. Soon after the baby is born, she gives up her rights to it to the adoptive parent or parents.

The surrogacy contract relies on the fact that the woman's mind is in control of her body and that she can simply follow the directives of the mind and give up the baby after delivery just as she agreed to do in the contract. The assumption is that the womb can be rented out for nine months and then vacated without complications. The contract, however, fails to take into account the enormous changes that occur in the body-mind of the woman who carries the child and the ways in which she may change her body-mind about the decisions she agreed to in the contract.

If we see adoption of a fetus as the involvement of the whole woman and as the start of a relationship, it becomes much more difficult to assume that how one feels and thinks about the pregnancy at or before conception will be the same later on in the pregnancy or after birth. Analyzing this situation using the patriarchal model, the woman ought to be able to simply sign the papers and in nine months fulfill her end of the contract. In that model what happens during pregnancy, as we discussed earlier, is just waiting; the important things are conception and birth. Bodily changes may be acknowledged but none that need invalidate the contract, which after all is enforceable in a court of law. Dichotomous thinking tells us that a woman should be able to simply do as she promised and give up the baby. But we see cases like the Marybeth Whitehead case, in which the surrogate mother did change her mind about giving the baby up.

Certain feminists are quick to reject the implications that a pregnant woman is not in control of her actions and cannot make a valid contract. Because women have been seen for centuries as less rational than men, many feminists are loath to admit "weakness" here. That a particular woman is irrational, emotional and unstable may be generalized to all women. However, rather than jumping on the bandwagon of reaction, we should look at what enforcing the contract signifies.

When we insist on specific performance of a surrogacy contract, after the mother changes her body-mind about wanting to give the baby up, we are devaluing that relationship between the mother and baby which is the sacred part in our model and siding with the law (the mind). If adopting a fetus is about starting up a relationship between birth mother and fetus, whether a mother can give up the child or not will depend on the nature of the relationship that has developed, combined with all of the other factors in a woman's life: her health, her financial status, how many other children she has, how she dealt with the budding relationship. Sometimes it is possible to separate from a relationship knowing all along that one will have to do so in the end. And sometimes despite one's best arguments against it, a relationship is formed that becomes essential to one's well-being and cannot be simply severed without causing great harm to the participants.

In any event, what happens with the relationship that has formed between her and the baby should be up to the mother. Whether she is the biological mother of the baby (that is whether it was her egg that was fertilized) or not, the woman who carried the baby is the person with whom the baby has a relationship; it should be up to her whether that relationship is severed, continued on with her as primary nurturer or continued on a shared basis. If she decides to give the baby up for adoption after birth, that is her choice. She, too, however, should be discouraged from thinking of the baby as her property; rather, she should think of whether she is able and willing to nurture the relationship.

Again, the difference lies in how we view pregnancy. If we see it as the formation of an object, a baby, inside an object womb, the emphasis is on the product of the womb, a product that can be bought and sold. Relationships, however, are a different matter. Relationships cannot be bought and sold in the same way as a product. The way we analyze them is much more complicated, requiring acknowledgment of what alterity exists and the others involved in the decisions. If the state is involved at all it should not be to insist on specific performance of a surrogacy contract, but rather to bolster the woman's alterity in any way possible.

I have heard numerous anti-abortion advocates suggest that it is simple for a woman to decide against abortion, go through with a pregnancy and then give the baby up for adoption. Some anti-abortionists say it is easier to give up a baby one has carried for nine months than to abort it at an early stage in the pregnancy. To make this a more attractive option, they emphasize the idea that if the baby is not shown to the mother, bonding will not occur and the separation may happen without great affect on the woman's life. This standpoint is closer to men's experience—if they do not see the baby, they will not become attached to it. If pregnancy is viewed as a relationship, however, that kind of thinking is ridiculous. For the mother, seeing the baby is just one of many steps, albeit an important one, already taken to bond with or avoid bonding with the baby. By the time a woman allows birth, she has had to establish some kind of a relationship with the baby whether she is planning to give it up or not. The involvement of the body-mind is there, acknowledged or not. The woman may try to tell herself (have her mind tell her body) that she is having none of it—that she is not bonding. She may be very practiced and expert at separating her mind from her body and controlling her feelings.

However, it is just as likely that no matter how much she swears to herself not to get involved with the fetus, when something lives with her as closely as does a baby for nine months, a relationship will develop. Fetal adoption changes the woman. She is not merely a womb walking around with a baby growing in it. She is a whole body-mind and a part of her body is growing and developing into something that gradually takes on its own personality. At the very least her whole body goes through the pregnancy and goes through many changes, and it is pretty certain that her mind, no matter how she tries to control it, can change in relationship to the fetus as well.

This is not to say that women should never carry a baby to term that they are planning to give up for adoption. But it does mean that this giving up is not akin to taking out an appendix. Giving up a baby for adoption must be taken seriously, must be seen as the severing of an ongoing relationship. Sometimes the mother may be relieved to give it up but often a mixture of feelings is involved. Practical circumstances may demand that she give it up while her body-mind feels ambivalent and torn.

If we take a woman-centered approach to pregnancy, in counseling a woman as to whether to have an abortion or give up her baby for adoption, we must speak about these complicating factors and not minimize the trouble a mother may have when it comes time to give up the baby. A broken relationship is much harder to take emotionally than one that was never entered into. When the bond that forms is unanticipated, the woman will have a harder time healing herself after she has the baby.

I agree with Rothman who calls for a limited period of time after the baby is born for the birth mother to change her mind about adoption (255). Her feelings about the relationship may turn out to be totally different from what was anticipated and there should be room for that possibility. Also there should be more choices than simply giving the child up. The possibility of shared parenting where the mother shares responsibility for the baby or where she relinquishes her rights but chooses to see the baby and have an aunt-like relationship should be available.

That said, I do not mean to minimize the role of the adoptive parents who, even without the running start of a relationship formed during pregnancy, can begin connecting with the child whenever they are given the chance to become its parents. My thought is that after a limited period of time, the relationship would be assumed to have been formed with the adoptive parents and the birth mother would no longer have any standing to change her mind and ask for the baby back. The laws ought to be weighted heavily in favor of what is best for the child. The person with whom the child has formed a relationship, regardless of genetic ties or a contract signed before the birth, ought to be the person the courts favor.

In this model, surrogacy would not be encouraged. There would always be a risk that the birth mother would change her mind during or after the birth and the would-be adoptive parents would be left holding the empty cradle. But as our technologies allow us to get closer to making babies through in-vitro fertilization, we should think about what a devalued mother/womb looks like.

Rich couples who do not want to engage in the messiness of pregnancy but want to live on genetically, could always use their own sperm and egg and implant it into a woman (probably one who needed the money) to have a baby for them. The class implications of this are explosive. A longstanding and similar issue is the use of nannies from different races and classes, whereby such an important thing as nurturance becomes a product to be sold to the upper classes. Are we devaluing and objectifying the child, the nurturer, the relationship that is child raising, or all three?

I would rather that we as a society make it more acceptable to raise children who are already in the world and eliminate the class disparities among people so that a poor woman could not be forced through economics to have a baby or to nurture someone else's baby at the expense of her own. Better to focus on relationships and the ramifications of being connected to one another than to deepen the chasms already among us. To focus on relationship is to take away the urgency of ownership of genes and to see that the most important contribution to be made is to be connected to each other, to each other's children and to the quality of all of our lives.

I feel for parents who want children and cannot have them by themselves; but I also feel for the children who have already been born who are being raised in a series of foster homes or in institutions. We need to change those laws that exclude many potential adoptive parents, so that as many children as possible are adopted and can begin successful permanent relationships with families.

Infancy and Child Raising

Let us talk briefly about what happens after a baby is born and is being brought up by a mother, father or other parent, friend or lover of the mother, grandmother or grandfather or adoptive parents. This period of infancy is crucial in the development of the child's psyche and we must not underestimate the amount or kinds of information that are processed and picked up by the infant. Here the child begins to learn sex roles and develops a sexual identity of her own. What I am particularly concerned with during this stage is the primary caregiver, who is usually female, and who I will call the "mother" for convenience. For our purposes a mother is a person who has primary responsibility for the nurturance and socialization of the child and could be male or female. Traditionally, that role has been reserved for women but men are capable of doing that work as well. I will refer to the mother as "she."

How does the mother perceive herself; how is she perceived by others; and how does that affect the development of sexual identity in the infant? This issue is complex and deserves much more attention than I can give it here. Using the Between model, I would like to merely identify some problems and suggest how we might look at them differently.

We have already seen how a pregnant woman is treated if she goes to a traditional medical doctor. The emphasis has been on the baby, on making sure that the baby is safe and well and delivered from the woman's body without mishap. Until just recently most hospitals took the baby away from the mother right after birth, placed it in a nursery and set up a regimented schedule. Perhaps due to the influence of midwifery, more and more hospitals have begun recognize that cycles and rhythms have already been established between the mother and the infant and have created the option of the baby "rooming in" with the mother. It is not as if the infant just popped into the world from nowhere when it had been living in relationship with the mother for nine months, having already formed patterns of sleeping and waking with her.

As stated earlier, from the beginning we concern ourselves mainly with the baby to the exclusion of the mother. The biological mother is simply the body from which the infant came and bodies do not have much standing in our thinking. Rather, we expect the mother, because of her sheer dedication to the baby, to do all sorts of sacrificing of herself for the baby. And generally speaking she does those things. When the baby cries, she is there in a flash; when the baby wants to eat, she is there to present it with a nipple. She is with the baby or within reach of it around the clock for some time. The mother is expected to do these things and to enjoy doing them; she is to be utterly unselfish for the sake of her baby. We expect not only that she be able to do these things but we also demand that she do them willingly and with joy or risk being labeled a bad mother.

And sometimes she does thoroughly enjoy it. The mother volunteers for this martyrdom for the cause of her precious baby. She prides herself on being selfless and devoted. However, in other cases this enjoyment is at best forced for many reasons. For instance, she may have other children who are also demanding her time and she has only so much to go around and becomes completely worn out. The baby wakes her up at all hours; she cannot get enough sleep; she is irritable and on top of that has to feel guilty if she begrudges the child anything. Often she is terrified of doing something wrong that she, of course, will be blamed for as long as her child lives. She feels the entire responsibility for the child on her shoulders. Even if her partner is helpful and does his/her share of the diaper changing and rocking the baby in the middle of the night, the mother still feels the final burden on her to produce a perfect child.

The readers know the routine, the story, the expectations. Everyday we hear the phrase, "Didn't your mama teach you manners?" and a hundred variations on the theme. It all comes back to the mother—the good, the bad and the indifferent. The common theme, however, is that the mother is not to be "for herself." The children come first, then the spouse since he can also feel neglected by the extra demands on her time, then finally she can think about herself if she has the time and energy left over. Her own desires are pushed aside for those of her spouse and child. She exists for them. You have heard the stories of what a mother will do to protect her children; she will become physically strong, emotionally together, assertive or aggressive, whatever it takes to keep her child from harm. But it is not OK if she uses these same resources for herself.

She must stay in the bottom half of the dichotomy, the nurturing object, there for others. But it is almost impossible for her to stay there and still get done what must be done. Mothering takes an enormous amount of energy, focus and skill. She needs to have some power in her life or end up crazy. Consequently, she takes power where she can get it. Often, especially if she has little alterity of her own, having power means getting it through power-over, turning the dichotomy on its head and making the infant take the lower position. She then has power-over the infant and her power depends on maintaining that position. She can tell the child what to do; punish it if it does not do her bidding; withhold love if it does not do as she wants.

In my estimation it is a rare mother who is able to stay out of this trap. Often she has no other power source and to get her needs met must get power where she can. After she has so selflessly stayed out of the power position for this infant from the time of conception or adoption to the age where the infant has some identity of its own, she must, for her own survival, get some power back.

When the choices are power-over or power-under (self-sacrifice), we are forced into destructive situations. If the mother takes on the power-over position, she makes the child into something that she needs it to be. The child goes from being loved in the Between and having its alterity encouraged, to the opposite, to a severing of that connection and the placement on the down side of the mother's dichotomy. That is a violent move, a ripping apart, a splitting through our most cherished place.

I want to emphasize here that I am not blaming the mother for this move. Her behavior is forced on her by a constantly impending checkmate of complete powerlessness. We as a society must take responsibility for forcing her moves, for forcing her to behave in this way, for setting up the game with the wrong goals in mind.

I am simplifying here, of course, but I do it to recognize and question the dilemma that is motherhood. There are thousands of permutations of the relationships between parents and their babies. I rely on the readers to look at their own experiences and the studies they know of in the area of childhood development with an eye toward how dichotomous thinking has affected their outcomes. My point is not to outline all of those but to give you salient examples to help you in applying Between thinking in your own situations and those you have encountered.

The goal in fetal adoption, motherhood and infancy should be to cultivate thriving Betweens, where love and creativity dwell, where we are connected body and mind, ourselves and our habitat, and each of us to the other. The last thing we want, then, is for the mother to be put in the position of power-under or for that matter power-over. If the mother is, throughout her pregnancy, thought of as an object, as a womb, and the concentration is on the subject baby, the mother is in the power-under position.

Imagine for a moment the Between model without women having alterity. Mothers are expected to be in the Between, nurturing and taking care of the child, loving the child with no alterity from which to enter the Between. They are somehow supposed to simply exist in the Between, providing all of those wonderful things that exist there while having no basis from which to enter this area. The mother knows that it is important to love her child without condition, that she create magic for it, that she encourage its alterity and development; and yet she is supposed to carry out this task from a place of disconnectedness from her own self. In fact, she is supposed to carry out this task in a society which has devalued that very place. I cannot imagine how this is even possible. She is aware of the Between on some level because she has just experienced it during pregnancy or after birth while the child was totally dependent on her. And some mothers describe it as the most intensely satisfying feeling they have ever had.

To live in the Between without a strong alterity for support puts one at the mercy of the other entity in the relationship. Living at the mercy of others can be enough to drive a person mad or it can drive them to seek predictable power in a dichotomous way. I look around at my friends who have small children and I see the pendulum swinging between these two extremes. I see mothers who feel as if they are going crazy, who love their children but feel that the more they love them, the more impossible the situation becomes. And I see them raging, sometimes at their kids and sometimes at their husbands, and sometimes at me for not having had kids. They feel powerless and out of control. Meanwhile, they are trying to live ungrounded in the Between in non-linearity, irrationality and unpredictability. They feel the love that is there; they feel the joy and the connection that is there; and they feel crazy, both because they as women have little alterity and because society gives no credence to those qualities.

We see the power-over models used in both emotional and physical child abuse. And we see women living in the Between with weak alterity who end up in mental hospitals, unable to cope with a world out of their control. One cannot live entirely in the Between without alterity; it is too out of control. There is depression in the Between when there is no place of retreat, no center to steady one. The Other always appears to be in control, battering the person against the rocks as the tides change. Nothing is solid.

Another possibility is that one finds a center outside of oneself. For some it is religion. There is a safe place, a place of answers which would keep a person away from the chaos of the Between and might restrain the urges for power-over. Sometimes this works. Religion can perhaps provide some answers, some solidity to temper the blows for the mother and the children as well. Other times, though, it can become just one more form of domination, power-over and a way to stifle the alterity of the child and parent.

Let me give a concrete example here that I am familiar with. A devout, Christian mother whom we will call Beatrice had five children. She basically gave up her own pursuits to get married and have children. Her husband was the sole wage earner at least for the first 15 years of their marriage. He was involved only peripherally in their lives. The mother did a lot of self-sacrificing for her kids, making them clothes, feeding them before she herself was fed. She thought of herself last. She took on the role of doing everything for her kids. She staked her life on the children turning out the way she had planned. Their alterity, if it did not coincide with her plan, was too much for her because hers was not strong. She had sacrificed herself but in so doing tried to get power through the children, and over them. Her power, her sense of self, depended on her children.

Beatrice got a part-time job when the youngest child was about 10, and things improved. She then had a way to develop her own resources and gain her sense of self back. She was no less interested in the children's welfare but she was not so interested in having them succeed for her. Still it was easy to fall back into old patterns, easy for both her and her children.

Her girl children went through a period where they blamed her for not behaving differently because since she was of their gender, she served as their role model. The children could see her self-sacrifice that, though it provided them with clothes and food and a comfortable environment, did little to build their self-esteem and alterity. The girls found themselves learning how to live in the bottom half of the dichotomy because Beatrice modeled how to live there; but it was not what they wanted to learn. If the girls had had a choice, they would have perhaps chosen other paths.

Mothers of daughters walk a fine line in raising their girls. On the one hand, they want their girls to succeed in an increasingly competitive world, and on the other, they want to support the girls in becoming their authentic selves. These two roads often seem to lead in entirely different directions. Elizabeth Debold, Marie Wilson and Idelisse Malave in *Mother Daughter Revolution* (1993) state, "Women can begin changing mother daughter relationships only if they look beyond the relationship and see how it is shaped by the demands and threats of the dominant patriarchy of the white middle class, as well as by the other patriarchies in which women live" (7).

And what were the boys in our example learning? In large measure they learned that women exist for them. They learned how to relate to that kind of giving, how to make the most of it. Seeing someone exist for others only, does not inspire emulation but it does inspire the desire for developing an association with someone who will.

Beatrice also feared the Between because of its uncertainty, its lack of mooring—her children learned to fear it, too—even as they longed for it. And the mistakes are repeated through the generations as the choices remain in two extremes: to use power-over or to dwell in the Between without strong alterity.

What I outline here is never all or nothing. We search for power and alterity and control all of our lives and we find varying combinations of it that will work for us. My point is not to justify or blame the combinations we have found to deal with our lives. But we need to realize that these are not our only choices. We humans have forced this situation on ourselves and we also can change it. By diagnosing the problem using the Between model, we can see a direction for change.

We get nowhere by blaming the mother for her choice in a hopeless double bind. First we back her up against the wall and then we get all worked up when she lashes out at us. We conveniently forget about how we backed her into the corner and we simply describe her behavior as angry or bitter and we blame her. But her behavior is simply a way to survive. It is only a symptom of a much larger problem that family therapy and 12 step programs cannot begin to come to terms with. These are societal problems, structural problems, philosophical splits that must be healed.

We as a society must examine our behavior that backs her into the corner. How do we stop this cycle? How do we think differently? Families are a key place to work since here children are developing their identities and we are reproducing dichotomous thinking and domination as the preferred form of power. In a society that values the Between, giving birth would be valued, not as a biological thing (and therefore taken for granted and devalued as "body") but as an integral part of the continuance of the human race. Just as there is an optimal context for health and ethics, there is an optimal context for birthing and raising children. And it requires the cooperation of the whole society.

The Between experienced with mother and fetus is the only guaranteed Between we know. If it was weak, we crave more always and look with blame at mother for not giving it to us. If it was strong, we got a taste of something so good that we seek it wherever we can and perhaps not finding it we look back nostalgically at mother or blame her for cutting us off at some point in our lives. How do we go about strengthening the Between and strengthening our alterity so that we can get access to the Between without fear and without being swallowed up?

What can women do and what can men do? We have different tasks. In the next chapter, I will imagine ways out of the dilemmas we are in. These may be the final chapters of this book but they are only the beginning of the dialogue. Hopefully you, too, will enter the discussion with experiences from your own lives. I encourage you to read the last chapters and then go out and write last chapters of your own.

11
Jamming the Machinery
of the Dichotomy Model

"The issue is not one of elaborating a new theory of which woman would be the *subject* or the *object*, but of jamming the machinery itself, of suspending its pretension to the production of a truth and of a meaning that are excessively univocal." (Irigaray, *This Sex* 78)

Our job is to tear down the destructive dichotomous structures but at the same time to build something else to take their place. I recommend that we do these tasks simultaneously—eventually the old structures will weaken enough and our combined weight in the new way of thinking will be substantial enough to tip the balance from power-over to immanent power.

In this chapter, I draw on the ideas of French philosopher Luce Irigaray to help me with theory; I will translate her theory into concrete ideas for action. At various points in the book, I have discussed the difficulties language can pose. Part of the reason Irigaray's ideas are so difficult to grasp is that much of what needs to be understood cannot be stated in a direct, straightforward way in the languages of patriarchy. To accept language at face value is to accept the dichotomous relations of things and to accept that once something is named, it is forever after the same, a solid, a fixed entity.

Irigaray would say that one of the first positive steps to take is to "jam the machinery" of patriarchy—that is, refuse the categories, overflow the banks, step over the boundaries, expose dichotomies by living as a whole body-mind.

Liquefy language, get it off the rocks and flowing into the cracks between, allowing names to be temporary, not solidified, not forever stuck. Remember the fire and water and air that have been neglected for us to appear solid.

Write and paint fire, floods, swelling, movement, the space of air, of nothing and of all. Of blood, the sanctity of it, of menstrual blood, the sacred flows, a god who bleeds (Ntozake Shange, *A Daughter's Geography*). Speak as subjects when objects are expected. Situate ourselves in the excess, in the Between. Wherever woman is defined as a lack, as negative in comparison with man, exceed that category.

Make room for the both at the same time, the expression of more than one. It is the rubbing together in the Between that we want, the always-changing, creative part which requires recognition and honor. It can never be only one thing—no capital letters need apply (e.g. Truth, Justice, Freedom).

Keep in body-mind that this work ought to engage us right now and not merely tap into some future-guilt trip, i.e., if I do not go to this demonstration or send money to save this or that species, something awful will happen. Bewhole the past and the future. They are not worlds apart, they are united by the Between which is this moment. The future is not somewhere distant; it is happening right now; we should consider what our actions do for us right now, in the moment in which we live— between the past and the future.

For instance, refuse to think: "We must work now and put aside our own individual desires and needs until after the revolution when we will have our perfect society." Instead, recognize that there will be difficult parts of this journey, roads we will not want to take; but at the same time there are the parts that are bursting to laugh, play, and not take any of it too seriously. That mix will free and motivate us to continue without burnout, without future-guilt.

And keep a sense of humor about this work since, when we look at the old worn out thinking, much of it will look ridiculous—especially if we are already invested in a new way of thinking. We want to tear down without drawing away too much of the energy required to build our own new ways. But where we can, we just slow down the "progress" of the old ways, point out their contradictions, parody them. Just keep throwing out the dichotomies when we see them, bewhole them. Speak, write, paint paradoxes that under rules of logic cannot *be*. Write about doing and not-doing, being and not-being, me and you, the two of us and the one of us.

Our job, then, is not to find a different Truth, to replace, for instance, men's Truth with women's. It is to jam the machinery of thinking that says there can only be *one*—that we can rid ourselves of ambiguity by defining A and not-A, men and women, as mutually exclusive. Stay limber, swim if you can, but do not stay in the trap of the One. Do not stop with turning the dichotomies on their heads but bewhole them.

Play with Language

"What is called for instead is an examination of the *operation of the 'grammar'* of each figure of discourse, its syntactic laws or requirements, its imaginary configurations, its metaphoric networks, and also, of course, what it does not articulate at the level of utterance: *its silences.*" (Irigaray, *This Sex* 75)

One of the first things we can do is to play with language, throw curves, refuse dichotomy talk. Is this "just play" or is it serious work? To answer a question like that we must first bewhole it.

Some think that playing with language is not a revolutionary act. I disagree. Poets are often revolutionaries because they make us think about how language actually structures our thinking and confines us; and they show us ways to break free.

But one does not have to be a poet to play with language. Simple reminders of the absurdities of language can help. We can refuse the pronoun game ("he" this and "he" that) and we can rename, reclaiming the power of language.

In the 70's I experienced the power of language when I stopped referring to myself as "girl" and started calling myself "woman." It was not simply semantics as some may charge; rather, it was a change in consciousness. At first I had a terrible time using the word "woman" without cringing and turning red—I felt like a liar. I could not simply exchange "woman" for "girl" without changing the way I thought about myself. The label "girl" had done its job; it had made me feel young and irresponsible—too young to act with initiative and too powerless to be independent. Changing the word meant I had to change the way I thought about myself and acknowledge my responsibility for and role in the world.

Using sexist language is not merely semantics. It may be semantics but it is not *merely*. Each time exclusive language is used, it perpetuates the dichotomy and the hierarchy. Each time inclusive language is used deliberately, it makes us conscious of the reality of exclusion of women from positions of power and action. For instance, saying "the scientist...she" jolts us into remembering that for so long women have not been scientists, and the image evoked by the word is invariably male— that is, until we take it upon ourselves to change that perception which must surely come before a change in our reality can be achieved. Such linguistic changes open our body-minds to the fact that a woman can be in a position of power, can be the subject of a life.

We underuse that power of naming.

For instance, instead of saying "chair" consistently, "chairman" is often used to refer to a man who is chairing and "chair" or "chairperson" is used to refer to a woman. Our tendency is to make the distinction rather than take the opportunity each and every time the term is used to make a statement about the possibilities. A man might be chair today but tomorrow a woman could be there instead. The term "chairman" needs to disappear from our language. And the same with a whole host of other terms like stewardess, mailman, fisherman, laundrywoman, garbageman, salesman, freshman, etc.

And play with pronouns. When we say, for instance, in playing with kids—"the dinosaur...she"—we play with language. It is correct grammatically and it shines a light on our assumptions. We can sprinkle "she's" throughout our speeches and writings and point out every white male "universal." When we see references in the newspaper to "the neighbor and his wife," make a point of saying, "I hope the neighbor and her husband felt similarly; surely she did not." When we see "women and people of color" written, we should ask, "Are women of color women or not?"

Al Young wrote a poem back in the early seventies entitled "Loneliness" included in his *Collected Poems: 1956-1990* (1992). The poem starts, "The poet is a dreamer" and I am with him, feeling myself a poet and a dreamer. But then he writes,

> "Should he put his white tie on
> with his black shirt
> & pass himself off as a docile gangster
> for the very last time?" (57)

He goes on in the poem to talk about watching women and such, and it is clear that he means the poet to be male, not to be a universal "he" at all. And he is using it as a personification of loneliness. A simple change of the article "the" to "this" (hence, "This poet is a dreamer") would take this poem from its attempt to be universal, to reference to a single poet, an embodied male poet. It may make the poet feel less grand, but without the change, women are left out of the category "poet" altogether.

Though I chose this example to illustrate my point, I could have chosen any number of other poems, novels, articles, etc. since this was and still is the norm. We need to think about the gender and race of the images we conjure up and not assume that they will be inclusive.

Pointing these instances out, not using them ourselves, uncovering the assumptions, are things we can do without expending a lot of energy; but they constantly create a new consciousness both in ourselves and in others. For me this awareness has been difficult. I, along with many of you, have spent much of my life believing that the "universals" included me, going along with it, laughing at sexist jokes as if I were not the butt of the joke—trying to be one of the boys. It is a cold dose of reality to notice the ways in which these "jokes" are by no means universal and are instead props for the hierarchy of dichotomization.

Listen to "Objects" Speak

"Woman has lost control of the production of her own image, lost control to those whose production of these images is neither innocent nor benevolent, but obedient to imperatives which are both capitalist and phallocentric. In sum, women experience a twofold alienation in the production of our own persons: The beings we are to be are merely bodily beings; nor can we control the shape and nature these bodies are to take." (Bartky, *Femininity and Domination* 42)

A. Refuse the Status of Women as Objects

Specifically, women must help each other refuse to be objects of exchange among men, as only mothers of boys, as only sex objects for men, as defined through males' eyes. Think of the myriad ways that women are categorized as objects and the ways women themselves play into that. All of us must challenge women's depiction as mindless bodies, controlled, manipulated, mutilated, starved, carved, compared, criticized, faked, silenced, shamed, sacrificed, suffocated, frozen, masochistic, body-matter, food for bodies and minds of men, objects of consumption.

There are countless examples. For instance, the bride gives up her father's name for her husband's name. The woman is the property of, and is named by, the man she is with. Seemingly small traditions such as

men taking women out to dinner or buying their fiancées an engagement ring, or many other such traditions give credence to the notion
that it is women who are for sale and men who are the buyers.

Women are consumed. They are consumed in the bedroom, they are
consumed in the nursery; they are consumed in the dining room; they
are consumed on the streets and in corporate boardrooms. Anytime
women are seen only through the eyes of the consuming male without
alterity, women are consumed.

Women who are on the bottom of the dichotomy are drained of
their own self worth and alterity and their substance is fed to the dominant sex. Men are not simply subjects while women are objects; instead
men are subjects at the expense of and as parasites on women. Most
often this is not consciously done, and consequently requires that the
consumption be brought to consciousness.

How do we resist this insidious idea that women are here to be consumed as objects? We begin by beginning. Men and women have different roles to play in this resistance. For women to become subjects, they
cannot turn to men once again to speak for them or take action for
them. And men need to become aware of their objectification of women
and stop it.

For women there is much work in this area that does not directly
involve men's changing. Instead it involves women's recognizing their
own power and refusing to give it away. Sounds easy, right? Women
have to become subjects in the face of debilitating objectification of their
bodies and themselves. A major reason women continue to act as objects
is that it is familiar; and if they are successful, they gain a certain kind of
indirect power. Sometimes they do it because of the threat of physical
violence. And many women have been convinced that this is the way to
get power and self-esteem. Women may not be able to directly change
men's gazing at them as if they were chocolate cheesecake; but women
can change their own acceptance of and complicity with that gaze.

Women can change the way they look at themselves, and therefore
some of the ways they behave, without huge structural changes. Women
can start today—not, "as soon as I get tenure," or "as soon as I get my
Ph.D.," or "as soon as I am in a stable relationship," or "as soon as I find
a decent paying job," etc.

Women have been defined as a "lack" for so long that they believe it
themselves. Whether they feel it yet or not, women need to begin to exceed those boundaries, overflow them, flood them with their fluid. They
must speak as subjects where objects are expected, situate themselves

in the Between, in the excess, in the not-one-or-the-other. Irigaray in referring to women states, "Rigorously speaking, she cannot be identified either as one person, or as two. She resists all adequate definition" (*This Sex* 26).

The image that comes to mind is that what women must do is turn and face a different direction, one of their own choosing, instead of engaging once again in the back and forth, up and down with men. When Brazen left the emperor's castle, she did not waste energy trying to get back in; she organized people to begin to build something new. The project, then, is to decide which direction to face and then to trailblaze like crazy. Turn away from the self-critical and societal-critical mirrors which always show women what they lack as objects, and face the wide open space of your own uncharted territory. Explore your interests and priorities and begin to be the subject of your own life.

Another route of change is to constantly point out the assumptions that are made about women. First we must see what those assumptions are. Let me give an example. Suppose I am having a discussion with someone about not having an intimate relationship and she says, "If you just lost about 15 pounds, men would be lining up to meet you." My suggestion is to stand this thinking on its head, to exceed the categories laid out for me as a woman. There are a number of assumptions in this statement that should be pointed out. One, that I am after "finding a man." Another is that to "get a man" I must look the part of an attractive object and therefore I must fit a standard object size. To say, for instance, "It is not *my* desire to lose 15 pounds—that is someone else's desire. Men can line up wherever they want; I care about how I feel, what I desire, and food may be part of what I desire. I am not going to work toward fitting a male ideal. That I have done all my life, which has left me with a bad feeling about myself. My desire is to feel whole in myself and to see if someone out there brings that out in me—it may not be a man; it may not be sexual; it may be sexual and it may be with a woman. Let's talk about my desire as a woman, a subject—let's talk about what *I* want."

Exceed the category of object and exceed the category of heterosexuality.

B. Women Speak Their Pleasure

The reference to women speaking their pleasure is connected to the idea that the object speaks; but it is more specific in that what is spoken about is pleasure, sexual and otherwise. Women have barely scratched the surface here since for the most part they have followed models of sexuality set up by men. The domination-submission and build-up and release models are seen across sexual preferences and pervade our thinking about sexuality.

Psychoanalysts and society at large have given very little attention to women's pleasure but instead have focused on male sexuality as the norm. Women's sexuality has been seen as lacking something, namely the penis. The silence of women's sexuality is shocking. From the silence of female statues, to women painted on canvasses, to women in pornography, women are assigned a place of silence in sexual discourse. Bodies and women do not speak, they are spoken about.

What would women speaking from their bodies wish to express about pleasure? It would undoubtedly not be the same thing that men have come up with. My hope is that women would not see sex as removed from everyday life, put in the bedroom and locked up for special times; rather, they might want sex to be more integrated into life in the form of sensuality and care for others: sensuality as nurturance, as feeding, as mutual respect for the alterity of the other.

I say it *may* be this or that because I have no way of knowing and because I would not want women's vision to be carved in stone, but rather open to endless possibilities. To stand where I am and make predictions about how women would feel about bewholed sexuality is to presume that what is today will be the same next week; and also to presume my vision to prevail over others whose visions are all needed in creating a present that integrates all. I would call for circles of women to begin to talk of these things; to begin to take their sexuality back from Freud and his ilk and to assert their own passions and pleasures.

I have heard critiques of trying to "purify" or make sex "politically correct" and how it takes the passion and spontaneity out of it. But that argument feels like a justification of the status quo, and women in general have not benefited from the status quo in matters of sexuality. They have been forced into reactive positions and have surprisingly still managed to salvage some pleasure in sex. Feminist activist Mariana Valverde in her book *Sex, Power and Pleasure* (1987) states, "Women's purpose is to actualize goals or ideals or desires that did not originate with them. In this sense it is correct to say with Freud that female desire is the 'dark continent,' the great unknown of Western culture" (158).

Women have on occasion been allowed to have desires, but only in the context of male desire. Although in the lesbian community much has been done around this issue, it has yet to reach the mainstream. In its dichotomized position, women's sexuality and desire is pale and unexplored. As with everything else, by allowing the dichotomy to rule we amputate the best of both men and women and we totally repress women's pleasures. Men's individuality and desire, too, is limited by the dichotomy but at least their limitations fit them into a dichotomized structure that gives them position and sexual power-over. It may be difficult for men to give up those privileges for the sake of something they have not experienced. For women, in a sense, it is easier to give up their already marginalized position as they have much to gain in terms of self-expression.

Valverde continues, "Because all desire has been conceptualized and experienced as primarily masculine, it is difficult to sort out which aspects of masculine desire are rooted in patriarchal domination, and which have been appropriated by masculinity but belong to the human species at large" (166). It is only by bewholing sexuality and moving beyond the domination paradigm that we can break out of those role limitations. Both men's and women's pleasures would be greatly expanded if we related to each other as whole people, whole body-minds and moved away from domination as turn-on to entering the Between as turn-on. The experimentation seems well worth the effort.

Taking the penis out of a position of centrality to sex would in itself free up expressions of sexuality that have until now been repressed. I compare it to becoming a vegetarian. Before I became a vegetarian I had no idea how many creative and delicious ways there were to fix vegetables and grains. Vegetables were an afterthought, a diversion, something that was required to "balance" a meal at best, when the central feature was the meat. All of a sudden, without meat, I was free to experiment with vegetables I had never even heard of before. The vegetables had always been there, of course, but because I was so preoccupied with finding and cooking the right meat, I had no energy, time, or inclination to worry much about the vegetables.

I think of the first Thanksgiving meal I cooked without a turkey. I was able to concentrate my efforts on the colors, textures, flavors, spices and combinations of vegetables and grains. Some traditional things that I enjoyed, like cranberries and mashed potatoes, I used again, but I could experiment wildly with the rest of the meal using black beans, orange beets, sweet pumpkin, eggplant, rosemary, sage and wild rice. It took more time and was a stretch for my imagination but I was pleased with the process. The next year's meal became easier knowing that I could do it with flair but most importantly with choice.

I am not suggesting here that we have to eliminate the penis from sexuality although if some feel the need to do that, fine. Many lesbians have no need to find a substitute penis or a substitute dominator. What we need to eliminate is the hierarchy that pulls energy out of women's desires and puts it into the domination of one sex's programmed desires. What I am suggesting is that we allow room for female sexuality to express itself, to show its multiplicity and variety and that we consciously move toward an inclusive sexuality that does not define itself by the turkey (no offense intended).

What would emerge from a female imaginary, a female body-mind that may be different from a male one? Our bodies do differ in ways that could make what we have to express qualitatively different. What effect does menstruation, lactation, giving birth, and menopause have on the psyche and the development of alterity? Additionally, women have the clitoris, a sexual organ that is not necessarily connected to procreation—what effect might that have? We might have to be prepared for lengthier erotic sessions that are not necessarily confined to the bedroom. Part of the experience might actually be growing the vegetables and picking and preparing them (so to speak). I would venture to guess that women's sexuality will turn out to be much more varied and unpredictable than what is currently considered acceptable. Could women and men actually think about what it is that they want without penis-centric assumptions and without male eroticism's claims of ownership? It is something else we can get started on right away.

When half of the population is assigned object status from before the moment of birth, we can expect to witness a lopsided, impoverished society. And when men continue to hold the speaking positions, women's subject status is undermined, no matter what the men are saying.

C. Women Exceed the Category of Mother

This subject was discussed in the motherhood chapter so I will not go into detail here. On one hand we must elevate the role of mother in order to give it support and status. Irigaray suggests that we "learn once again to respect life and nourishment. Which means gaining respect for the mother and nature. We often forget that not all debts can be paid by money alone and that not all nourishment can be bought" (*je, tu, nous* 47).

But, on the other hand, women need to know in their bones that they are not required to be mothers to express themselves. "It wouldn't be a bad thing, nowadays, if we improved the conditions of natural and spiritual life so as to deal with procreation in a reasonable manner. It seems to me that one of the spiritual tasks for our time is to ask ourselves what the future holds for existing children rather than blindly jumping on the bandwagon of having them. Learning to like your self, your sex, the other sex, their particular or common creations—isn't this what we need at the very least to reach some sense, socially, here and now?" (Irigaray, *je, tu, nous* 104). Challenging compulsory motherhood is a step in this direction.

D. Women and Men as "Aljects"

I use the word "subject" only because I have not been able to come up with a different word for what I mean. Keep in mind, however, that when women become subjects, the whole landscape of subject/object must change; the dichotomy is healed. To understand this, picture the dichotomy model with women as objects cut off from their subjecthood able to function only in the lower part of the dichotomy. Then picture it bewholed, moving into the Between model of object-subject.

Subjects as we currently know them take up lots of room in the world and use up too many of the world's resources. I would hate to see what our habitat would look like if we were all emperors. What I envision, instead, is a bewholed future where we all occupy a position that incorporates features of both our current subject and our current object. People then are never only objects to someone else's subject but are both at the same time. We are subjects of our own lives while at the same time we are objects in others' lives; but there is no way to separate or isolate us as objects simply existing for someone else or as subjects with no relation to or dependence on others. I have considered calling that position an "alject" (combining alterity with the suffix "ject").

For men the project is different than for women. For men, particularly white men, the project is to see themselves as objects as well as subjects and to recognize their interdependence particularly with those who have played the role of object to their subject, namely women; but also men of color. It may mean playing a more receptive, a more object-like role at times; it certainly means becoming aware of the ways in which men treat women solely as objects—in their banter, in their assumptions about who does what in a marriage, in their denial of that part of themselves that is not emperor but has room for allowing others to lead.

A peer relationship must be established between men and women and what is involved is quite simple. Men must listen to women, give up some of their stage time to women and then not walk away saying, "this is women's stuff," but sit down, take a deep breath and listen to women's stories and women's wisdom. Men must stop treating women like objects over which they have power. Additionally, men must take responsibility for their own bodies, for getting to know them and for caring for them.

Challenge Separation on Account of Difference

"All the modes of oppression—psychological, political, and economic—and the kinds of alienation they generate serve to maintain a vast system of privilege—privilege of race, of sex, and of class. Every mode of oppression within the system has its own part to play, but each serves to support and to maintain the others." (Bartky 32)

Earlier in the book we talked about the additional dichotomization of ethnic and racial groups, people with disabilities, women who do not fit a beauty and/or weight standard, people with varying sexual preferences, people from lower classes, and just generally people who do not fit a standard. Along with women gaining subject status must come the elimination of institutionalized racism and all of the other "isms." Disembodiment of universals has allowed us to pursue a course of isms without easy detection. In the name of "all are created equal," we have firmly entrenched and frozen the imaginary with the symbolic of white, able-bodied heterosexual men of the upper classes. To undo that, we must bewhole our body-minds and hear each other's stories and experiences so that we can create new structures that bend and flow with the wisdom of all of our experience. These separations must all be challenged and eliminated.

Though women have experienced much separation and various kinds of oppression based on their differences, what they all have in common is oppression as females, exploitation of their bodies and denial of their desires. The patriarchy would like to see women continue to be separated on the basis of race and class and ethnicity. But the key to the end of women's oppression is the same as the key to ending class and race oppression. We must stop separation and domination and work on a model of respect for alterity in whatever form it may take.

As discussed earlier it may be that men of color, women, the differently abled, lesbians and gay men, etc. will initially want to maintain separate groups, sanctuaries away from the people who have traditionally had power-over them so that they will feel safe enough to reveal, develop and strengthen their alterities. But we should all understand that at some point, even if sanctuaries remain, we must unite through our various oppressions to dismantle the dichotomies.

We see this conflict between sanctuary groups and universals played out on our college campuses now as the unreality of the so-called universal is being shown. The bastions of power accuse those who challenge the "universal" of being petty, intellectually sloppy, and divisive. Multi-culturalism is ridiculed and attacked for tearing up the fabric of our society. The fabric that is tearing, however—and there is fabric tearing—is the fabric made of the threads of one color, one class, one sex. We feel the divisiveness and the pain of separation because we have lived under the illusion of universality for so long that we strongly believe it exists. We say, yes, there are differences but can we not concentrate on our commonality as human beings? What we look to once again is a sameness of mind only. Are we not all the same under the skin?

No, because there is no "under the skin." We are whole human beings and we must not be deluded by the fallacy we have lived with for centuries that we can exist apart from our skin. The cloth made of one thread must be torn. We must recognize our particularities before we can begin to lose the idea that our alterities have ever been included. We must then work toward their inclusion.

In California, where the economy is worsening, there is a push to get rid of immigrants—cut off services, report and deport, close up the border. But borders are arbitrary categories which eliminate the Between. This country's relationship to other countries has the potential for all of the creativity and richness that the Betweens among people bring. But again we are being urged to cut off, split apart and use power-over instead of immanent power.

The differences among us are always there to be exploited by the emperors whenever there is a viable threat to the system of power-over. There is always someone else to fight, someone else who is taking the power and the money away from "us." As long as the splits go unquestioned, we are encouraged to fight among ourselves for the increasingly small supply of available power-over while the power-over hierarchy itself goes on and on.

The ecology movement has sprung up to awaken people to the critical nature of our relationship to our habitat. In order to eliminate the human/habitat split, people in some branches of that movement, such as the deep ecology movement, often talk of how humans must see ourselves as one with everything in the universe. Our selves must expand to include the trees, the sky and the deer. This approach is also similar to some Eastern philosophies. "They [some Eastern philosophers] suggest that our sense of self can expand to include aspects of both the mind and the world that we usually regard as 'other' or 'not me.'"[28] These philosophies include the notion of the unity of the universe.

The approach in this book contrasts somewhat with that notion because the "expansion of self" and the "unity" models do not adequately deal with difference; they assume that all of our interests are identical. These models gloss over and ignore or deny difference: different interests, different needs, different experiences. What I advocate is not an expansion of self to include others, or the parallel expansions of men to include women, whites to include people of color, or mind to include body. Rather, what I am calling for is both the acknowledgment of the alterity of all entities in the universe and at the same time the understanding that we are all connected by our Betweens.

The vision is not that "We" invite "you" to join "Our" programs as has happened with primarily white groups in the name of diversity. Rather, required is a change in the program and in the power structure to a shared power arrangement that does not continue to rely on the Us and Them dichotomy and power-over model. We cannot celebrate difference while the power imbalance remains and while we are unwilling to listen to each other's painful and joyful stories. The Between model gives us a way to see both our sameness and our difference. We are going to have conflict, places where our differences entail wanting the same resources on a planet that has limited resources. However, the conflict, the different interests, are something to be feared and repressed only if we allow the mentality of dichotomy and power-over to shape our destinies.

If we seek to win, to come out on top, we are still playing by the rules of the power-over society. What we must search for is immanent power, that power which lies directly in the Between, in the area of the stirring of interests, in the area of richness and diversity. By fearing it and going away from it, we lose its power and our power. Our inclination to assert our rights, our separate interests and to constantly emphasize that aspect of ourselves, moves us away from immanent power into the realm of the power-over. Sometimes such a movement is needed for survival in a world that is run on power-over. But in so many other ways, by understanding immanent power, by refusing to remain in the power-over mode, we can begin to change the way the world thinks about itself.

Blur Categories

Samuel Butler, writing in the late 1800's, stated the problem with categories in this way:

"Everything must be studied from the point of view of itself, as near as we can get to this, and from the point of view of its relations, as near as we can get to them. If we try to see it absolutely in itself, unalloyed with relations, we shall find, by and by, that we have, as it were, whittled it away. If we try to see it in its relations to the bitter end, we shall find that there is no corner of the universe into which it does not enter. Either way the thing eludes us if we try to grasp it with the horny hands of language and conscious thought." (*Selections From the Note-Books* 149)

If we allow categories too narrowly to define us, we restrict ourselves needlessly.

Language and logic are linked in a way that makes it hard to talk of one without the other. As I touched on earlier in the book, language names things and defines them as dichotomies and the rules of logic keep them in their places. If the categories are not so easily assigned or if they start blurring into one another, the rules of logic cannot hope to keep them apart. Dichotomies start to look ridiculously old fashioned, like a hoop skirt, impractical and oppressive.

In 1980 I worked as a crew leader in the U.S. census in Hawaii. There the racial and ethnic distinctions were beginning to weaken. It was fun to watch the trauma this breakdown created in the bureaucracy. Those exasperating little circles on the census forms were supposed to be serious, and yet so many people in Hawaii could not pick out one racial or ethnic group to identify with. They were inclined to fill in three or four of the circles indicating the categories—Filipino, Hispanic, Japanese, Samoan and so on, which, of course, the computers could not have handled. Did they not know that a person was one thing or another, but never more than one? Well, no, that had not been their experience.

Census headquarters in Honolulu informed the workers that we had to narrow down the answer to one ethnicity and they gave us formulas for doing so. First, ask, "What race is your mother?" If that, too, must be answered with a couple of circles darkened in, then ask, "Which ethnicity do you identify with?" and if there is still confusion then ask the same question about the mother. And finally, "Just do the best you can but give us only forms with one circle darkened." Conditions such as these herald the beginning of the breakdown of racial dichotomies.

Without rock solid categories, the hierarchy is hard pressed to ensure that certain groups continue to maintain power-over certain other groups.

Are not many of us interracial entities *a priori*? Who said that if you have a drop of "black blood" (and what is that?) then you are black? Without such pseudo-definitions, the continuum could be restored with every mix possible represented and the recognition that "purity" is an impossibility—what could it possibly mean and by whose definition? "Purity" and universals go hand in hand and should now be recognized for what they are—disembodied abstractions fabricated by people who have power-over. I am suggesting that we exceed these artificial categories. Using the term "people of color" is consistent with this idea. It is a self-definition and it defies such categorizations within groups. Perhaps we should all use it.

My saying that I am a woman of color nullifies the idea that there is a "white," or a place of "purity" that speaks with "universality." I have been in groups who were doing diversity work and for the "white" people it was difficult to say what ethnicity they were. They had a tendency to want to say that they were just regular, nothing special—no ethnicity at all. This parallels men's thinking that they are not speaking from a gendered point of view but from a view that transcends gender. The group in power idealizes and universalizes its experience and makes everyone else's experiences "other." Those in the power-over group must resist this temptation because it reinforces hierarchical power-over.

In certain contexts, then, we must all be people of color. I do not say this to disregard the oppressions that certain groups have suffered and continue to suffer, but to resist a forced division that is based on an artificial standard and those different from it. In certain contexts this resistance would be counterproductive, e.g., in the case of affirmative action, where inequities are being artificially corrected and such categories are necessary—or to resist the melting pot mentality where cultural differences are essentially erased. But if in other instances such as the census, surveys, and most importantly in our own body-minds, so-called white people thought of themselves as people of color, they would be consciously refusing to be part of a white/non-white division.

There is still much debate in, for instance, the African American community about the best way to proceed. Should a writer be identified as an African American writer or as a writer, period? Particularity has been used historically to ghettoize people of color. But to do away with particularity before dealing with the white male standard is counterproductive. Rather than debating whether to be embodied or not, those "others" should be spending their time exposing the body in the white male standard. Once it falls, the rest of us are free to fill the gaps with our unique particularities.

The other huge category related to blurring lines is gender, i.e., sexual identification and "masculine" versus "feminine" traits and behaviors. As Australian philosopher Moira Gatens states, the French feminists Luce Irigaray and Helene Cixous conclude that not only are women "*oppressed* in educational, legal, or economic terms, but also the *feminine* is *repressed*" (*Feminism and Philosophy* 113). Thus, not only are the genders dichotomized and made oppositional but so are certain qualities. When the French feminists speak of the "feminine," they do not mean those qualities that have traditionally been associated with women and which come out of a dichotomized worldview. What they refer to are the qualities that would emerge from the female body-mind if women were given subject status. But because women have for so long been in the object category, the qualities that might predominate in women in general are also unheard, not utilized and largely unknown.

As we mentioned earlier, although Irigaray tries to steer clear of speculating on what those "feminine" characteristics might be, she does draw parallels between women and fluidity and men and solidity. Since we have seen what the male imaginary has come up with in terms of language, logic, economics, political systems, philosophy, science, marriage, motherhood and sexuality, etc., we may be able to detect a predisposition in men—or more accurately, those in power-over positions— toward drawing boundaries, making distinctions and predictions. The element that seems to be missing from our institutions and our language is water. Water lends itself much less to strict boundaries. Water is also much less predictable, with turbulent flows being chaotic instead of linear.

Because we are so far from hearing from sexual difference and also far now from what men's imaginaries might be capable of if they had not been frozen into power-over dichotomies and hierarchies, I am reluctant to hazard too many guesses here. Rather than speculate about what we ultimately might find out about sexual differences in general, I want to make sure that we do not skip the step of particularity, the alterity of each individual that is separate from the issue of gender. Both men and women need experience and practice with relationships based on a Between model first, before any such generalizations could ever be drawn with any accuracy. Women have not had subjectivity, a prerequisite for the expression of alterity. And men have had a platform but not the ability to express difference nor their particular body-minds, and as a result, their range, too, has been stunted.

Our work now is to let alterity, experience, knowledge, creativity, bodily desires and pleasure emerge from each of us; and to do that we must be released from the strict categorization of male and female, masculine and feminine (in the traditional sense of the word). A deliberate jamming of the so-called requirements of this gender or that—of the clothing, the language, the jobs, the interests, the sexuality, the desires, the expectations—is called for.

In the area of sexual attraction, for instance, it cannot be assumed that someone will unequivocally be attracted to the opposite sex. What, after all is the *opposite* sex but a forced dichotomy between "male" and "female?"

The existence of homosexuality destabilizes the strict dichotomy. Recently discussion has centered on whether these sexual identities are choices or whether they are genetic. Some gays and lesbians argue that homosexuality is not a choice and therefore should not be punished or marginalized. However, even apart from the preposterous notion that homosexuality should be punished if it *were* a choice, the assertion that gayness is genetic returns to perpetuating an artificial dichotomization—one must be either gay or straight. Such an assertion promotes the idea that biology is the sole determinant of behavior, rather than recognizing the role both biology and culture, mind and body, inextricably play. Whether we support the genetic theory or not, the very existence of gays and lesbians challenges the status quo because it forces us not to make assumptions about people based solely on their gender. And it may be that for the present, further dichotomization is necessary in the struggle for civil rights for gays and lesbians, a very necessary struggle. It should not, however, be seen as an endpoint.

Perhaps what happens when we bewhole sexual attraction is a certain kind of bisexuality, though I dislike that term because it implies only two where I would like to see the opening for more choices. Attraction is made up of many factors, only a few of which are based on the actual genitalia a person comes equipped with. Sexuality would look much different if we allowed for the Between which is equivalent to allowing for a chance combination any of the possible things that could comprise attraction.

In our current way of thinking, people are expected to know beforehand to whom they are attracted. We are even encouraged to come up with fantasies of ideal mates and then deliberately seek out someone with those qualities, e.g. physical qualities or ideals, like the boy or girl next door. This kind of categorization generally rules out as possible sexual partners people of other genders, races, religions, ethnicities, body types, ages and abilities—and as a result our choices become severely limited. The process is similar to the way we choose our food. Our minds, which have been influenced by television, advertising, religion, novels, etc., set up for us what or whom we ought to crave, or be attracted to, and our body-minds readily accept these externally imposed desiderata.

Ideally, sexual attraction ought to be arrived at through both the Between of body and mind and that of biology and culture. However, if we wished to identify as strictly gay or straight, we could choose to live mainly that way. Likewise, members of certain racial or ethnic groups or economic classes could rule out attraction to anyone outside of those categories. But some of the strongest, most loving relationships I know of resist all of these categories of sameness. If people were willing to let go of the categorizations, admit their blurred nature, they might find themselves happily attracted to any number of individuals who did not fit their preconceived preferences.

By bewholing ourselves, we allow for whatever is in our body-mind to emerge as we enter the Between with an other. When we make a rule that we must declare in advance who we are, and to whom we will be attracted, we force ourselves into boxes created by a dichotomized society. It may be that our own particular mix has very little straight or very little gay; and therefore the people we will most likely be attracted to might be of a similar mix. On the other hand, we might find that attraction would depend on the alterities of the individuals we encountered in our lifetimes, in ways we could not have predicted.

Human beings do not possess just two mutually exclusive and exhaustive sexual identities. The range of possibilities is endless and changing all the time. I heard a friend of mine use the phrase "cardio-sexual"—instead of homosexual, bisexual or heterosexual—meaning "to follows one's heart"—or one's Between. This term could include blurring of all sorts of categories, not just gender. Maybe we should call it Between-sexual. We allow ourselves to enter both the Between of our own body-mind (so we do not allow our minds to determine what our bodies ought to feel) and the Between of ourselves and an other.

For a person to have discovered attraction to the same sex, they must have allowed themselves to enter that Between at least once. For heterosexuals that letting go might never have happened. Adrienne Rich in her essay "Compulsory Heterosexuality and Lesbian Existence" (1980) describes this phenomenon as compulsory heterosexuality—heterosexuality by default. If one does not choose, one rules out the possibilities.

But even if one discovers attraction to the same sex and chooses to live a gay lifestyle, often the lesson learned is that one is now in a "different" category, i.e. gay or lesbian. Often the categories themselves are not examined with suspicion. I would like to see the dichotomies themselves bewholed.

Keep in mind, too, that an identity is not something that is set for life at age 2 or 3 (or any other age) but is in constant flux, especially if one is open to it. Alterity changes with one's experiences, and the mix in the Between changes, depending on who the other is. A person's sexual identity (which I consider to be more than gender preference but includes all of the other preferences I mentioned above) comes from genes, from experience, from context, from any number of places. When that identity comes up against another's identity which, too, was formed by different circumstances, we can only wait and see how the two coincide.

Another instance where blurring occurs is with transgendered people. The blurring I am talking about is most effective while the body has not been tampered with and still retains the original gender, but the body-mind has assumed the opposite gender. Some feel that they need hormones and an operation to correct the situation in which they feel trapped in the body of the wrong gender. But unfortunately, after such an enormous expenditure of energy, and money and pain, they still remain trapped in the dichotomous male/female power structure.

It is a shame that our society leaves no room for men to be as "feminine" (whatever that is) as they want to be and for women to be as "masculine," that it forces a person to feel that the only way to fit in and be comfortable in his/her body is to mutilate it, change it, feed it hormones and coerce it to be the way the mind wants it to be.

Once in the early seventies, I was out walking with a friend on a busy street in Philadelphia. We passed by a person who could have been male or female, who had long hair, was not wearing make-up, had on loose clothing and walked with a savvy confidence and a little wiggle. Though we had only a fleeting glimpse of this person, the fact that we could not immediately assign a label of male or female froze us in our tracks. My friend, who wanted to refer to this person in our conversation, had to figure out the right pronoun decisively before we could go on. There was no room for ambivalence, no living and letting live with ambiguity, but a demand for certainty.

What kind of certainty is that? It is an illusion of certainty in my friend's mind. When she had decided which sex this person was and had enough rationale for it, she could continue; having concluded that the person was indeed a woman, she went on to make judgments about "her." She commented on the inappropriateness of "her" walk and that "she" did not wear make-up and was not pretty. She even went so far as to comment that with some effort the "woman" could be pretty and was obviously suffering from some mental problem since "she" did not try to be more attractive. All of these judgments were made simply so that my friend could comfortably keep her grip on "reality."

I cannot help but wonder what life would be like if we allowed ourselves the luxury of ambivalence, so that people were free to express themselves as they see fit, rather than having to fit into assumptions others make about them. The male/female example is just one of many, but it is the most basic distinction that is demanded, even by our language.

There seems to be an unwritten code particularly with regard to gender that keeps many of us in line—that we ourselves have the responsibility for defining ourselves to others in no uncertain terms. Thus, we see many women on the street at night terrified of rape but still dressing to make sure everyone knows they are women, with earrings, skirts, high heels, a purse and perfume. Writer and activist Marilyn Frye has stated that, "Constant sex-identification both defines and maintains the caste boundary without which there could not be a dominance-subordinance structure" (*The Politics of Reality* 33). The clear demarcation between male and female is crucial to the maintenance of power by men. The taboo on ambiguity is so strong that women often put themselves in danger in order to comply with it.

Similarly, there are women and men who do not comply with those taboos who are under constant attack for their refusal to follow the lines of sexual stereotyping. Women who dress in leather and walk with defiance are called names in the street, spit on and harassed. Men who wear dresses or act "feminine" are laughed at, ridiculed and beat up. In spite of those assaults, boundary blurrers daily perform courageous and important work confronting the prisons of "masculine" and "feminine."

Some, like female impersonators, often take on these roles for the comic effect. It is funny to mimic devalued traits and caricature them. The reverse is not as "funny" because it is not so out of the question— women take on male characteristics routinely to fit into a male dominated society (note the rarity of male impersonators). Those who voluntarily choose to take on "feminine" qualities hold up a mirror to the sexual stereotypes. I am often offended by the way the female impersonators ridicule women, taking on what I consider to be their worst qualities, namely the contortion of themselves into desirable, flirtatious objects; however, these caricatures can serve to further highlight the absurdity of strict masculine and feminine separation.

The movie *The Crying Game* (1992) is an excellent portrayal of life in the realm of blurred boundaries. I would encourage more films of that nature and I would encourage those who have the courage to live with the ambiguity of blurring to do so. Allies—that is, people not affiliated with a particular oppressed group who commit themselves to giving support to that group wherever possible—who do not live in the blurred area can continually question assumptions that go unnoticed every day about what it is to live in a man's body or a woman's body, or in any particular body.

Over-generalization and fear of the continuum force us to pass for what we are not if we can, and to deny the desires of our body-minds. This denial restricts our choices. Actively blurring the categories will in the long run free us from the shame of not fitting specified categories. We can then stop forcing ourselves to fit what our minds and society tell us we must, and begin realizing our alterity, our particularity and our possibilities.

Embody Viewpoints

"It is the male subject which is most familiar to the student of modern philosophy. It is this self which is most often presented in philosophical works as the *human* being because it is this self which is presented as, in essence, sexually neutral. The agency of this subject is closely connected to its ability to separate itself from and dominate nature." (Gatens 5)

Another way to jam the machinery of the production of "truth" is to put body, experience, perspective, and context back into the discourse. Truth can never be only one thing. Everything is changing and nothing is so solid in its boundaries as to have no Between. If we accept a Between model, we will realize that there is nothing that is solidly unchanging. Therefore, anything that purports to be true for all times, in all places is exaggerated and is generally spoken from a place of power-over.

Everywhere we go we must continuously uncover the bodies of men in the discourse. Bring your pick, shovel and a strong stomach (these bodies have been here for such a *long* time!). As we discussed earlier, ideas claiming universality through language are actually based on white male experience and perspective. The subjects we study are for the most part in *mind* fields.

We can talk about and expose the bodies of writers, artists, historians, scientists, advertisers, politicians, makers of constitutions and laws. Instead of struggling internally to make ourselves believe that women and men of color were meant to be included, we can struggle outwardly to show how they are not. In all our subjects we can look for the bodies, look for the women. "The necessity to be disembodied begs the question of the implicit maleness of the labourer, the citizen, the ethical person" (Gatens 6). Much writing is an attempt to hide from and cover up a basic fear of women, bodies and mortality; once embodied, its shaking knees can be seen clearly.

In philosophy classes we must ask, "How did Descartes 'think and therefore be' without a mother?" Or ask about Plato's Republic, not in the abstract but by putting particular bodies in there. Pretend a guardian is a woman and see how she fits in. Are wives kept in common for her? The rewards for bravery her choice of women? When she gets pregnant or has her period, what does she do?

In religion we must ask, "Why does our God not bleed, not become pregnant, not nurse?" In medicine ask, "How can you cure only my body, separate and mechanistic, when it is my body-mind, my relationships and my habitat that are ill?"[29] In science ask, "How did the scientist's own biases and perspective both frame the question and alter the results of the experiment?" In ethics ask, "From whose perspective is this so-called universal 'fair and just,' and at whose expense is it levied?" In government ask, "What do the men look like who are created equal?" In mass culture ask, "What is the sex of the viewer, what is her perspective?" In psychology ask, "What is the experience of this individual, in this body now; and how can therapy heal our connections, not just our 'minds'?" In language ask, "What is the gender of the subject and what are we assuming about the object?" In logic ask, "How useful is a technique that relies on forced categories like A and not-A when in reality there may be no such clear cut distinctions?" In history ask, "And what were the women and the men of color doing?" In literature ask, "What is the support system for these characters—who built the houses; who cooked the food; who supplied the natural resources for these characters? And what color and gender are the heroes in these 'universal' stories?" In environmental science ask, "Whose environment are we studying and who has the final say?" In nutrition ask, "What kind of body was in the experiments: white, male, moneyed, aware or unaware of who picked the food, how much and what kinds of pesticides were used and how the food got there?" In agriculture ask, "What effect does this crop have on those who come into contact with it, those who pick it, those who eat it, and what about a few years from now?" In social science ask, "What was the perspective of the observer, what kind of people were studied, what was their gender and who interpreted the data?" In the marketplace ask, "Who produced these things, where, for how much, and in whose interest is it that I buy them?"

When we read poetry and novels, view paintings, sculpture, and movies, notice—and later comment on—who are the objects and who are the subjects. From whose point of view is this beauty or justice or desire?

I am reminded of the movie *Thelma and Louise* (1991). Why did this movie disturb so many people? Generally, men thought it was nothing special or that it was shallow; and many women responded to it enthusiastically. That movie was one of the few in which women were real subjects, actors in their own interests; men were peripheral to the pursuits of these women. It was not perfect but it was revolutionary in its own way. Marilyn French writes of *Thelma and Louise* that "it breaks two major taboos: it shows men at war on women, and women retaliating against men" (*The War Against Women* 173). It took a fairly familiar genre, the rebels against something, and changed the gender of the rebels without thereby changing the thrust of the movie.

When the rebels were women, people became stirred up. The old models did not work. For some women it was the first movie of its sort that they could relate to as the main characters. For men it was the first one where they could not. It points out the gendered nature of all of those other celluloid rebels. They were not just rebels without causes— they were male rebels without causes.

The strategy of embodiment, then, points out these things constantly, brings them out of the closet, shines a light on them. Women need to refuse to take on identification with the emperor. If they do not take it on, they may not want to go to most movies that are made. Good.

One thing men might do as they speak is to refrain from universalizing their positions but instead to reclaim their own bodies and their own positions in the world. Here is an example of which there are thousands daily. We read in the paper "The U.S. showed strength in bombing Iraq." The embodied position would read that a white male representative elected by those few people of the United States who bothered to vote, showed military strength when he ordered the bombing of a small nation of people of color who had no way to defend themselves. At least once the statement is embodied, we see that real people were hurt and that they were hurt by a person who was elected by people, not by an abstract ideology or entity. We have done so much to remain disembodied and distant and euphemize our actions, that by reclaiming the body we also reclaim responsibility for our actions and our humanity.

We need to ask "whose truth, whose justice, whose right, whose wrong, whose rights, whose pain, whose death?" Show the viewpoint. Point out the speaker and those who benefit and those who do not. Where we desire objectivity we must work instead toward locating our truths in the world where they are and must remain. We want to know what is right and what is wrong; but first we must see the circumstances from as many viewpoints as we can and then make a decision. There is a right and a wrong but it is embodied; and it is different for different people in different places. It is not discovered by remaining outside the situation and looking down at it; or by making rules that apply to all situations and all people; rather it is created by staying inside, listening to all sides and working together to resolve differences. Respect for our own alterity and that of others is the only rule. The further outside the situation one is, the less one can know and the more one imposes one's own increasingly inappropriate viewpoint on the situation.

Once we embody the many areas in our life, we can begin to see that each of our perspectives is as valid as the one that has been chosen as the One and Only. We can also see that ours is not the only perspective that exists; and we will need dialogue to learn about others.

Challenge Pornography

"More blood...Passivity, and more specifically penetration, are always represented as painful. Pain as a necessary component of pleasure: that of the male who penetrates, that of the male or female who is penetrated. *What fantasy of a closed, solid, virginal body to be forced open* underlies such a representation, and such a practice, of sexuality? In this view, the body's pleasure always results from a forced entry—preferably bloody—into an *enclosure. A property?* By whom, for whom, is that property constituted? Which man (or men) does this quasi crime against property concern? Even though it is most often committed on women's bodies." (Irigaray, *This Sex* 201)

What about so-called pornographic images and representations? In pornography we see, for the most part, the representation of women as objects being dominated, humiliated and used by men. In the framework used in this book, I define pornography as the sexualization of the splitting of mind from body, male from female, and/or self from other; the disregard for the alterity of oneself or another; and the subsequent abuse of sexual power-over, particularly over women and children. My definition includes more than just violent depictions of sex and must be thought of in the larger context of the array of cultural images representing men and women.

The power represented comes from splitting men from women, self from other, body from mind, and body parts from the body. To focus on a certain kind of pornography takes our energy away from the harmful effects of what at first glance might seem more innocuous. I include in my definition, for instance, much of what is common in advertising, television, movies and almost every romance novel ever written.

The cultural images of power-over sex so bombard us that at times we feel helpless to stop it. We are called prudes if we speak out against it. We are accused of hating our bodies and being against pleasure. But the fight against pornography and power-over sex is not a fight against the pleasures of the body. In fact, many who fight it are merely trying to salvage the body-mind, our connections to each other and to our habitat—to uncover where the lasting, quality pleasures of our body-minds lay and to make them sacred.

What is called for is education and activism. We need to discuss the effects of these images and look at the real lives of those involved in the making of the images. Similarly, we cannot ignore the dangers of censorship to our freedom of speech. If we could see that these two positions, censorship and freedom of speech, are not dichotomous but rather are connected and overlap we could see that, while they look contradictory, some of the arguments for each side are true.

Pornography hurts women in very specific, embodied ways. We cannot ignore the effects some of these images have on real women and men. Since there is so much power and money in the pornography industry, it hardly seems fair to equate corporate freedom to speak with the speech of individuals. Corporations have always had more "freedom" of speech because speech, if it is to be effective and widespread, is rarely free.

There are also studies that show a direct link between certain kinds of pornography and violence against women. In the pornography industry alone, there are ongoing abuses of women. Women are often coerced into participating with no guarantees that they will get paid properly. Because there is so much money being made in the industry and because so much of it is treated by our "puritanical" society as if it is not there, cover-ups of such abuses are rampant. And pornography does not just hurt the women who are involved in making it. It encourages the perpetration of the ideology of that women are objects and that violence against them is "normal."

However, it is extremely difficult to write a law that does not rely on the good judgment of the people enforcing it; and we cannot always count on good judgment. Censorship can be used against women. For instance, Mariana Valverde cites an example where the Toronto police confiscated a feminist art exhibit on display in a bookstore window and charged the artists with obscenity (143).

Another problem with passing legislation on the issue of pornography is that agreement as to what is and what is not harmful to alterity is difficult to define. Everyone has a different view of what is harmful. What results sometimes is that anything dealing with the body is labeled pornographic. This approach defeats itself since it further splits mind from body in trying to save them from being split. If everything associated with the body is considered obscene, how then can we conduct the dialogues we need to reunite the two split parts, the body and the mind? The body has an alterity that is perfectly natural and free and unproblematic but, of course, we can never know what that is separated from culture. All we can do is try to hear its alterity and change the power-over culture so that it does not separate the body out as evil and something to be transcended but lives together with it in cooperation and respect.

There may be some laws that are useful, which try to stop pornography at the level of its objectification and use of women. I visited Nicaragua about five years after the Sandinista revolution. They had passed a law stating that women's bodies could not be used gratuitously to sell products. They simply made it against the law to use the kinds of billboards and advertisements we are bombarded with daily in which women's bodies are exploited to get the consumer's attention and to sell products. There are gray areas even here, of course, but precedence already exists in regulating the promotion of certain kinds of products (like illegal drugs or cigarettes on television). But by attacking the problem at the level of advertising, we are not keeping a product from being sold but limiting the way it can be presented. Granted, it does not necessarily come out of a raised consciousness of the population and in Nicaragua other forms of objectification in comics and beauty contests went on unscathed. Still, it is a start.

Valverde also suggests some actions that might be taken short of censorship, such as boycotting bookstores who sell "offensive" magazines, putting graffiti over billboards, etc. (143); at the same time we must commit ourselves to strengthening women's alterity. We should encourage both discussions about bodies, desire, who has the power and who is making the money from the production of these images, and direct action in response to all forms of perpetuating the objectification of women. Part of creating alterity is an empowerment of women and a re-definition of the erotic.

Some will argue that women have the right to do whatever they want with their bodies and if they want to sell them, expose them, pose them, it is their right to do so. However, in the abstract rights game where power-over is the mode, women always lose because women are equated with bodies and bodies have no rights, no power. Women *may* get remuneration for their acts but the price they themselves pay in loss of immanent power is great. And these acts do not just harm her but every woman and girl on the planet who may become targets of power-over and abuse. It is not safe to be a woman or a girl—they are seen as expendable, disposable, as targets of twisted eroticism. Until that changes, we cannot sit placidly by as those images are bartered and sold, as women and girls are bartered and sold for huge profits.

For men the project is to stop putting their economic resources into pornography. Be insulted by its degradation of women and thereby its degradation of all who are linked and connected to it. Do not go along with the jokes, the pin ups, the insults, the sexual harassment of women. Stop endorsing this method of relating by splitting and dominating. Men must deconstruct their base of self-esteem, de-program from the images that have been etched in their minds and reinforced in their bodies through orgasm.

Men are caught in a vicious circle. Luce Irigaray writes, "*What is it that eludes pleasure this way, making the repetition compulsion so tyrannical?* Leaving a categorical imperative to dictate the pursuit of some pleasure that is never used up? For physical exhaustion alone determines the stopping-point of the scene, not the attainment of a more exhaustive pleasure. Such a pleasure in fact becomes increasingly rare and costly: the master requires more and more of it for his enjoyment. Pornography is the *reign of the series*. One more time, one more 'victim,' one more blow, one more death…" (*This Sex* 202).

Men must begin to understand their psychological needs for domination and control even when that threatens their identities as men. Those identities are built at the expense of others and must be refused.[30]

Next time one of these issues comes up try to break out of thinking dichotomously. Try to reconcile the body and the mind, the concrete and the abstract, men and women. The concerns of the body and of women are by no means lesser concerns, and they in fact lead us to seeing possible ways to start healing the mind/body split instead of "fixing" it with more of the same.

12
Fabricating the Between—
What Threads are Missing?

Women's Alterity Building

"When women want to escape from exploitation, they do not merely destroy a few 'prejudices,' they disrupt the entire order of dominant values, economic, social, moral, and sexual. They call into question all existing theory, all language, inasmuch as these are monopolized by men and men alone. They challenge *the very foundation of our social and cultural order*, whose organization has been prescribed by the patriarchal system." (Irigaray, *This Sex* 165)

I would advocate forming circles of women as an avenue toward change.[31] The role such circles can play is to help build the alterity of each participant. The circle becomes the container for self-expression, for trusted listeners and for mirrors. It is a place where women can move into the Between of women, a place as yet uncharted. To some these groups might sound apolitical. To me, they are one of the most political actions women can take.

The groups I envision are similar to the consciousness raising groups of the 70's—but taken one step further. Getting together to identify problems women shared was good (though it stopped short of being inclusive enough of women of color and women of varying classes). It is a worthy goal to recognize that women are not isolated and to see the personal as political; but women need to support each other, not just to see what is wrong with society, but to create visions for the future and to change their internalized object status.

These groups of women must help each other beyond the stage where women see themselves only as victims, and move into the area of speech and expression of desires as subjects. We must ask what Deena Metzger asks in her workshops, "What has our experience, our particular story prepared us for?" Stepping out the role of victim and object where possible, women can seek their own course, their own destination, not predetermined by the hierarchical, dichotomous structure. This step, of course, is not always possible in the context in which many women live their lives—with abusive men, as single mothers, in poverty. However, within the circle of women is a place of safety where each of us can take that next step.

These groups should be as diverse as possible from the beginning so that we can check each other on our grasp of the "truth." By exposing our diversity and uncovering the shame we have internalized about who we are, we further the project. We can break patterns of self-oppression and dependency on sameness—break patterns of fearing the other. Women can begin speaking about their desires—not about desires to be more beautiful objects—but about their desires for expression, sensuality and compassion—a different sort of world. Women can articulate what that world might look like and what it is they want. They can tell their stories and listen to those of others. They can bewhole experience and when they need to, make up new language.

Authors Jill McLean Taylor, Carol Gilligan and Amy M. Sullivan, after conducting extensive interviews with young girls of diverse backgrounds, state in their book *Between Voice and Silence* (1995), "To break a cycle of repetition, it becomes necessary at some point to go past the edge of the familiar and enter a place that is truly unknown. To open oneself to change, to feel the hope that such an opening brings, means also to become vulnerable to the reenactments of past hurts and betrayals. To feel the hope that change is possible creates the most intense psychological vulnerability. But in the absence of the willingness to risk relationship—the experience of really hearing and taking the other's voice into oneself—the talking just goes on and on, because in the absence of relationship, change is impossible" (209).

The emphasis here is on intentionally changing a repetitive cycle instead of falling back into ways of being that reinforce the status quo and the silencing of women as subjects. My vision of these circles of women is that they limit the swapping of notes on which diets work, which ways to starve ourselves next, which plastic surgeons we recommend, or anything that in general encourages women to see each other as objects to be compared to each other. A tendency in women's groups is to discuss just those things, since we are all trapped in them to some degree. When women get caught up in discussions about how to lose weight, they tend to make an assumption that everyone has a desire to lose weight in order to be more attractive or to feel good about themselves. We must talk about those assumptions instead. Sandra Lee Bartky states, "The numerous exploitations of the fashion-beauty complex must be exposed at every opportunity and its idiotic image-mongering held up to a ridicule so relentless that that incorporation into the self on which it depends will become increasingly untenable. As part of our practice, we must create a new witness, a collective significant Other, integrated into the self but nourished and strengthened from without, from a revolutionary feminist community" (43). My suggestion is that the groups purposefully move beyond commiseration as victims in order to become for each other that "collective significant Other."

That kind of discussion is more difficult, brings in more feelings, stirs up bigger problems and is less easy to solve or to quantify; but those are the issues that need to be addressed. The difference is to focus on what women desire as desiring beings and not how to make themselves more desirable.

Someone may say to the group, "How can I feel good about myself when I weigh too much? I do not want this for anyone else but for me. It's not that I want a man; it's that I want to feel good about myself." A question might be, "What would it take for you to feel good about yourself?" She might answer, "I would feel good if I lost 15 pounds." This answer is classic. It has immobilized more women and women's groups than any other kind of answer. Literally the rest of her life could be spent thinking about her relation to that 15 pounds.

We must be careful then not to fall into the trap of thinking that this request is different because it has to do with how the woman feels about herself. Of course she will feel better about herself in this cultural context. Women have been trained so carefully by our society with its fashion-beauty industry to construct their self-image on what they look like. It becomes a vicious circle; it is exhausting, meaningless and harmful. Instead of asking how the woman can value herself within the framework already in place—that is, that her self-image is based on how she looks—I suggest that the group look at changing the framework, figuring out ways to deal with shame that do not play directly into the hands of the power structure—to reject the image of beauty that brings on the shame. To ask "How can we reconstruct our self-images so that we are not batted about by everyone who happens to have an opinion about how we look, including ourselves?" To ask, "Where is our immanent power here and how can we maximize that?"

Women's focus on their object status is archaic and destructive; there are better ways to spend time and energy. Women and men have been developing techniques for doing just that for a while now. We know it feels good and right but we have not known its value and importance to the project of transformation of a society so far removed from its roots, its life force, its immanent power. Groups of women tap into their own body-minds and their unconscious and in so doing bring awareness and voice to the female of the species. Because talking "rationally" and from the head often repeats the same patterns, women need to dig deeper, to a place that is pre-verbal.

Thus in the groups women must work on ways to bypass language and communicate with each other on other levels. Anna Freud in her foreword to Marion Milner's book *On Not Being Able to Paint* (1957) stated, "The creative process in art… 'remains within the realm in which unknown affects and impulses find their outlet, through the way in which the artist arranges his (sic) medium to form harmonies of shapes, colours or sounds'; whether deliberate action is affected or not is the last issue, the main achievement is, according to the author, a joining of the split between mind and body that can so easily result from trying to limit thinking to thinking only in words" (xiv). Following I will outline a few suggestions for groups in that regard. I encourage you to add to these in a creative exploration of the Between of your body-minds, much of which remains as yet unconscious.

1. Try painting either individually or in collaboration. The point of these exercises is not to produce "great art" (though it may be) but to communicate from a place that is not normally reached through speaking together in a linear way. Colors and shapes bring out parts of us that we did not before have access to. Often meaning arises during the process or after the piece is done.

Collaborations[32] take creativity one step further by accessing one's own body-mind while at the same time attempting to enter the Between with someone else. It requires a letting go of ego involvement and control over how the painting will look. What emerges is an effort to combine subject/object, to be active and passive in turns and to do it non-verbally. My experience has been that having another set of creative eyes and hands multiplies the possibilities that I alone may have designed.

People learn to trust formal logic to give them their picture of the world; this reliance on logic gives them a false picture of the world of human feeling Milner states, "And the result is that whole areas of their experience become cut off from the integrative influence of reflective thinking. What they are essentially in need of is a setting in which it is safe to indulge in reverie, safe to permit a con-fusion of 'me' and 'not-me'" (*On Not Being Able To Paint* 165). The groups give women a place of safety where this experimentation can take place. With art in particular we can break up old patterns and ways of thinking about ourselves that are individualistic rather then relational. We can explore the areas that used to be considered not-me but can now be seen as part of me, as part of the Between.

Because we have been so split off from our bodies, some exercises can help us to get in touch with messages our bodies might be sending to us. An exercise I did recently was to draw an outline of my body (someone else did that while I laid on the paper) and then to decorate it through painting, collage, glitter, etc.[33] This was a way to tap into feelings about the body that were not necessarily conscious. As I decorated different parts of the body, I tuned into those areas to see how they were feeling. We can think of ways to honor our bodies with drawings, decoration and just in general paying attention.

2. Dancing together in a place of trust bypasses immediately the verbal and the "head" stuff and moves us into our bodies. Recently I danced in such a place at Women's Alliance Solstice Camp in the foothills of the Sierras. Dancing to the drumming of Barbara Borden, a well-known Bay Area drummer, and others, I gave up conscious control of my movements and allowed the music to move my body directly, music to body-mind with no interference. Because of my balance problems, I have rarely allowed myself to give up worries about how I looked. I have had negative feedback on my dancing since I was small. I normally worry that I will fall or be laughed at. However, my daily work with my body-mind in swimming, walking and exercise has not been in vain and has helped me in many ways to loosen up the rigid control my mind wants to have over my body.

3. Drumming, playing music and/or singing are also ways to tap into an unconscious place. A friend of mine recently told me that though she did not play any kind of musical instrument, she found learning to drum practical for her since it did not involve learning notes. But it got her to a state of consciousness that I would call the Between. She

described it as taking concentration and attention while at the same time relaxing into the rhythms. When she slipped into either conscious thought about what she was doing, she started messing up the rhythms, or if she completely left off attending to what she was doing, she also got lost. Perhaps she was accessing both the Between of her body-mind and the Between of herself and the music.

4. Another way to get to the unconscious is through writing. Here I am not talking about linear, academic writing but about writing that comes directly from our body-minds without censorship. Natalie Goldberg has described a method of "wild mind" writing.[34] Her method is quite simple—the writer starts with a line or phrase and then writes whatever comes to mind, keeping the pen moving and not crossing anything out. Cecile Moochnik, a teacher I had in Berkeley, gathers people together to write in the Goldberg style. She sets the stage by reading poetry or short prose and then has the group begin writing a timed writing piece. The pieces are read out loud to the group and when the reader is finished, the listeners say back to the writer what they heard that had stayed with them or was meaningful to them. The result is nothing short of magic. First, we write whatever comes to mind from the unconscious, with often surprising results. Then to share that with others and to have them listen intently to it gives us a method for expression that is rarely possible in our daily lives.

We all too infrequently access the unconscious, the Between of our body-minds. Another rarity is a safe, non-judgmental place to speak and be heard, where our alterity is respected. We give ourselves the permission to enter into the Between with the others in the class who are not just witnesses but are part of the writing itself. Often certain words will appear in several of the pieces as if these were words somehow in the air in the room for anyone to pick up. As a participant, I feel as if I am not only practicing my writing but also learning how to get into my body-mind and how to listen to others.

5. I would suggest forming dream groups so that our dreams are not lost to us. Even if you already write down your dreams and work with them, I would recommend talking about them in a group. The group process helps give one the perspective necessary to see things that would otherwise be missed. Also the group is helpful because sometimes dreams do not seem to have a message just for the dreamer but have what appears to be a larger message that should be shared with others.

I am in a dream group in which sometimes it is hard to remember whose dream was whose, or sometimes a character from one dream can comment on the characters in other dreams. Since we are an all-women's group, themes for women in general seem to emerge. The connections and messages can change our everyday lives for the better. We must learn to pay attention to the "non-rational," the non-linear messages that we come across which will enrich our lives and charm us.

If you are unable to be in a dream group, write the dreams down anyway so that your unconscious knows that you are paying attention to it and taking it seriously. It is similar to the writing group. If your body-mind knows the thoughts will be written down or spoken out loud, there is a better chance of tapping into it.

6. Another area of work is that of learning to enter the Between of ourselves and all other entities in our habitat. The most obvious way to do this is, of course, to go outside and spend time walking, smelling the flowers, hugging trees, lying on the earth, watching sunsets, listening to birds, and learning about the animals, plants and land areas around you. What we humans so often have had to do in order to have an excuse to be involved with nature was to kill something. To sit by a stream, we get out our fishing rod and fish, to wander in the woods, we take out our guns and hunt. We must learn to just sit and just wander without having to *do* something to assert our dominance over the creatures around us.

As I sit here writing in a cabin in the woods in Northern California, I am amazed by the response of my whole self to the closeness of nature. I am much more in tune with the weather and the changes in light. I find I have bodily responses to some weather, for instance, just before it begins to rain, I feel irritable and out of sorts and when the rain begins, I relax. In the city I do not realize how much I need the contact with my habitat—I almost forget I have a habitat. Here I am reminded of whom I share this planet with and the connection feels good.

We all need to learn the best ways for us to reach our unconscious and the Betweens in our lives. Access to the Between of body-mind is critical for our physical and mental health because, as we discussed earlier in the book, it is here that healing lies. Music, art and dance are not some kind of amusement to make our day go by faster and they are not adjuncts to a happy life. They are an integral part of creating the Between.

This work is vital in a society built on a male imaginary to the exclusion of a female imaginary. Here is where sexual difference matters intensely and where it is not the same for groups of men to reach the unconscious as it is for groups of women. Think of the imaginary and the symbolic and their relationship in Western thought and then think of how women are not only repressed but are taught a male symbolic with all of its ideas about the value of women.

Women's role in this is not to clamor to be included in the male way of doing things. It is, rather, to create something new—not simply to tear down but to create visions for the future.

Alterity of Body

"Sexual differences have of course been exaggerated into the stereotypes and oppressive social policies associated with biological determinism, but the truth in the stereotypes is that different kinds of bodies give us different raw materials for artfully constructing our viewpoints on life." (Don Johnson, *Body* 61)

What are some ways to integrate our body-minds, to be more aware of our bodies' needs and wants? Our bodies give us meaningful information and change our perspective on life. Living with a male body is different from living with a female body, living with a disabled body is different from living with an able body, living with a sick and/or dying body is different from living in a healthy body. Somatics professor and author Don Johnson writes, "People born with structural anomalies or serious illness, such as cerebral palsy or polio, often develop a perspective on life that leads them to notice aspects of reality that pass by the rest of us" (61). We should not discount the differences these experiences teach us about life.

We need to listen to our bodies, acknowledge that we are body-minds and not minds-who-own-bodies, and begin to respect the alterity of our body-minds. That means demanding attention to the body's needs in many areas that currently ignore such needs. For instance, I have attended philosophy conferences where bodies are completely forgotten or denied. No breaks are scheduled in three hour sessions; we are seated in uncomfortable chairs; and we sit there trying to be the universal mind and meanwhile find we can hardly sit still.

We need to call body needs to the attention of the planners and the attendees of conferences and other public meetings. Accessibility is an issue in more ways than what we commonly consider. Conference planners should always be aware of the special needs of people who may attend. For instance, not all of us have Herculean bladders and not all of us have backs which are made for straight backed chairs or feet that can be comfortable resting on the ground in conventional style. Additionally, the use of perfumes and scented products makes some people very ill. Advance conference materials should expressly ask people to refrain from wearing those products so that the conference will be accessible to all.

Do not try to pass as mind-only in public places. Do not try to make yourself fit the standard; rather, make the places accessible to more people. Passing only plays into the hands of the hierarchy and mind/body split and makes us feel ashamed of our bodily needs. The emperor has a body, too and so does everyone in those stuffy rooms.

We also need to learn about how our bodies work so that we do not so readily hand them over to someone else to fix when something goes wrong. We will know when something is wrong if we are familiar with the way our bodies normally work and are alerted to different sensations. I have begun keeping a body journal and that has heightened my awareness. Not only am I in touch with my body when I am writing in it but I also find myself making mental notes throughout the day about things I will enter later. It is a way of becoming more aware. Through my records, I am also able to see patterns of health and find out what is normal for me and what is not. Often when we rely on doctors to tell us what is normal, they apply an average to us, something that may not be at all applicable to our particular bodies.

When I exhibit various symptoms, I note them and mention what I have been eating; later I can go back and see the patterns and make changes. I also keep track of the cycles of my period, the moon, the weather. I can see corresponding patterns in my sexuality, moods and overall health. The journal teaches me more than I imagined I could understand about my body's functioning. Now when I go to a health professional I do not have to guess at when the start of my last menstrual period was or when I started to feel a symptom. I have this documented. But even more importantly, I can know these things for myself and for my own diagnosis of what I may need to change without ever seeing a "professional."

Try to catch yourself when you are dissociating from your body. I found that the way I meditated, I ignored my body. If my body were uncomfortable, I would ignore that and tell myself to transcend that pain and find a higher truth. Now I do not want a higher truth if it means leaving my body behind. Now I involve my body in the meditation by touching it and moving as I meditate. I meditate when I swim, keeping track of how my body feels in the water and also what my mind is doing and how they are connected. For me that is where spirituality is, in the connections.

We cannot leave this section without mentioning the part schools should play here. As I said earlier in the book, singing, dancing, gym and movement are not just frill subjects. We need to start children at young ages thinking about their body and its needs and attending to them. We need to make sure that students learn about the body and are tuned into it. This means less regimentation at school and more physical involvement. It means tailoring the program to meet the alterity needs of the students and teachers. The body must not be thought of as a "problem" needing correction and control while we concentrate on the students' minds. Integration of embodiment into the curriculum and raising the status of bodies is called for in schools.

It is imperative that we recognize that a universal, disembodied standard is an illusion and thus an impossibility for people of alterity to fit. Often when we as a society struggle with issues such as how to equalize the pay of men of color and women, we argue that all people are the same in their minds, that bodies should not be a factor in our determinations about promotion and pay. That argument might apply if we did not have entrenched in our system a white male standard which, stated or not, determines where people are placed on a pay and promotion scale. A person's success depends on how well they fit that standard. Refusing to engage in a discussion about individual differences, whether they are based on gender, race, height, weight, religion, health, or physical ability, glosses over the fact that we are all different and few of us are comfortable fitting our bodily reality into a standard based on a particular body.

My point here is that we should not strive to make our workplaces enforce a white male standard, but should strive to have our differences acknowledged and dealt with. If we go on saying that any of us should and can do exactly the same as job as every other one, we will never have an adequate way to deal with pregnancy, paternity and maternity leave, compassionate leave, child care problems, illness, or physical disability. We are different and we will require differing treatment in order to have equitable results. Many would rather continue to assert that we are all the same because they fear that otherwise treatment will be unfair; there will be unequal pay and promotion. I understand that fear but do not think it will be helped by ignoring difference.

We cannot progress to a place of fairness unless our individual differences are acknowledged and the standard body is exposed. Are we willing to look the other way, away from the hierarchy as it exists, implicitly determining how we are treated? Or can we expose the situation and work toward incorporating and acknowledging difference? We need a system in which our individual needs can be met and respected. We cannot get there by ignoring and repressing our individual needs and desires.

Resist the attempts to make you think of your body as an object, as a piece of inert clay to be molded to the shape your mind ordains it to be. Instead try to tune in to the messages the body sends you, from the cramp in your leg to the callus on your foot to the desire for certain kinds of food. Tune in to it and learn to discern what are emotional needs or created needs and what is an appetite that should simply be satisfied.

Alterity of Our Habitat

Food

In this section I would like to talk about how to break patterns we have developed over many years. I will give a few examples of the reassessment we can make. Those skills can then be generalized to apply to any situation we encounter. To break patterns, we must first become aware of their existence and the choices we make unconsciously every day.

An example of a pattern that can be broken through awareness is the way we relate to our food. We often treat our food as simply affecting our bodies, entirely separated from our minds. If we ate with our body-minds, we would have to be mindful (body-mindful?) of what went into our food. If we ate meat, we would have to be aware of where the animals came from, how they were treated and how they were killed. In most cases of meat eating, the animal eaten was raised and fed in an inhumane way so that the producer could make the highest possible profit. We often ignore the fact that what we eat comes from dead animals. Author Carol Adams states, "After death, cows become roast beef, steak, hamburger…" (*The Sexual Politics of Meat* 47-48). Euphemisms allow us to go on eating dead animals without body-mindfulness.

Minds should not tell bodies what to eat and what not to eat based on an abstract principle such as, "killing animals is wrong." But by the same token, we should not eat without thought. We should pay close attention to what our body wants and needs and attend to how our food got to us, the resources spent to produce it, the suffering caused, the treatment of the workers involved in bringing it to us, the damage to the habitat that resulted from the production. Being aware of these things as we eat is an attempt to integrate ourselves into our habitat and not to treat everything outside our skins as fair game for our use.

Breaking this pattern is difficult work because it involves our lives so intimately and because we are encouraged on all fronts not to think about what we are eating. Adams writes, "Because of the dominant discourse which approves of meat eating, we are forced to take the knowledge that we are consuming dead animals and accept it, ignore it, neutralize it, repress it. What are the costs of this? What are the implications of repressing facts about the absent referent whose death enables meat eating?" (186-187). The absent referent enables us to bypass our own body's responses to what we are eating, as for instance, the fact that we eat dead animals is kept under wraps. Not dealing with the implications of embodiment, both our own and the food we eat, are what we as a culture have done for centuries.

Would body-mindfulness spoil the taste and enjoyment of food? In some cases, yes, it would. If we became aware and stayed aware of how animals are being treated in this world, we would probably stop wanting to eat them. Our stomachs might churn at the thought of the suffering and distress we cause fellow creatures in our habitat. If we were aware of our connections, it would not be so easy to fry up that steak because we would be frying up a part of ourselves.

Taste is never in a vacuum; our society teaches us to forget, to ignore the sources and to divorce our senses from our awareness so that we will eat anything that is presented as pleasurable to the senses. Liking the taste of something has many factors built in, including habits, mass marketing and what everyone else is doing. The mind/body split has been very helpful in keeping what we eat separate from what we know. We promote senseless sensing.

Even when we try to eat what is "good" for us, we do it on the basis of mind over body. If we eat something that is not good for us we think we are hurting only our bodies which can be corrected by exercising or purging ourselves. We overeat not because our body wants more and more food but because we do not have the slightest idea what our body needs or wants. If we have a history of dieting, we may eat out of a legitimate feeling of being starved and deprived. When we deprive the body of what it needs, like delicious food, it must do all sorts of things to compensate and we lose the familiarity with it we once had. Our mind can force feed or force starve our bodies under the guise of what is "good" for it or what will give the mind some feeling of control or nurturance.

Part of respecting the alterity of the other is learning something about them and how they function. Part of respecting your own alterity is being able to work from a place of body-mind where you act not just out of pure emotions or out of pure rationality but reason and emotion combined—bewholed. Some say they need meat for the protein or because they like the taste. John Robbins, in *Diet for a New America* (1987), states that studies have shown that Americans overeat protein and overconsumption in itself can cause problems. One such problem is that too much protein interferes with the absorption of calcium and can be a cause of osteoporosis (189-196). Many of our nutritional studies have been sponsored by the beef or dairy industries and as such cannot be trusted. For most people a vegetarian diet is much healthier than one with meat in it. Take away the fallacy that meat is necessary and you are freer to eat what is healthy and what you like, not based on old programmed patterns but based on how your body-mind actually feels. When you also factor in the alterity of the animal or plant, the taste will change.

When we eat meat we are also eating the hormones and secretions that the animal produced as a result of the conditions of its life and death. If we are aware of those things, the meat is bound to be less appetizing. Knowing more about how vegetables are raised can also change how we eat. If we know that certain vegetables are grown by plastering them and all who work with them with pesticides, those vegetables will be less appetizing. We can look for vegetables grown organically where possible. We need to become knowledgeable about how our food is grown and raised because by eating it we endorse and ingest the methods used.

We know that by eating animals we are allowing grain that could go to feed hungry people to go instead to the animals we raise for our consumption. Those animals that we breed, particularly cows, mutilate the hillsides, the streams and the ozone layer, by producing the "emission of three of the four global warming gases—methane, carbon monoxide and nitrous oxides" (Rifkin, *Beyond Beef* 223). The alterity of the land is often not considered. Most methods of agriculture are not based on the organic model and have detrimental effects on the land. We must be aware of the sources and methods for producing all of our food.

Try staying aware as you eat vegetables. If you are using an abstract formula about life, you may hesitate to eat anything that had to be killed for you to eat. However, if you become familiar with how the vegetable was grown and harvested and you are comfortable with those methods, you can eat in appreciation of what the plant and the farm worker who grew it are giving to you. The plant world tends to evoke images of tending, nurturing, slow evolutionary change, and harmony with the seasons. Rifkin states, "We have substituted mechanism for organism, utilitarianism for spiritualism, and market values for community standards, turning ourselves from beings to resources" (*Beyond Beef* 287).

We do not think of the Between when we buy packaged food and then throw away the packaging and what is leftover as if our habitat were simply here for our exploitation. Part of being aware of where food comes from is thinking about what happens to that which we cannot eat. We should all have access to a compost pile where we our leftovers could go back to the soil for its nourishment. We should take only what we need and can use and the rest should be returned to the soil. We are in it together and we must take care of each other. Our habitat provides for us; we must provide for it.

Eating body-mindfully is not something we need to wait until after the revolution to change; it is something that we can start doing right this minute. Certainly for some of us it is harder to get good food than for others; sometimes it costs more or is just not available in the neighborhoods in which we live. Luckily more and more cities are sponsoring farmers' markets in downtown areas which provide organic, low-cost fresh produce. Also, there are more and more Community Supported Agriculture projects starting up where one can either buy shares in an organic farm or become a subscriber and receive a weekly box of vegetables. We can all make *some* changes in the direction of becoming more body-mindful, right now.

There is no cut and dry answer to what you should eat. Rather the answer will come from your body-mindfulness; it will not be the same for every person. When we feel the connection of our food to our nurturance, to our survival and to our pleasure rather than as an assertion of the right of humans to eat anything they please, we will eat differently and behave differently in the world.

Some assert that in hunting and killing their food they feel their connection to the animals. But it seems that we humans, operating out of a domination mode, are free to use weapons developed by minds to distance us from the other animals and to kill them with a feeling of conquest and victory rather than an awareness that part of us was just killed as well. What is it that drives us (and it is mostly men) to hunt? The pleasure is in stalking and killing the animals, feeling superior to them, exercising cunning and power-over them. Hunting in a society that does not need meat to survive encourages the domination mode of thinking and has nothing to do with us feeling our connectedness. We play out the same scenes of domination of human over habitat over and over.

Those peoples who do kill animals because it is necessary for their survival have a very different attitude toward killing them. They do not kill for thrill but out of necessity. They do not hunt to show their prowess and manliness, but with dread and sorrow, aware of sacrificing their connections.

Listening To Our Habitat

Of course, we need major changes in our local, regional, state and federal policies, but major changes in our attitudes and behavior can occur before those larger policy changes and can indeed begin to force those larger changes. We can start right now by seeking wholeness in our body-minds, in our relations with others and our habitat. By bringing into consciousness that in each act, we are connected, our behavior will change. When will we learn that caring about others, caring about our habitat and caring about ourselves are all part of the same struggle? We must stop thinking that our interests are diametrically opposed and in competition with those of others.

The idea that we will win and our habitat will lose; that I will win and you will lose; that my mind will win and my body will lose, are all absurd. Life is not a battle to see who is more powerful and who can win. We all know that in reality there is ultimately no way to win that battle.

Then what *is* our goal? For me it is simply living in harmony with others and my surroundings, taking only what I need and giving back as much as I can—and being happy, feeling whole and unrestrained by splits and walls.

Practicing body-mindfulness in relation to our habitat, as in our own selves, goes against the grain of practically everything we have been taught. Embedded in our language is always the separation between ourselves and the earth; rarely does it evoke our connections. We live on the "earth" and not in it or with it. And still the "it" remains. What words teach us about what part is both of us? We see pictures of the earth as a big blue ball and we feel distanced from it, giving us the illusion that it is different and apart from us. Constant attention and work are required to become aware of the connections which our society tries so hard to sever.

We will need to enter into dialogue with our habitat. How? Where we have grown accustomed to relying on verbal communications, we will have to try something else—using all of our senses. We can use touch (lie flat out on the earth); we can use smell to sense whether or not animals are being treated with care; we can use taste to tell whether what we are eating is good for us. Again these are not senses removed from the mind but rather infused with it. The taste of something is very much affected by all of the factors that brought it to us and how it will make our body feel later.

We can develop relationships with animals, not necessarily pets that we "own" but also the other creatures in our habitat that we basically ignore.

We seem unable to acknowledge our connections and our dependency on other creatures and on the land. Humans and the environment—humans on top and severed from the environment, and the environment lumped together as "other," as non-human, and defined through human eyes, through the use value it has to humans. My partner and I were out walking in Lassen Volcanic National Park and we ran into a man who lives near there. We all looked over at a mountain that we could see had been clear-cut and he said, "Well, I guess it's OK because I never planned to hike over there anyway."

Until we understand that our split reality is not reality, that all creatures and mountains and plants have alterity and are connected to us through the Between, we will never solve so-called environmental problems. We have to recognize that our place is *in* our habitat, not above it and we must see how our actions affect everyone else.

Non-European societies such as the Native Americans have traditionally had a relationship with their habitat that recognizes symbiosis. What is done to the world by each part of it is acknowledged to affect every other part and therefore must be considered in any plans humans make. They realize that entire populations of animals cannot be slaughtered without a huge effect on the functioning of the whole ecosystem. What is recognized is that a give and take within the habitat maintains a balance in which we can all thrive.

We U.S.ers think that if we can control the habitat we will save ourselves. We must turn instead to wholeness that requires radical changes in our self-images, all of our relationships, our language, our ethics and what we conceive of as the meaning of our lives. If we continue to conceptualize our habitat as separate from us, we will not understand the kind of re-framing that is necessary. We cannot respond to this emergency call with business as usual. We must respond in a new way, not merely for the sake of the "earth" and not merely for our own sake, but for the sake of us all.

Proactive change is needed and that means changing now our way of being in the world, not merely reacting to every crisis that pops up. When we see garbage ships circling the globe for a place to dump, we think of recycling; when the ozone layer sprouts holes we think about outlawing spray cans; when tankers spill oil, we cry for double hulled ships; when nuclear power plants and research facilities can no longer contain their wastes, we frantically search for a place to stash it, at least for a while; when the last of the old growth redwoods are threatened by logging, we try to save the spotted owl and the trees. How many fingers can we stick in the dam we built between ourselves and our habitat, until it weakens and falls? How many emergency calls from the other inhabitants will it take until our response is timely and commensurate with the seriousness of the plea?

Recycling is good; saving the spotted owl is good, banning chlorofluorocarbons is good but none of these stop-gap measures will ever solve our most threatening problems. We need a dismantling of the dam between us and our habitat and we need a new way to see ourselves in relation to it. We need a way to listen and respond to each other and we cannot do that as preoccupied as we are with sticking fingers in the dam. I am calling on our ability to respond to the cries, stifled as they now are behind the dam. With each step and each breath, we are connected to our habitat and it to us; we must strive for awareness of those ties.

On an individual level we make decisions every day which add to the problems of our habitat. The attitude is often expressed that "I am not going to change my habits because no one else seems to be doing it and whatever I save, they use up." I spoke to a man on the street in San Francisco during a drought in the Bay area. He said that he does not bother to save water because he knows that tourists come to the City and take hour-long showers. The feeling that we are all alone in conserving can be an overwhelming feeling. But the feeling that you are doing all that you personally can do to conserve no matter what anyone else is doing, is also a strong feeling, and a positive one. Changing one's attitude toward personal habits with an eye on the reason for it, can bring you the openness to find your place in the cosmos, a place of reciprocity. More and more of us are changing our thinking and our actions and someday, if we are lucky, that will add up to enough.

It does matter whether we drive our own personal cars everywhere or try whenever possible, even when it takes twice as long, to ride public transportation. The decision to jump in the car to go somewhere should not be automatic. The buses and trains are not there to ride only if one is too poor to own a car; they are there to offer us a way to contribute to the well being of the planet instead of taking away from it. Sometimes, of course, our systems being what they are, there is no other way to get where we are going other than to drive. And sometimes we will ride a bike or take a bus. But in our world we make these choices every day and can feel empowered by being conscious of it—not to guilt trip ourselves each time we drive, but to pat ourselves on the back for having considered the alternatives in good faith.

Some things feel so small that one might wonder whether they are worth doing—such things as carrying a re-usable cup instead of using a Styrofoam cup when you travel, or buying primarily used clothing. For the purpose of living in the Between, of living life in that place of respect for others and for the planet, every small gesture which encourages connection adds to our lives. And these gestures empower others to do the same thing. However, there will be people who respond to such gestures with hostility, feeling that an attitude and actions different from theirs automatically constitutes a critique of their lives.

That response is difficult to manage but often the people who are the most hostile are the ones who are closest to understanding the rightness of the action and may at some later time try it. Our lives are all complex and we need to recognize the lack of societal support for thinking like part of a whole.

The society itself is built on a split from our habitat and consequently all of our responses seem inadequate and piecemeal. But the shift of consciousness is on its way; it is just a matter of time until enough people are living in the new attitude. Anything, no matter how small, which moves more of our energy and our engagement over to the other side of the teeter-totter helps make that shift possible.

On all of these issues I recognize that my way of thinking and feeling about the world might be different from someone else's who is standing in a different place. The best we can do is to act out of a place that is not dichotomizing the world, out of cooperation and not domination. Resolution would take discussion, dialogue and a forum where people could speak from their body-minds, from the place where we are connected.

The correct method is not always clear and there is no one right way for all time. However, what is clear is the method we use to decide how to proceed, the method of paying attention to the body-minds and experiences of all of us.

Conclusion:
Beyond Ethics to Body Politics

Over the years, the emperor has learned many ways to keep us from exposing his body. He continues to make us believe in our inferiority if we cannot see his clothes, his point of view. He has thoroughly convinced us that bodies are bad and must be overcome by whatever means are necessary.

Our society is a quagmire of conflicts, violence, environmental degradation, racism, sexism, homophobia, image madness, consumerism and greed, government hypocrisy, lies and confusion. In this atmosphere some lament the loss of "family values"—virtues of honesty, hard work, women staying at home, the nuclear family and so forth. But the power of the nuclear family in Western culture has always been based on splits of men from women, mind from body and public from private spheres.

A return to split values does not deal with our core problems. People talk of getting back to basics, back to a time when things were simpler and when people refrained from injuring each other. But I cannot think of a time when this was true unless we are again taking on the perspective of the emperor and are mainly concerned about his wealth and happiness. From an African American viewpoint, going back does not seem idyllic unless we go all the way back before slavery (this is not a date I have heard mentioned by the family values lobbyists). Certainly from women's point of view this regression is not without its share of problems. What are the feelings we recollect with such nostalgia?

Perhaps what we remember are those earliest connections to our mothers while we were still in the womb, even if those connections did not last long after we were born. There is an impetus, a compulsion, to recover that loss, and many strive to redress it through capturing women in the home and keeping them there as object/mothers and by asserting control over all women, but especially pregnant women (witness the abortion debates). The impulse is to demand that women be available to the society to compensate for the anchor that has been lost. But the Lost Mother or Nanny is as much a fairy tale as the High and Mighty Emperor: they are illusory and yet we continually waste our time on search and recover missions, much like the search for the Holy Grail. Can't we see that the Lost Mother is meant to be a prototype, the first in a long series of loving and blessed connections that we can have with so many in our habitat, from dragonfly to redwood, from creamy butternut squash to peanuts, from hummingbird to deer, from our own selves to a series of dear human friends?

There are those who feel that our problems require a system of ethics to live by—a set of moral traffic rules that would tell everyone when and how to stop and go. The theory is that a system of ethics would supply the restraint that humans need, else they will act out of self-interest, greed and disregard for the feelings and well being of others. I argue in this book that our traditional systems of ethics will not help; we need a fundamental change of consciousness and language to create a culture and institutions that will enable us to reconstitute the wholeness that has been fragmented.

Our present problems are not of recent origin. In this book I have traced the roots back to their origin in classical Greek thinking. There we saw how a survival instinct that includes a dread of dying and sickness produced a craving for immortality. Since only the body was seen to sicken and die, it was natural to feel an abhorrence for that body and a desire for what was unchanging and immortal, i.e. perfection—qualities which were felt to reside in the mind. Since women were more visibly tied to the body by the fact that they gave birth, they became identified with body, whereas men identified themselves with mind. Thus arose the concept of hierarchical dichotomies that value one part (mind, male) over another (body, female).

These dichotomies provided an ideal tool for the elite few to develop and maintain power over others and have remained strong in our thinking, language and institutions up to the present. Over the ensuing centuries, this power tool has been applied in virtually every field.

Religion always confers a special power on its priests and shamans because by definition they have special connections to the eternal and unchanging higher power. Early Christian theologians lost no time in taking over this tool of philosophy; they conferred on philosophy the title "handmaiden of religion." And we saw how these pre-Christian philosophies and theories of knowledge were pressed into service for the advancement of sacerdotal power. We saw this process epitomized by the belief in a supreme deity housed in a transcendent dematerialized white male body. Religion idealized the pure, unchanging and eternal, and the body—and everything associated with it—became not only abhorrent or frightening, but sinful and wicked; and as such was to be scourged and suppressed.

In science we saw how the aim was to separate ourselves from our bodies and our habitat to more perfectly observe and control them. The things that could be assimilated and understood by the human mind became equated with perfection—e.g., the circle could be understood in terms of Euclidean geometry, whereas an ellipse exhibits more complex mathematical properties; consequently those who insisted that the earth travels in an elliptical orbit were condemned as heretics. Further developments have shown the reality around us to be more and more difficult for mathematics to encompass. We have Goedel's incompleteness theorem, Heisenberg's uncertainty principle, quantum physics, chaos theory. We live in a world of asymptotes, not absolutes.

In medicine the process of fragmentation of the body-mind went even further. Not only was body isolated from mind but parts of the body were isolated from each other as specialization was carried to further and further extremes. Only recently has this trend been found to be so detrimental that a reversal has taken place; the field of general practice is now accorded equal status and respect with the other specialties. There is a slight but growing tendency to "listen to the whole patient," i.e., the body-mind.

Living within a capitalist economic system that requires the ownership and utilization of more and more resources, both human and otherwise, has created further divisiveness. The exercise of power by the few over the many is crucial to its continuance. On the production side of capitalism, we saw that workers' bodies can be bought and regimented in much the same way as the machines which assist in the generation of capital. In the workplace the best body is one which has no special needs but rather can perform in a "standard" way.

We saw that the body which best fits that standard and is rewarded most highly is the white male body. We also looked at how vulnerable a mind split from a body is to the incessant advertising required to create ever-new needs to consume. The shame that is created by not fitting a standard also plays right into the hands of advertisers who want people to try still one more way to fit in.

In law and politics, we saw how the public sphere was built on and defined by its opposition to the private sphere. The goal in the public sphere was to leave behind particularity for the "universal" good. Thus the physical body—and women—were relegated to the private sphere. In the early days of this country, this meant that only those who fit the standard body, i.e., white male property owners, were included in the founding documents, which were at least in part an attempt to ratify the status quo of the propertied.

The mind/body split gives those in power the justification for war, for slavery, for imperialism, and for evangelism. The mind/body split allows "us" to think that "we" have access to the "Universal" and "True" and "Right" way of the world. Anyone who does not know or pay homage to "our" God, our system of economics, our politics, our power-over mode of business is savage, immoral and/or wrong.

"We" think that our power-over systems of knowledge and science and technology show that we are right. And in a power-over sense they do: we have the largest and most destructive weapons in the world.

We have seen the detrimental effects that the hierarchical dichotomization has had on mind, body, men and women. In our systems of knowledge, instead of disembodiment and universality, we have institutionalized one very embodied point of view (that of the group which has the most power-over, white upper class males) as the universal one. The attempt to sever our knowledge from body and perspective and values is impossible because we live in our bodies and in our habitat at all times.

Body and women have been harmed by being put into object status and having no place from which to be heard. Human qualities associated with the female have been devalued and repressed. Men, too, have been hurt by having to cut off vital parts of themselves to conform to the standard. They are forced into power-over modes that remove them from their own bodies, from other people and from their habitat.

With the introduction of the Between model I have presented a new paradigm for moving us away from that split madness toward wholeness. It is made up of two interlinking circles. I propose that anything or anyone who has been dichotomized can be re-conceptualized through the use of this model.

Splitting ourselves is not just a benign and gentle act like pulling out a splinter; rather, it is the most violent act possible if the Between model accurately describes reality. We, in fact, slice ourselves through our most sacred, life-giving part, the part where we are connected to each other. Jeremy Rifkin in his book *Algeny* (1984) calls this act "desacralization." He states, "Humanity cannot afford to acknowledge all of the blood that it spills and the destruction it inflicts on the world in its effort to perpetuate itself…. Desacralization is the psychic process humanity employs to drain its prey of aliveness in order to make it palatable. It is our way of convincing ourselves that there is no fundamental likeness between us and other living things. For it is always more difficult to kill and incorporate things that one identifies with. The desacralization process allows human beings to repudiate the intimate relationship and likeness that exist between ourselves and all other things that live" (50-53).

Dichotomization is a way of desacralizing the world. No longer do we need to pay attention to our connections, that which is sacred. We then must rely on making dysbodied rules about how to behave because we cannot consult ourselves as whole and connected humans.

But the systems of ethics we devise, which operate on the assumption that we are dichotomized and pronounce "universal" principles of right and wrong, are not systems of ethics at all; they are a system of anesthetics (Irigaray, *Elemental Passions* 55). Once we are split from our bodies and each other, we are anesthetized and can no longer feel; of course we are then in grave danger of doing the "wrong" thing. The amputated foot still itches but we have no way of scratching it. When we can no longer feel and respond to those around us, we need an artificial system, a crutch to lean on to tell us what to do next.

The only reason we need a system of ethics to tell us how to behave is that we have already entered into and endorsed the most unethical behavior of all, behaving as if each of us are completely separate from our bodies, each other and the habitat. When we restore those connections so as to act from a place of wholeness, we will be able to see how we must act, situation by situation. We will have many more resources to draw on because we will enter a dialogue from a place of strength and alterity into the rich Betweens.

At a Women's Solstice Camp in Grass Valley, California, Deena Metzger gave a talk called "Healing the Body Politic and the Planet" (1992). In it she stated that we must create a context for health, a place where health is inevitable. I am saying a similar thing about wholeness. Our task in searching for wholeness will be to create a context of wholeness. That context is a society in which each particular entity has the power to express itself and to be heard in all of its alterity and in which no one viewpoint is standard and imposed on all the others, where we no longer operate from the notion that we are all separate and that our relationships are those of dominator/object and owner/owned.

The actual work we must do to become whole ethical people has nothing to do with formulating abstract rules of right or wrong or moving up a hierarchy of moral behavior; it has to do with becoming skilled in the integration of our bodies and minds, how to listen to the others in our habitat, including those who are not using a verbal language.

We explored ways to shift our consciousnesses toward wholeness, where our decisions can be made based on relationship and not on dichotomy and power-over. We looked at the women's and men's movements to see what parts of them fit with this different worldview. We then went on to show an application of the Between model to institutions as well as movements. We looked at the institution of motherhood and the issues surrounding it: pregnancy, abortion, adoption, surrogacy and infancy. When these issues are reframed from the perspective of relationship rather than power-over and ownership, they take on new meaning.

A large portion of the book is devoted to practical suggestions for making the changes I advocate. Some of these include ways to push on weaknesses in the present system, refusing to go along with dichotomization: by playing with language; blurring the categories and challenging separations on account of difference; embodying viewpoints; listening to "objects" speak; by women refusing object status; women speaking their pleasure; women exceeding the category of mother; and women acting as subject-objects with men as object-subjects.

Also important are envisioning and beginning to take the steps to construct the Between model: ways to strengthen alterity, particularly that of women, body and earth which have so long been in the object category and unheard.

Connection is not something we can force any one group of people to provide; it is not something that can be forced at all. We cannot continue to compel women to be responsible for making connections for the rest of us. What we need is to be certain that women and all others in a power-under position are encouraged to discover, retrieve, and develop their alterity so that all of us can live ethically, so that we can live in thriving Betweens. A return to a time of even more entrenched splits between men and women is not a path to the so-called Promised Land.

But the longing is real—the longing is real. Even while we repeatedly split ourselves up like nuclear fission, one reaction following the next, without time to breathe, we desperately seek and grasp after any-thing we can find that is whole or suspected of being whole. We have split ourselves from the soil, the air, the waters of this land, from our food, from each other and from our own bodies. We are thirsty for im-manent power, for a way for our whole selves to be seen so that we can live fully without shame for the parts of us that don't fit a standard.

One of the keys to strengthening our own alterity is to explore our uniquenesses, our perspectives, our experiences and feelings, our sto-ries, so that we are ready to enter into the Between in good faith, with a commitment to listening and dialogue. But having a strong alterity in isolation from everyone else will not be enough. We need to make sure that all women and also men of color have a place to stand and that voices which have been silent are heard; and we have to make sure that everyone and everything in our habitat has alterity and standing in any decisions that we make. That is what I call body politics.

Some of the expression of alterity cannot merely be verbal, cannot exclusively use a language that is itself hopelessly dichotomized. We will have to learn other ways to communicate and perhaps that is more a process of remembering than learning anew. We were all pre-verbal once and many of us have tried to communicate without words at vari-ous times throughout our lives. This work has room for many talents.

Many of these suggestions are things that we can do right now with-out systemic change, but which will lead inevitably to larger change. Change must occur in our body-minds, in the social and political set-ting and in the way we relate to our habitat. We must work on all of these levels at once.

When we start making our decisions from a place of body-mind interacting with other body-minds, we may feel a letting go of ego. It is not a letting go of particularity, however, but a strengthening of particu-larity which creates in us the strength to let go of me and mine and see the places that are shared with you and yours. True, we are then giving up control; the Between cannot be controlled. But we are by no means giving up our power; rather we are realizing our immanent power in the very process of letting go.

At the end of our fairy tale, when the emperor's toe begins to move in time with the music, this is not the Holy Spirit coming down from on high and entering his toe—this is the Spirit of the Whole that had been there all along but was split into tiny fragments. And still there was enough power to move his toe. That is immanent power which, if nurtured, will continue to grow until it is capable of powering him to seek out more and more connections.

The toe beginning to move in time with the music is a ritual act that can be incorporated into the service of the whole. Similarly, in our own small ways we can incorporate rituals that, while in themselves seemingly insignificant, are sacred acts. I have in mind that we faithfully and regularly, with an intent to feed the whole, ritualize the acts of taking bottles, cans and newspapers to recycling centers; contributing "garbage" to the compost pile; taking public transportation or bicycling wherever possible; supporting organic farms, eating and growing our food body-mindfully; and generally working toward liberty and alterity for all beings. When done in time with the music and out of awareness of our connections, such acts are just like the movement of the emperor's big toe—they are harbingers of a shift in consciousness. As more and more of us move in time with the music, not concerning ourselves with emperor time, the shift will begin to happen; it starts as lowly as the tapping of your toe.

This may feel mystical and in a way it is; it is ancient, unpredictable, powerful and bigger than our individual selves are. If this book has caused even one toe to let go and move into the Between, we will all have succeeded.

Notes

1 Joy Harjo, a Muskogee poet, has called this the "over-culture" (poetry reading at Laney College in Oakland, California, August 8, 1992).

2 Thank you to Mary Berg for this insightful suggestion.

3 Throughout this book I critique language and its effects; I want to be clear about my own usages. When speaking about women I use the pronoun "they" instead of "we" for reasons similar to those cited in Casey Miller and Kate Swift's *Word and Women* (xxi). Since my ideas have the tendency to divide the sexes in the short term, though the long-term desire is to unite them, I need the distance "they" provides. The "we" will be used to refer to all of humankind but not to a part of it with which men readers could not identify. I sometimes use the "universal" she to parody the use of the "universal" he and as a convenience instead of using the more awkward s/he.

4 Joan Jacobs Brumberg writes in *Fasting Girls* (1989): "Anyone who has worked with anorectics or read the critical literature understands that food refusal becomes increasingly involuntary as the physiological process of emaciation unfolds" (36). Brumberg states further, "I find the model of 'addiction to starvation' particularly compelling because when we think about anorexia nervosa in this way, there is room for incorporating biological, psychological and cultural components" (38).

5 For a detailed analysis of the linkage between the public and private and men and women in political philosophy, please see Carole Pateman, *The Disorder of Women* (1989).

6 See discussion of witches as healers, scientists and midwives in the pamphlet *Witches, Midwives and Nurses: a History of Women Healers* by Barbara Ehrenreich and Deirdre English (1973).

7 For further discussion see Douglas R. Hofstadter, *Metamagical Themes* (1986).

8 The Bohemian Grove is an ultra-exclusive and heavily guarded retreat in Northern California where the male power elite gather, ostensibly to "let their hair down," but actually to reinforce their power base.

9 For further information see Helena Norberg-Hodge, *Ancient Futures: Learning From Ladakh* (1991).

10 See Immanuel Kant's *Groundwork of the Metaphysics of Morals* for a precedent-setting example of what I refer to here.

11 For an exception to this rule, see Lorraine Code's *Epistemic Responsibility* (1987).

12 An aside about philosophers who do not think that ethics belongs in philosophy. One argument I have heard for this point of view is that ethics is subjective, a matter of taste and therefore not a subject that philosophy in its search for objective truth cares to deal with. In other words, ethics can never be "pure" enough for philosophy and for Truth. Here I treat ethics like any other part of philosophy; I do not relegate it to the lower half of the dichotomy with body and women.

13 See the work of feminist ethicists: Claudia Card, Sara Rudick, Sarah Hoagland, Rita Manning, Nel Noddings, Marti Kheel, etc.

14 Bertrand Russell, *Principia Mathematica* (1908). Bertrand Russell described this paradox as the set of all sets which do not contain themselves, and thus does not contain itself, so cannot contain all sets.

15 See for instance the concept of the "veil of ignorance" put forward by John Rawls in *A Theory of Justice* (1971).

16 See Jeremy Rifkin's *Beyond Beef* (1992) for an insightful discussion of all of the issues surrounding the cattle culture.

17 See Jessie Carney Smith and Robert L. Johns, *Statistical Record of Black America* (1995). People of color are disproportionately represented in the military and this becomes even more disproportionate in the ranks of enlisted personnel who are the main casualties in war.

18 In the terms used in this book, I define pornography as the eroticization of the splitting of mind from body, male from female, and/or self from other; the disregard for the alterity of oneself or another; and the subsequent use of sexual power-over, particularly over women and children.

19 For one example see studies done by Nancy Niedzielski at University of California, Santa Barbara presented at the Berkeley Women and Language Conference on April 5, 1992. She reported that 94% of boys and 50% of girls studied did not envision girls when the pronoun in reading materials was masculine.

20 See Erik H. Erikson, *Identity, Youth and Crisis* (1968). The eight stages he describes are: 1) trust vs. mistrust; 2) autonomy vs. shame, guilt; 3) initiative vs. guilt; 4) industry vs. inferiority; 5) identity vs. identity confusion; 6) intimacy vs. isolation; 7) generativity vs. stagnation; and 8) integrity vs. despair (94-95).

21 For an insightful discussion of McClintock's work, see Evelyn Fox Keller, *A Feeling for the Organism: The Life and Work of Barbara McClintock* (1983).

22 Deena Metzger, Speech given to the Women's Alliance Solstice Camp, June 19, 1992.

23 For more discussion of this issue see the conclusion of *Words of Power: A Feminist Reading of the History of Logic* by Andrea Nye (1990).

24 Essentialism in feminist writing is defined as "the view that females (or males) have an essential nature (e.g. nurturing and caring versus being aggressive and selfish) as opposed to differing by a variety of accidental or contingent features brought about by social forces" (Blackburn, *The Oxnard Dictionary of Philosophy* 125).

25 The Promise Keepers is a Christian group that was founded by Bill McCartney in 1991. They sponsor rallies in which men admit to having broken promises: that they have been insensitive, abandoned children, engaged in racial hatred,

supported pornography, and beat their wives. The September 3, 1997 issue of *Time* magazine cites that their numbers have grown from 4200 in 1991 to 1.1 million in six years.

26 Major splits were caused in the feminist movement over the importance of motherhood. Some feminists came out against it and others who were mothers themselves felt targeted as having less commitment to the cause as a result.

27 According to *The Amicus Journal* (Winter 1994), population growth is by far the worst threat to the global environment not in Africa and Asia but in the U.S. Our annual population growth has an impact on global warming about equal to China's and India's combined—and two and one half times bigger than Africa's (20).

28 See *The Encyclopedia of Psychology* by Roger Walsh, under the heading "Transpersonal Psychology" (qtd. in Warwick Fox, *Toward a Transpersonal Ecology* 299).

29 Elizabeth Roberts, June 18, 1993, Women's Solstice Camp, Grass Valley, California.

30 If male sexual identity is a social and political construction inextricably linked to male supremacy, then, John Stoltenberg (1990) argues, we must consider the implications of "refusing to be a man."

31 I would also encourage circles of men to get together to work on ways to tear down the dichotomous structure, to explore their connections to each other and to their habitat, to explore their alterity and to confront violence against women and against each other. It is, however, imperative that women begin to work on building alterity and step into leadership roles. Since women have been completely cut off from expression as subjects they need to find ways to express themselves as subject-objects. Although I speak in this section specifically of activities for women's circles, men too, could benefit from doing similar work.

32 Thanks to teacher, friend and artist Claudia Wolz who taught me about collaboration.

33 Patricia Waters, an art therapist, led this group at Women's Alliance Solstice Camp, June, 1993.

34 See Natalie Goldberg, *Wild Mind: Living the Writer's Life* (1990).

Bibliography

Adams, Carol J. *The Sexual Politics of Meat: A Feminist-Vegetarian Critical Theory*. New York: Continuum, 1990.

Aquinas, Thomas. *Supplement to Summa Theologica*. Trans. The Fathers of the English Dominican Province. New York: Benziger Bros., 1947.

Bartky, Sandra Lee. *Femininity and Domination*. New York and London: Routledge, 1990.

Beauvoir, Simone de. *The Second Sex*. Trans. H.M. Parshley. New York: Random House, 1974.

Bennett, William and Joel Gurin. *The Dieter's Dilemma*. New York: Basic Books, 1982.

Berman, Ruth. "From Aristotle's Dualism to Materialist Dialectics: Feminist Transformation of Science and Society." *Gender/Body/Knowledge*. Eds. Allison M. Jaggar and Susan R. Bordo. New Brunswick: Rutgers UP, 1989. 224-255.

Berry, Thomas. *The Dream of the Earth*. San Francisco: Sierra Club Books, 1988.

Blackburn, Simon. *The Oxnard Dictionary of Philosophy*. Oxford and New York: Oxford University Press, 1994.

Bly, Robert. *Iron John: A Book About Men*. Reading, MA: Addison-Wesley, 1990.

Braverman, Harry. *Labor and Monopoly Capital: The Degradation of Work in the Twentieth Century*. New York: Monthly Review Press, 1974.

Bruch, Hilde. *Eating Disorders: Obesity, Anorexia, and the Person Within*. New York: Basic Books, 1973.

Brumberg, Joan Jacobs. *Fasting Girls: The History of Anorexia Nervosa*. Canada: Penguin Books Canada, 1989.

Butler, Samuel. *Selections From the Note-Books*. Great Britain: The Travelers' Library, 1950.

Butler, Judith. "Gender Trouble, Feminist Theory, and Psychoanalytic Discourse." *Feminism/Postmodernism*. Ed. Linda J. Nicholson. New York: Routledge, 1990. 324-340.

Capra, Fritjof. *The Turning Point*. New York: Bantam Books, 1983.

Card, Claudia. "Caring and Evil." *Hypatia* (Spring 1990): 101-108.

Chapkis, Wendy. *Beauty Secrets: Women and the Politics of Appearance*. Boston: South End Press, 1986.

Chodorow, Nancy. *The Reproduction of Mothering: Psychoanalysis and the Sociology of Gender*. Berkeley and Los Angeles: University of California Press, 1978.

Code, Lorraine. *Epistemic Responsibility*. Hanover and London: University Press of New England, 1987.

Daly, Mary. *Gyn\Ecology: The Metaphysics of Radical Feminism*. Boston: Beacon Press, 1978.

Debold, Elizabeth, Marie Wilson, and Idelisse Malave. *Mother Daughter Revolution: From Betrayal to Power*. Reading, Massachusetts: Addison-Wesley Publishing Company, 1993.

Descartes, Rene. *The Philosophical Writings of Descartes, Vol. II*. Trans. John Cottingham, Robert Stoothoff and Douglas Murdoch. Cambridge: Cambridge UP, 1984.

Eckholm, Erik. "Disappearing Species: The Social Challenge." *Worldwatch Paper 22*. Washington, DC: Worldwatch Institute, June 1978.

Ehrenreich, Barbara and Deirdre English. *Witches, Midwives and Nurses: a History of Women Healers*. New York: The Feminist Press, 1973.

Eisler, Riane. *The Chalice and the Blade: Our History, Our Future*. San Francisco: Harper & Row, 1987.

Erikson, Erik H. *Identity, Youth and Crisis*. New York: Norton, 1968.

Firestone, Shulamith. *The Dialectic of Sex: The Case for Feminist Revolution*. New York: Bantam Books, 1971.

Foucault, Michel. *Discipline and Punish: The Birth of the Prison*. Trans. Alan Sheridan. New York: Vintage Books, 1979.

Fox, Warwick. *Toward a Transpersonal Ecology*. Boston and London: Shambhala, 1990.

Frankenberg, Ruth. *White Women, Race Matters: The Social Construction of Whiteness*. Minneapolis: University of Minnesota Press, 1993.

French, Marilyn. *The War Against Women*. New York: Ballantine Books, 1992.

Freud, Anna. Foreword. *On Not Being Able to Paint*. By Marion Milner (a.k.a. Joanna Field). Los Angeles: Jeremy Tarcher, 1957.

Fromm, Erich. "The Erich Fromm Theory of Aggression." *New York Times Magazine*, 27 February 1972.

Frye, Marilyn. *Politics of Reality*. Freedom, California: The Crossing Press, 1983.

Funk & Wagnalls. *Standard College Dictionary*. New York: Harcourt, Brace & World, 1963.

Gatens, Moira. *Feminism and Philosophy: Perspectives on Difference and Equality*. Bloomington and Indianapolis: Indiana UP, 1991.

Gilligan, Carol. *In a Different Voice*. Cambridge: Harvard UP, 1982.

Gleick, James. *Chaos: Making a New Science*. New York: Viking, 1987.

Goldberg, Natalie. *Wild Mind: Living the Writer's Life*. New York: Bantam, 1990.

___. *Writing Down the Bones*. Boston: Shambhala, 1986.

Grosz, Elizabeth. *Sexual Subversions: Three French Feminists.* Winchester, Mass.: Unwin Hyman, 1989.

Hanh, Thich Nhat. *Peace is Every Step.* Ed. Arnold Kotler. New York: Bantam Books, 1991.

Harding, Christopher, ed. *Wingspan: Inside the Men's Movement.* New York: St. Martin's Press, 1992.

Hartley, Ruth E. "Sex-Role Pressures and the Socialization of the Male Child." *Psychological Reports* 5 (1959): 457-68.

Hayles, N. Katherine. *Chaos Bound.* Ithaca and London: Cornell UP, 1990.

Hochschild, Arlie. *The Second Shift.* New York: Avon Books, 1989.

Hofstadter, Douglas R. *Metamagical Themes.* New York: Bantam Books, 1986.

Irigaray, Luce. *Elemental Passions.* 1982. Trans. Joanne Collie and Judith Still. New York: Routledge, 1992.

___. *je, tu, nous: Toward a Culture of Difference.* 1990. Trans. Alison Martin. New York: Routledge, 1993.

___. *Speculum of the Other Woman.* 1974. Trans. Gillian C. Gill. Ithaca, New York: Cornell UP, 1985.

___. *This Sex Which is Not One.* 1977. Trans. Catherine Porter. Ithaca, NY: Cornell UP, 1985.

Johnson, Don. *Body.* Boston: Beacon Press, 1983.

Johnson, Sonia. *Going Out of Our Minds.* Freedom, California: The Crossing Press, 1987.

Kant, Immanuel. *Groundwork of the Metaphysics of Morals.* New York: Harper and Row, 1964.

Keller, Evelyn Fox. *A Feeling for the Organism: The Life and Work of Barbara McClintock.* New York: Freeman, 1983.

___. *Reflections on Gender and Science.* New Haven and London: Yale UP, 1985.

Kheel, Marti. "From Healing Herbs to Deadly Drugs." *Healing the Wounds: The Promise of Ecofeminism.* Ed. Judith Plant. Philadelphia: New Society Publishers, 1989. 96-111.

Knowles, John H. *Doing Better and Feeling Worse: Health in the United States.* New York: Norton and Co., 1977.

Kohlberg, Lawrence. *The Philosophy of Moral Development: Moral Stages and the Idea of Justice.* San Francisco: Harper and Row, 1981.

Kristeva, Julia. "Woman Can Never Be Defined." *New French Feminisms.* Eds. Elaine Marks and Isabelle de Courtivron. New York: Schoken Books, 1981. 137-141.

Merchant, Carolyn. *The Death of Nature: Women, Ecology and the Scientific Revolution.* San Francisco: Harper & Row, 1980.

Miller, Casey and Kate Swift. *Words and Women.* New York: HarperCollins, 1991.

Milner, Marion (a.k.a. Joanna Field). *On Not Being Able to Paint.* Los Angeles: Jeremy Tarcher, 1957.

Natural Resources Defense Council. *The Amicus Journal.* Winter 1994.

Nicolis, Gregoire. "Physics of far-from equilibrium systems and self-organization." *The New Physics.* Ed. Davies. New York: Cambridge UP, 1989. 316-347.

Nilsen, Alleen Pace. "Grammatical Gender and Its Relationship to the Equal Treatment of Males and Females in Children's Books." Diss. University of Iowa, 1973.

Noddings, Nel. *Caring: a Feminist Approach to Ethics and Moral Education.* Berkeley: University of California Press, 1984.

Norberg-Hodge, Helena. *Ancient Futures: Learning From Ladakh.* San Francisco: Sierra Club, 1991.

Nye, Andrea. *Words of Power: A Feminist Reading of the History of Logic.* New York and London: Routledge, 1990.

Oxford Universal Dictionary. 3rd edition. Oxford: The Clarendon Press, 1955.

Pateman, Carole. *The Disorder of Women: Democracy, Feminism and Political Theory.* Stanford: Stanford UP, 1989.

Plato. *Phaedo.* Trans. G.M.A. Grube. Indianapolis: Hackett, 1977.

___. *The Republic of Plato.* Trans. Francis MacDonald Cornford. London, Oxford, New York: Oxford UP, 1945.

Prigogine, Ilya and Isabelle Stengers. *Order out of Chaos.* New York: Bantam Books, 1984.

Rawls, John. *A Theory of Justice.* Cambridge: Harvard UP, 1971.

Rich, Adrienne. "Compulsory Heterosexuality and Lesbian Existence." *Signs* 5.4 (Summer 1980): 631-660.

Rifkin, Jeremy. *Algeny.* Middlesex, England: Penguin Books, 1983.

___. *Beyond Beef.* New York: Dutton, 1992.

Roach, Catherine. "Loving Your Mother: On the Woman-Nature Relationship." *Hypatia* 6.1 (Spring 1991): 46-59.

Robbins, John. *Diet for a New America.* Walpole, New Hampshire: StillPoint Publishing, 1987.

Rothman, Barbara Katz. *Recreating Motherhood.* New York: W.W. Norton, 1990.

Ruether, Rosemary Radford. "Misogynism and the Virginal Feminine in the Fathers of the Church." *Religion and Sexism: Images of Women in the Jewish and Christian Traditions* Ed. Rosemary Radford Ruether. New York: Simon and Schuster, 1974. 150-183.

Russell, Bertrand and Alfred North Whitehead. *Principia Mathematica.* Cambridge: University Press, 1908.

Schmidt, Michael A., Lendon H. Smith and Keith W. Sehnert. *Beyond Antibiotics.* Berkeley: North Atlantic Books, 1993.

Schott, Robin May. *Cognition and Eros: A Critique of the Kantian Paradigm*. Boston: Beacon Press, 1988.

Smith, Jessie Carney and Robert L. Johns, eds. *Statistical Record of Black America*. New York: Gale Research Company, 1995.

Shange, Ntozake. "We Need a God Who Bleeds Now." *A Daughter's Geography*. New York: St. Martin's Press, 1983.

Spretnak, Charlene. "Treating the Symptoms, Ignoring the Cause." *Women Respond to the Men's Movement*. Ed. Kay Leigh Hagan. San Francisco: HarperCollins, 1992. 169-175.

Starhawk. *Dreaming the Dark: Magic, Sex and Politics*. Boston: Beacon Press, 1982.

Stern, Daniel. *The First Relationship, Mother and Infant*. Cambridge: Harvard UP, 1977.

Stoltenberg, John. *Refusing to be a Man: Essays on Sex and Justice*. New York: Meridian, 1990.

Tavris, Carol. *The Mismeasure of Woman*. New York: Touchstone. 1992.

Taylor, Jill McLean, Carol Gilligan and Amy M. Sullivan. *Between Voice and Silence: Women and Girls, Race and Relationship*. Cambridge, Massachusetts: Harvard UP, 1995.

U. S. Department of Commerce. *Statistical Abstract of the United States* 1996, Economic and Statistics Administration, Bureau of Census, 116th edition.

Valverde, Mariana. *Sex, Power and Pleasure*. Philadelphia: New Society Publishers, 1987.

Webster's New World Dictionary. Warner Books Edition. New York: Warner Books, 1987.

Whitford, Margaret. *Luce Irigaray: Philosophy in the Feminine*. London and New York: Routledge, 1991.

Wolf, Naomi. *The Beauty Myth*. New York: Anchor Books, 1991.

Yalom, Marilyn. *A History of the Breast*. New York: Alfred A. Knopf, 1997.

Young, Al. *Collected Poems 1956-1990*. Berkeley: Creative Arts Book Company, 1992.

References for Further Reading

Women and Philosophy

Anzaldua, Gloria, ed. *Making Face, Making Soul = Haciendo Caras: Creative and Critical Perspectives by Women of Color*. San Francisco: Aunt Lute Foundation Books, 1990.

Beauvoir, Simone de. *The Second Sex*. Trans. H.M. Parshley. New York: Random House, 1974.

Daly, Mary. *Gyn/Ecology: The Metaethics of Radical Feminism*. Boston: Beacon Press, 1990.

Dinnerstein, Dorothy. *The Mermaid and the Minotaur: Sexual Arrangements and Human Malaise*. New York: HarperCollins, 1976.

Donovan, Josephine. *Feminist Theory: The Intellectual Traditions of American Feminism*. New York: Continuum, 1985.

Firestone, Shulamith. *The Dialectic of Sex: The Case for Feminist Revolution*. New York: Bantam Books, 1970.

Frye, Marilyn. *The Politics of Reality: Essays in Feminist Theory*. Freedom, California: The Crossing Press, 1983.

___. *Willful Virgin*. Freedom, California: The Crossing Press, 1992.

Gatens, Moira. *Feminism and Philosophy: Perspectives on Difference and Equality*. Bloomington and Indianapolis: Indiana UP, 1991.

Gould, Carol and Marx W. Wartofsky, eds. *Women and Philosophy: Toward a Theory of Liberation*. New York: G. P. Putnam's Sons, 1976.

Grosz, Elizabeth. *Space, Time and Perversion*. New York: Routledge, 1995.

hooks, bell. *FEMINIST THEORY: from margin to center*. Boston: South End Press, 1984.

___. *Talking back: thinking feminist, thinking black*. Boston: South End Press, 1989.

Keller, Catherine. *From a Broken Web: Separation, Sexism and Self*. Boston: Beacon Press, 1986.

Lloyd, Genevieve. *The Man of Reason: "Male" and "Female" in Western Philosophy*. Minneapolis: University of Minnesota Press, 1984.

Massey, Marilyn Chapin. *Feminine Soul: The Fate of an Ideal*. Boston: Beacon Press, 1985.

Mohanty, Chandra Talpade, Ann Russon, and Lourdes Torres, eds. *Third World Women and the Politics of Feminism*. Bloomington and Indianapolis: Indiana UP, 1991.

Oliver, Kelly. *Womanizing Nietzsche: Philosophy's Relation of the "Feminine"*. New York: Routledge, 1995.

Russell, Dora. *The Dora Russell Reader: 57 Years of Writing and Journalism, 1925-1982*. London: Pandora Press, 1983.

Schott, Robin May. *Cognition and Eros: A Critique of the Kantian Paradigm*. Boston: Beacon Press, 1988.

Spelman, Elizabeth V. *The Inessential Woman: Problems of Exclusion in Feminist Thought*. Boston: Beacon Press, 1988.

Women and Moral Theory

Card, Claudia, ed. *Feminist Ethics*. Lawrence, Kansas: Kansas UP, 1991.

French, Marilyn. *Beyond Power: On Women, Men and Morals*. New York: Ballantine Books, 1985.

Gilligan, Carol. *In a Different Voice*. Cambridge: Harvard UP, 1982.

Harrison, Beverly. *Making Connections: Essays in Feminist Social Ethics*. Boston: Beacon Press, 1985.

Kittay, Eva Feder and Diana T. Meyers, eds. *Women and Moral Theory*. New York: Rowman and Littlefield, 1987.

Manning, Rita C. *Speaking From the Heart: a Feminist Perspective on Ethics*. Lanham, Maryland: Rowman & Littlefield, 1992.

Noddings, Nel. *Caring: A Feminine Approach to Ethics & Moral Education*. Berkeley and Los Angeles: University of California Press, 1984.

___. *Women and Evil*. Berkeley and Los Angeles: University of California Press, 1989.

Pearsall, Marilyn, ed. *Women and Values: Readings in Recent Feminist Philosophy*. Belmont, California: Wadsworth, 1986.

Ruddick, Sara. *Maternal Thinking: Toward a Politics of Peace*. New York: Ballantine Books, 1989.

Political Philosophy

Bock, Gisela and Susan James, eds. *Beyond Equality and Difference: Citizenship, Feminist Politics and Female Subjectivity*. London and New York: Routledge, 1992.

Eisenstein, Zillah R. *The Color Of Gender: Regaining Democracy*. Berkeley and Los Angeles: University of California Press, 1994.

Frankenberg, Ruth. *White Women, Race Matters: The Social Construction of Whiteness*. Minneapolis: University of Minnesota Press, 1993.

hooks, bell. *Killing Rage: Ending Racism*. New York: Holt and Co., 1995.

Phillips, Anne, ed. *Feminism and Equality*. New York: New York UP, 1987.

Pateman, Carole. *The Disorder of Women: Democracy, Feminism and Political Theory*. Stanford: Stanford UP, 1989.

___. *The Sexual Contract*. Stanford: Stanford Universtiy Press, 1988.

Pateman, Carole and Elizabeth Gross, eds. *Feminist Challenges: Social and Political Theory*. Boston: Northeastern UP, 1986.

Walker, Alice. *Anything We Love Can Be Saved: A Writer's Activism*. New York: Random House, 1997.

Women and Religion

Christ, Carol. *Diving Deep and Surfacing: Women Writers on Spiritual Quest*. Boston: Beacon Press, 1988.

Christ, Carol and Judith Plaskow, eds. *Weaving the Visions: New Patterns in Feminist Spirituality*. San Francisco: Harper & Row, 1989.

Cooey, Paula M., Sharon Farmer and Mary Ellen Ross, eds. *Embodied Love: Sensuality and Relationship as Feminist Values*. New York: Harper & Row, 1987.

Daly, Mary. *Beyond God the Father: Toward a Philosophy of Women's Liberation*. 1973. Boston: Beacon Press, 1985.

Fiorenza, Elisabeth Schussler. *In Memory of Her: A Feminist Theological Reconstruction of Christian Origins*. New York: Crossroad, 1990.

Johnson, Sonia. *Going Out of Our Minds*. Freedom, California: The Crossing Press, 1987.

Morton, Nelle. *The Journey is Home*. Boston: Beacon Press, 1985.

Oches, Carol. *Behind the Sex of God: Toward a New Consciousness Transcending Matriarchy and Patriarchy*. Boston: Beacon Press, 1977.

Ruether, Rosemary Radford, ed. *Religion and Sexism*. New York: Simon and Schuster, 1974.

Women and Language

Daly, Mary and Jane Caputi. *Websters' First New Intergalactic Wickedary of the English Language*. Boston: Beacon Press, 1987.

Grahn, Judy. *Another Mother Tongue: Gay Words, Gay Worlds*. Boston: Beacon Press, 1984.

Henley, Nancy M. *Body Politics: Power, Sex & Non-Verbal Communication*. New York: Simon & Schuster, 1977.

Miller, Casey and Kate Swift. *Words and Women*. 1976. New York: HarperCollins, 1991.

Nye, Andrea. *Words of Power: A Feminist Reading of the History of Logic*. New York: Routledge, 1990.

Spender, Dale. *Man Made Language*. London: Routledge & Kegan Paul, 1980.

Tannen, Deborah. *You Just Don't Understand: Women and Men In Conversation*. New York: William Morrow, 1990.

Women and Body Image

Brown, Laura and Esther D. Rothblum, eds. *Overcoming Fear of Fat*. New York and London: Harrington Park Press, 1989.

Bruch, Hilde. *Conversations with Anorexics*. Eds. Danita Czyzewski and Melanie A. Suhr. New York: Basic Books, 1988.

___. *Eating Disorders: Obesity, Anorexia, and the Person Within*. New York: Basic Books, 1973.

Brumberg, Joan Jacobs. *Fasting Girls: The History of Anorexia Nervosa*. Canada: Penguin Books Canada, 1989.

Chapkis, Wendy. *Beauty Secrets: Women and the Politics of Appearance*. Boston: South End Press, 1986.

Chernin, Kim. *The Hungry Self: Women, Eating & Identity*. New York: Random House, 1985.

___. *The Obsession: Reflections on the Tyranny of Slenderness*. New York: Harper & Row, 1981.

Freedman, Rita. *Bodylove: Learning to Like Our Looks and Ourselves*. New York: Harper & Row, 1989.

Orbach, Susie. *Fat is a Feminist Issue*. New York: Berkley Books, 1979.

___. *Fat is a Feminist Issue II*. New York: Berkley Books, 1982.

Roth, Geneen. *Feeding the Hungry Heart: The Experience of Compulsive Eating*. New York: New American Library, 1983.

Schoenfelder, Lisa and Barb Wieser, eds. *Shadow on a Tightrope: Writings by Women on Fat Oppression*. San Francisco: Spinsters/Aunt Lute, 1983.

Szekely, Eva. *Never Too Thin*. Ontario, Canada: The Women's Press, 1988.

Wolf, Naomi. *The Beauty Myth*. New York: Anchor Books, 1991.

Yalom, Marilyn. *A History of the Breast*. New York: Alfred A. Knopf, 1997.

Food

Adams, Carol J. *The Sexual Politics of Meat: A Feminist-Vegetarian Critical Theory.* New York: Continuum, 1990.

Bennett, William and Joel Gurin. *The Dieter's Dilemma.* New York: Basic Books, 1982.

Barnard, Neal, M.D. *The Power of Your Plate.* Summertown, Tennessee: Book Publishing Co., 1990.

Klaper, Michael. *Vegan Nutrition: Pure and Simple.* Umatilla, Florida: Gentle World, 1988.

Rifkin, Jeremy. *Beyond Beef.* New York: Dutton, 1992.

Robbins, John. *Diet for a New America.* Walpole, New Hampshire: StillPoint Publishing, 1987.

Rosen, Steven. *Food for the Spirit: Vegetarianism and World Religions.* New York: Bala Books, 1987.

Body

Foster, Patricia, ed. *Minding the Body: Women Writers on Body and Soul.* New York: Doubleday, 1994.

Goldenberg, Naomi R. *Returning Words to Flesh: Feminism, Psychoanalysis, and the Resurrection of the Body.* Boston: Beacon Press, 1990.

Johnson, Don. *Body.* Boston: Beacon Press, 1983.

Kapit, Wynn and Lawrence M. Elson. *The Anatomy Coloring Book.* New York: Harper & Row, 1977.

Martin, Emily. *The Woman in the Body: A Cultural Analysis of Reproduction.* Boston: Beacon Press, 1987.

Olsen, Andrea with Caryn McHose. *BodyStories: A Guide to Experiential Anatomy.* Barrytown, New York: Station Hill Press, 1991.

Schmidt, Michael A., Lendon H. Smith and Keith W. Sehnert. *Beyond Antibiotics.* Berkeley: North Atlantic Books, 1993.

Steinman, Louise. *The Knowing Body: Elements of Contemporary Performance & Dance.* Boston & London: Shambhala, 1986.

Habitat

Berry, Thomas. *The Dream of the Earth.* San Francisco: Sierra Club Books, 1988

Carson, Rachael. *Silent Spring.* Greenwich, Connecticutt: Fawcett, 1962.

Collard, Andree with Joyce Contrucci. *Rape of the Wild: Man's Violence Against Animals and the Earth.* London: The Women's Press, 1988.

Devall, Bill. *Simple in Means, Rich in Ends*. Salt Lake City: Peregrine Smith Books, 1988.

Fox, Warwick. *Toward a Transpersonal Ecology*. Boston: Shambhala, 1990.

Mander, Jerry. *In the Absence of the Sacred: The Failure of Technology and the Survival of the Indian Nations*. San Francisco: Sierra Club Books, 1991.

Regan, Tom. *The Case for Animal Rights*. Berkeley, California: University of California Press, 1983.

Sessions, George and Bill Devall. *Deep Ecology*. Salt Lake City: Gibbs Smith, 1985.

Shiva, Vandana. *The Violence of the Green Revolution: Ecological Degradation and Political Conflict*. London: Zed Books, 1991.

Singer, Peter. *In Defense of Animals*. New York: Basil Blackwell, 1985.

`Ecofeminism

Adams, Carol. *Ecofeminism and the Sacred*. New York: Continuum Publication Group, 1994.

Bigwood, Carol. *Earth Muse: Feminism, Nature, and Art*. Philadelphia: Temple University Press, 1993.

Caldecott, Leonie, and Stephanie Leland, eds. *Reclaim the Earth: Women Speak Out for Life on Earth*. London: The Women's Press, 1983.

Collard, Andree with Contrucci, Joyce. *Rape of the Wild: Man's Violence Against Animals and the Earth*. London: The Women's Press, 1988.

Diamond, Irene. *Fertile Ground: Women, Earth and the Limits of Control*. Boston: Beacon Press, 1994.

Diamond, Irene and Gloria Feman Orenstein, eds. *Reweaving the World: The Emergence of Ecofeminism*. San Francisco: Sierra Club Books, 1990.

Gaard, Greta Claire. *Ecofeminism: Women, Animals, Nature (Ethics and Action)*. Philadelphia: Temple University Press, 1993.

Hypatia: A Journal of Feminist Philosophy. Special Issue on Ecological Feminism: 6.1 (Spring 1991).

King, Ynestra. *Ecofeminism and the Reenchantment of Nature*. Boston: Beacon Press, 1991.

Midgley, Mary. *Beast and Man: The Roots of Human Nature*. Ithaca, New York: Cornell University Press, 1978.

___. *Heart and Mind*. New York: St. Matrtin's Press, 1981.

Noske, Barbara. *Humans and Other Animals*. London: Pluto Press, 1989.

Plant, Judith, ed. *Healing the Wounds: The Promise of Ecofeminism*. Philadelphia: New Society Publishers, 1989.

Ruether, Rosemary Radford. *New Woman/New Earth: Sexist Ideologies and Human Liberation*. New York: Seabury Press, 1983.

Shiva, Vandana. *Staying Alive: Women, Ecology, and Survival in India*. London: Zed Books, 1988.

Shiva, Vandana and Maria Meis. *Ecofeminism*. London: Zed Books, 1993.

Sturgeon, Noel. *Ecofeminist Natures: Race, Gender, Feminist Theory and Political Action*. New York: Routledge, 1997.

Warren, Karen and Nisvan Erkal, eds. *Ecofeminism: Women, Culture, Nature*. Indianapolis: Indiana Universtiy Press, 1997.

Sexuality

Coward, Rosalind. *Female Desires: How They Are Sought, Bought and Packaged*. New York: Grove Weidenfeld, 1985.

D'emilio, John and Estelle B Freedman. *Intimate Matters: A History of Sexuality in America*. New York: Harper & Row, 1988.

Dworkin, Andrea. *Pornography: Men Possessing Women*. New York: Putnam's Sons, 1979.

Griffin, Susan. *Pornography and Silence: Culture's Revenge Against Nature*. New York: Harper & Row, 1981.

Ortner, Sherry B. and Harriet Whitehead, eds. *Sexual Meanings: The Cultural Construction of Gender and Sexuality*. New York: Cambridge University Press, 1981.

Snitow, Ann, Christine Stansell and Sharon Thompson, eds. *Powers of Desire: the Politics of Sexuality*. New York: Monthly Review Press, 1983.

Valverde, Mariana. *Sex, Power and Pleasure*. Philadelphia: New Society Publishers, 1987.

Women's Spirituality/Power

Adler, Margot. *Drawing Down the Moon: Witches, Druids, Goddess-worshippers, and Other Pagans in America Today*. Rev. ed. Boston: Beacon Press, 1986.

Allen, Paula Gunn. *The Sacred Hoop: Recovering the Feminine in American Indian Traditions*. Boston: Beacon Press, 1986.

Anderson, Sherry Ruth and Patricia Hopkins. *The Feminine Face of God: The Unfolding of the Sacred in Women*. New York: Bantam Books, 1992.

Bolen, Jean Shinoda. *Godesses in Every Woman: A New Psychology of Women*. New York: Harper & Row, 1984.

Olson, Carl, ed. *The Book of the Goddess, Past and Present: An Introduction to Her Religion*. New York: Crossroad, 1990.

Rosenwasser, Penny. *Visionary Voices: Women on Power*. San Francisco: Aunt Lute Books, 1992.

Sjöö, Monica and Barbara Mor. *The Great Cosmic Mother: Rediscovering the Religion of the Earth.* San Francisco: Harper& Row, 1987.

Spretnak, Charlene, ed. *The Politics of Women's Spirituality.* New York: Doubleday/Anchor, 1982.

Starhawk. *Dreaming the Dark: Magic, Sex and Politics.* Boston: Beacon Press, 1982.

___. *Truth or Dare: Encounters with Power, Authority, and Mystery.* San Francisco: Harper & Row, 1987.

Stone, Merlin. *Ancient Mirrors of Womanhood: A Treasury of Goddesses and Heroine Lore from Around the World.* Boston: Beacon Press, 1984.

___. *When God Was a Woman.* New York/London: Harvest/Harcourt Brace Jovanovich, 1976.

Taylor, Jill McLean, Carol Gilligan and Amy M. Sullivan. *Between Voice and Silence: Women and Girls, Race and Relationship.* Cambridge, Massachusetts: Harvard UP, 1995.

Walker, Alice. *Living By the Word: Selected Writings: 1973-1987.* San Diego: Harcourt Brace Jovanovich, 1988.

Domination/Power-over

Anzaldua, Gloria. *Borderlands/La Frontera: The New Mestiza.* San Francisco: Spinsters/Aunt Lute, 1987.

Anzaldua, Gloria, ed. *Making Face, Making Soul = Haciendo Caras: Creative and Critical Perspectives by Women of Color.* San Francisco: Aunt Lute Foundation Books, 1990.

Bartky, Sandra Lee. *Femininity and Domination: Studies in the Phenomenology of Oppression.* New York and London: Routledge, 1990.

Benjamin, Jessica. *Bonds of Love: Psychoanalysis, Feminism, and the Problem of Domination.* New York: Pantheon Books, 1988.

Dinnerstein, Dorothy. *The Mermaid and the Minotaur: Sexual Arrangements and Human Malaise.* New York: HarperPerennial, 1991.

Eisler, Riane. *The Chalice and the Blade: Our History, Our Future.* San Francisco: Harper & Row, 1987.

Ehrenreich, Barbara and Deirdre English. *Witches, Midwives and Nurses: a History of Women Healers.* New York: The Feminist Press, 1973.

Faludi, Susan. *Backlash: The Undeclared War against American Women.* New York: Crown Publishers, 1991.

Hester, Marianne. *Lewd Women & Wicked Witches: A Study of the Dynamics of Male Domination.* New York and London: Routledge, 1992.

Steinem, Gloria. *Moving Beyond Words.* New York: Simon & Schuster, 1994.

____. *Outrageous Acts and Everyday Rebellions*. 2nd Ed. New York: Henry Holt, 1995.

Tuan, Yui-Fu. *Dominance and Affection: The Making of Pets*. New Haven, Connecticut: Yale University Press, 1984.

Motherhood

Caplan, Paula J. *Don't Blame Mother: Mending the Mother-Daughter Relationship*. New York: Harper & Row, 1989.

Chodorow, Nancy. *The Reproduction of Mothering: Psychoanalysis and the Sociology of Gender*. Berkeley and Los Angeles: University of California Press, 1978.

Debold, Elizabeth, Marie Wilson, and Idelisse Malave. *Mother Daughter Revolution: From Betrayal to Power*. Reading, Massachusetts: Addison-Wesley, 1993.

Hochschild, Arlie. *The Second Shift*. New York: Avon, 1990.

O'Brien, Mary. *The Politics of Reproduction*. Boston: Routledge and Kegan Paul, 1981.

Rich, Adrienne. *Of Woman Born: Motherhood as Experience and Institution*. New York and London: W.W. Norton, 1976.

Rothman, Barbara Katz. *In Labor: Women and Power in the Birthplace*. New York and London: W.W. Norton, 1991.

____. *Recreating Motherhood: Ideology and Technology in a Patriarchal Society*. New York and London: W. W. Norton, 1989.

____. *The Tentative Pregnancy: Prenatal Diagnosis and the Future of Motherhood*. New York: Penguin, 1986.

Stern, Daniel. *The First Relationship, Infant and Mother*. Cambridge: Harvard UP, 1977.

Trebilcot, Joyce, ed. *Mothering: Essays in Feminist Theory*. New Jersey: Rowan & Allanheld, 1984.

New Paradigm Science

Capra, Fritjof. *The Tao of Physics*. 2nd ed. Boston: New Science Library, 1985.

____. *The Turning Point*. New York: Bantam Books, 1983.

Dossey, Larry. *Space, Time & Medicine*. Boston: New Science Library, 1982.

Easlea, Brian. *Fathering the Unthinkable: Masculinity, Scientists and the Nuclear Arms Race*. London: Pluto Press, 1983.

____. *Science and Sexual Oppression: Patriarchy's Confrontation with Women and Nature*. London: Weidenfeld and Nicholson, 1981.

____. *Witch-hunting, Magic and the New Philosophy: An Introduction to the Debates of the Scientific Revolution 1450-1750*. Sussex: Harvester Press, 1980.

Ella, Irene. *The Female Animal*. New York: Henry Holt, 1988.

Gleick, James. *Chaos: Making a New Science*. New York : Viking, 1987.

Haraway, Donna. *Simians, Cyborgs, and Women: The Reinvention of Nature*. New York: Routledge, Chapman and Hall, 1991.

Harding, Sandra. *The Science Question in Feminism*. Ithaca, New York: Cornell University Press, 1986.

Harding, Sandra and Jean F. O'Barr. *Sex and Scientific Inquiry*. Chicago: University of Chicago Press, 1986.

Hayles, N. Katherine. *Chaos Bound*. Ithaca and London: Cornell UP, 1990.

Jacobus, Mary, Evelyn Fox Keller, and Sally Shuttleworth, eds. *Body/Politics: Women and the Discourses of Science*. New York and London: Routledge, 1990.

Jaggar, Allison M. and Susan R. Bordo, eds. *Gender/Body/Knowledge*. New Brunswick: Rutgers UP, 1989.

Keller, Evelyn Fox. *A Feeling for the Organism: The Life and Work of Barbara McClintock*. New York: Freeman, 1983.

___. *Reflections of Gender and Science*. New Haven and London: Yale UP, 1985.

Keller, Evelyn Fox and Shuttleworth, Sally, eds. *Body/Politics: Women and the Discourses of Science*. New York and London: Routledge, 1990.

Merchant, Carolyn. *The Death of Nature: Women, Ecology and the Scientific Revolution*. San Francisco: Harper & Row, 1980.

Prigogine, Ilya and Isabelle Stengers. *Order Out of Chaos*. New York: Bantam Books, 1984.

Rifkin, Jeremy. *Algeny*. Middlesex, England: Penguin Books, 1983.

Shepherd, Linda Jean. *Lifting the Veil: The Feminine Face of Science*. Boston and London: Shambhala, 1993.

Tavris, Carol. *The Mismeasure of Women*. New York: Simon & Schuster, 1992.

French Feminism and Postmodernism

Allen, Jefner and Iris Marion Young, eds. *The Thinking Muse: Feminism and Modern French Philosophy*. Bloomington and Indianapolis: Indiana UP, 1989.

Cixous, Helene. *Writing Differences: Readings from the seminar of Helene Cixous*. Ed. Susan Sellers. Milton Keynes: Open UP, 1988.

Fuss, Diana. *Essentially Speaking: Feminism, Nature & Difference*. New York: Routledge, 1989.

Grosz, Elizabeth. *Sexual Subversions: Three French Feminists*. Winchester, Mass.: Unwin Hyman, 1989.

Irigaray, Luce. *Elemental Passions*. 1982. Trans. Joanne Collie and Judith Still. New York: Routledge, 1992.

___. *je, tu, nous: Toward a Culture of Difference.* 1990. Trans. Alison Martin. New York: Routledge, 1993.

___. *Marine Lover of Friedrich Nietzsche.* Trans. Gillian C. Gill. New York: Columbia UP, 1991.

___. *Sexes and Genealogies.* 1987. Trans. Gillian C. Gill. New York: Columbia UP, 1993.

___. *Speculum of the Other Woman.* 1974. Trans. Gillian C. Gill. Ithaca, New York: Cornell UP, 1985.

___. *This Sex Which is Not One.* 1977. Trans. Catherine Porter. Ithaca, NY: Cornell UP, 1985.

Marks, Elaine and Isabelle de Courtivron, eds. *New French Feminisms: an Anthology.* New York: Schocken Books, 1981.

Minh-ha, Trinh T. *Woman, Native, Other.* Bloomington and Indianapolis: Indiana UP, 1989.

Nicholson, Linda J., ed. *Feminism/Postmodernism.* New York and London: Routledge, 1990.

Whitford, Margaret, ed. *The Irigaray Reader.* Cambridge, Massachusetts: Basil Blackwell, 1991.

___. *Luce Irigaray: Philosophy in the Feminine.* London and New York: Routledge, 1991.

Men's Movement

Bly, Robert. *Iron John: A Book About Men.* Reading, MA: Addison-Wesley, 1990.

Hagan, Kay Leigh. *Women Respond to the Men's Movement: A Feminist Collection.* New York: Pandora, 1992.

Harding, Christopher, ed. *Wingspan: Inside the Men's Movement.* New York: St. Martin's Press, 1992.

Stoltenberg, John. *The End of Manhood.* New York: Dutton, 1993.

___. *Refusing to be a Man: Essays on Sex and Justice.* New York: Meridian, 1990.

Creativity

Goldberg, Natalie. *Writing Down the Bones.* Boston: Shambhala, 1986.

Mathieu, W. A. *The Listening Book. Discovering Your Own Music.* Boston and London: Shambhala, 1991.

Metzger, Deena. *Writing for Your Life: A Guide and Companion to the Inner Worlds.* New York: HarperCollins, 1992.

Milner, Marion. (a.k.a. Joanna Field). *On Not Being Able to Paint.* Los Angeles: Jeremy Tarcher, 1957.

Index

About the Author

© 1998 Cathy Cade

Elise Peeples was born the third of four preacher's kids. Currently she lives with her writer/publisher husband Adam David Miller in Berkeley, California. Elise holds degrees in psychology and philosophy, is a trained paralegal, and has practiced community mediation for 15 years. She is the Executive Director of Minding the Body, Inc., a California non-profit corporation addressing the issues of women, body image, and health. Her publication credits include numerous articles on mediation, philosophy, and the law, as well as book reviews, fiction and poetry.